JOE JORDAN
BEHIND THE DREAM

My Autobiography

JOE JORDAN
BEHIND THE DREAM

My Autobiography

JOE JORDAN

With James Lawton

Hodder & Stoughton

First published in Great Britain in 2004 by Hodder and Stoughton
A division of Hodder Headline

A CIP catalogue record for this title is available from the British Library

ISBN 0340 83586 9

Typeset in Galliard by Hewer Text Ltd, Edinburgh
Printed and bound by
Mackays of Chatham Ltd, Chatham, Kent

Hodder Headline's policy is to use papers that are natural, renewable
and recyclable products and made from wood grown in sustainable forests.
The logging and manufacturing processes are expected to conform to
the environmental regulations of the country of origin

Hodder and Stoughton Ltd
A division of Hodder Headline
338 Euston Road
London NW1 3BH

To my wife, Judith, who has always been there to support me,
my children Lucy, Andrew, Thomas and Caroline,
and my mother and father

CONTENTS

.

Acknowledgements   ix
Foreword by John Giles   xi
Prologue   xv

1   The boy from Cleland   1
2   The road of Purdie Kane   14
3   No easy rites of passage   27
4   The most painful business   43
5   Passing the tests   53
6   Jordan of Scotland   69
7   From Revie to Armfield via Clough   90
8   A state of flux   106
9   The Old Trafford experience   121
10   Life beyond the touchline   138
11   Something unaccountably mislaid   153
12   Welcome, Lo Squalo   170
13   A year in Verona   183
14   A third World Cup   193
15   Settling for the possible   206
16   A proper setting   218
17   A fine line   230

Epilogue   244
Index   247

ACKNOWLEDGEMENTS

Many thanks to James Lawton for his patience in listening to my story and his great skill in putting my thoughts into book form. Our many meetings were always a pleasure.

Photographic Acknowledgements

The author and publisher would like to thank the following for permission to reproduce photographs:

Associated Press, Colorsport, Empics/Peter Robinson, L'Equipe/ Offside, Getty Images/Hulton Archive, Mark Leech/Offside, McLean Museum & Art Gallery/Inverclyde Council, Mirrorpix, Popperfoto.com, Press Association, Sporting Pictures, TopFoto.

All other photographs are from private collections.

FOREWORD

WHEN Joe Jordan arrived at Leeds United from Scotland, he was a half-formed professional footballer, eighteen years old, quiet, intense, as nervous as a colt. You could see he still had a lot to do. Physically and mentally, he had to toughen up to make his way in an environment that gave few favours and had established levels of performance that had to be met, day in and day out. He was not by any means a certainty.

Some kids you know about straight away. They have an easy talent. You just hope they have the temperament to support their gifts, which is far from always the case. Joe didn't have that obvious, God-given ability but I do not say this to diminish him in any way, or his superb career at both club and international level – quite the contrary. By the force of his will and the honesty of his nature, Joe didn't make himself a good footballer, he made himself a great one.

As in many other aspects of life, in football greatness takes different forms. The special distinction of Joe Jordan was that he achieved every goal he set himself. He saw, maybe more clearly than any other young professional I ever came across in a playing career that stretched to more than twenty years, what he had to do – and he simply went out and did it.

Joe never ceased in his effort to understand the game and what his contribution could be. In the process, he made himself into one of the most honest and effective players I ever knew at the top of the game. One of the big controversies of his career, which dogged him long after he stopped playing, is that he deliberately handled a ball in a World Cup qualifying match against Wales at Anfield in 1977. The world says that he did, Joe says that he did not. I believe Joe, instinctively, because anything that Joe Jordan says is good enough for me. That's not something to say lightly but a declaration that has to spring from long experience of a man's instincts and character.

Players, inevitably, are the harshest judges of their peers. They know about image and the impact a player has had on the public, and then they know about the realities out on the field. They know the players who do all the hard things, who play for their team above all and are filled with what can only be called moral courage. Joe Jordan's physical courage became a legend in the game in Scotland, in England and in Italy, where he played for three years and confirmed all the fighting instincts he had first suggested when he arrived at Leeds and went about the task of proving himself under the critical gaze of old pros such as Billy Bremner, Jack Charlton and me. He also had that other, not so easily definable, courage that flows from the strongest hearts only. Joe went into the dangerous places, always probing to give his team an edge. He would make the run that hurt physically but was vital to the cause of the team. For midfielders, such as Billy Bremner and me, one of the great needs was for somebody willing to receive the ball and hold it under fierce pressure as you sought to build a productive attack. I never once looked up for Joe and found that he wasn't there. Joe covered the ground, took his punishment and never complained. He was ferocious in the air and on the ground. Don Revie adored him because he always knew that no going would be too heavy to prevent Joe Jordan doing his work and helping his team.

Sometimes, a rare thing can be said about a leading football player – that he is revered in equal measure by the fans and his fellow professionals. The fans always knew what they would get from Joe Jordan – fierce commitment, courage and a perfectly honed instinct for inflicting maximum damage on an opposing defence. At home he was known as Jaws. In Italy they called him The Shark. In dressing rooms up and down the land the assessment of Joe was less dramatic, but no less heart-felt. He was a real player and a real man. Among professionals – at least, those of that time in the game – there was no higher praise.

Joe Jordan represents standards that will be the most valuable as long as the game is played.

John Giles

PROLOGUE

Like any shrewd and careful Scotsman, I expect to leave my affairs in good order. I do not anticipate loose ends or untidiness of any kind – it would not be as I tried to live my life – but may be there is one issue I will never be able to resolve as a neat item of my legacy and that's the matter of where to bury my football heart. There are, after all, some compelling candidates. The great, thrilling bulk of the San Siro in Milan, rising out of the haze of a hot afternoon like some awe-inspiring basilica of the football religion, is one. Old Trafford is another, where the blood raced so strongly when you ran on to the field and the smell in your nostrils told you, 'This is football, this is the sweat and the blood of the game.' Then there's Elland Road, where I learned that, more important even than winning or losing, you always had to compete until you had given everything you had. Hampden Park is, of course, the other contender. Wherever I played football, the huge gaunt stadium was always the touchstone of my career, the place where I came home to show my people that I could still do the job.

Football has been both kind and cruel to me but I have not sought to dwell on the downturns of fortune while reliving my days as a player, coach and manager. I have made no attempt to settle old scores, other than accounting for what happened from my perspective, perhaps some would say my prejudice. I accept that in football, as in life, you are obliged to take the best on offer and live with the rest of it. All those perceived injustices that inflame you at the time have to be balanced against all that has lifted you to the stars.

If I could, I would single out the moment that lingers most powerfully in my mind when I look back across the years, but that would just be some trick or device. It wouldn't be true because there are too many things I cannot separate in terms of how they moved me at the time. It's not possible to distinguish between the thrill of a telephone call that told me I had been called up for the Scottish team, and the earlier one that brought me the news I was to pack my bags, leave my village and head south to England for a career in the big league. I worked with great intensity for the Scottish call. Soon afterwards I would be wearing the shirt once pulled on by the demi-gods of my youth. That was always the dream of dreams, the final stepping stone of the journey I was determined to launch from the little field in the village, which lay in the fold of low hills, near worked-out collieries and open cast mines. I had many helping hands on that journey and I hope in these pages all of them are given their proper due.

I had been operating at the top of the game for some time – had played in a European Cup final – when Sir Matt Busby walked into my house in Leeds at the head of a deputation from Manchester United. They had driven over the Pennines to make an offer for me that would break the British transfer record. The sight of Busby there in my house, talking to my father about the old days in Scotland, will always be with me, along with a thousand images of the game that I always believed would shape my life.

Where, on the great totem pole of memory, do I place that moment early in my eighteenth year when Bobby Collins, one of the great Scottish players, whispered in my ear in Morton's pokey dressing room the news that I been noticed by one of the most successful managers of the football ages; or scoring the goal that carried Scotland to their first World Cup in sixteen years and then going out on the town with Denis Law and Billy Bremner – the town of Glasgow, which for one night at least belonged to me. Where do I fit in being escorted from the San Siro by the carabinieri after scoring against AC Milan's most bitter rivals, and playing in not one but three World Cups for Scotland, and scoring in each of them? And what about my father in the winning dressing room, being showered in champagne – a drink not frequently bought let alone thrown away in our village – after I helped Leeds United to an FA Cup final?

Those were some of the times that I have always balanced against the moments when harsher realities intruded, moments that made you wonder if you would ever be so sure of yourself again. Examples? Yes, but where do we start? Perhaps being told, at the age of thirty-one and for the first time in my football life, that I was being moved on. For a little while I had the fear of every professional when he is told, in so many words, that the days are drawing in and something inside might die if it is not rekindled very quickly indeed. But what do you do? You keep running and fighting and hoping that the game will be at the centre of your life until the last possible moment.

In telling my story I've tried to emphasise what was always most important to me about football, priorities that I know well enough may have changed with the years, and more rapidly than the men who formed my career – great football men including Don Revie, Busby, Dave Sexton and Jock Stein – could ever have believed when they sent earlier generations of players out on to the field.

If fashions and values have changed dramatically, some things about football are, I believe, timeless. The challenge and the beauty of the game remain at the heart of it, still the same as when I first played deep into the dusk in winter and spring, summer and autumn when I was a boy in Scotland. Then, football was central to the life of my homeland. It shaped the dreams and ambitions of the young and the old alike. It had a compulsion that had nothing to do with the prospect of big earnings and celebrity. It had an appeal of its own and I hope, and doggedly believe, that one day that magic will flower again.

1

THE BOY FROM CLELAND

HE was a working man, anyone could see that, and if you didn't know differently, if you had just parachuted in, you would have said he was like any other in my home village of Cleland in Lanarkshire. He lived with his family in the flat above Kelly's Bar at the Cross, without any fuss or grandeur, and even though he was just off shift he was approaching the bus-stop on the balls of his feet.

He had his hat pulled down and he carried a wee Army-style knapsack on his shoulder. You could see the outline of his flask of tea. So why, when a schoolboy like me looked at him, did my blood pulse with so much pride? It was because I belonged to this man's tribe, and here was someone who in an extraordinary way was so much more than just another hard-working villager.

He had been a professional footballer, something that would have given him great status in my eyes, and those of almost all my friends, if he had merely worn the colours of one of the local Scottish league clubs. A man who wore the amber and claret of Motherwell, or the red diamond of Airdrie, was a star in his own right. He had made a mark beyond so many of his contemporaries, for whom playing football professionally was a dream that could make you ache. But this man at the bus-stop had occupied much more than that honourable ground. He was one of the great ones. He was Jimmy Delaney.

What he had done was all I ever dreamed of doing. He had scored a winning goal at Hampden Park in front of a crowd of 133,000, who had poured into the huge ground to celebrate the end of the Second World War and the re-start of the old one with England. He had won Cup-winners' medals with Celtic and with Manchester United. He had been idolised at Parkhead and was a key member of Sir Matt Busby's first great United team. That was the Busby who came from down the road in Bellshill, whose father had died in the battle of the Somme in the First World War and whose wife, before their marriage, had sifted coal at the pithead; the Busby who had played for Manchester City and Scotland, who wore a tweed jacket, smoked a pipe and had become an institution of the game while building up United from the bomb damage of another war and the ravages of the Munich air crash.

You could warm yourself on such glorious familiarity with the origins of great men. You could nurture your ambitions so much more hopefully because you breathed the same gritty air as Busby and Delaney.

Maybe today a schoolboy in Cleland might wonder why a man who had done so much was standing at a bus-stop with his knapsack, reflecting on another eight hours in the factory. He might question the whereabouts of the big car and the posh house and the villa in Spain. Not then, not in the world I inhabited, where football wasn't the means to a rich end, it was an end in itself. It wasn't your escape from the ghetto, it wasn't a lottery ticket and it didn't mean having a Ferrari and a Porsche on the double drive. Jock Stein was still riding a bus to Celtic Park and the man who captained his great team, Billy McNeill, was known as Caesar, not because of the drive and splendour of his leadership but because he was the only one who owned a car. Football was football, a basic part of life but also separate and maybe even holy in a way, and if it was exploited, the last place to assign guilt was the dressing room.

In those days, you couldn't have made a film like *Trainspotting* in Edinburgh or Glasgow or their environs. Drugs hadn't begun to do their vicious work in the tenements and the terraced houses of the big cities and the mining and steel villages, but the harsh conditions that facilitated their growth were in place all right. High expectations were not generally encouraged. You worked and in so many cases you drank, but while you were young you had a great and specific yearning – you wanted to be a football player.

Delaney had played with Celtic and United and Scotland and it didn't matter to me – or him, I always believed – that he was back in the crowd. What he had could never be taken away, and certainly it could never be measured in any material way.

He was a friend of my father, Frank, and I played on the Corn Patch – the village football field – with his son John and my cousin Joe Brennan. Delaney's eldest son, Patsy, ran the paper shop, and I reported to him every day to collect piles of the *Scottish Daily Express* and the *Daily Record* to deliver around the village. You could talk to Patsy about football as long as you liked. He had played with Alex Ferguson at Dunfermline before injury cut him down. His kid brother, cousin Joe, and me were inseparable. We played together on Saturday mornings and on Saturday afternoons we prayed together at St Mary's Catholic Church. After hours spent on the Corn Patch playing the game before the call for dinner, in the evening we went to the local dancehall in the hope of pulling a bird. Every day of my life I was reminded of what was possible – and, at the dance, maybe what was not. Football was always accessible, pulsating with a life that so quickly became central to my own.

My father told me all about Jimmy Delaney. When I was six or seven, he went down to Old Trafford to see his friend play and some time later he brought me a United shirt. It was one of the great treasures of my life. Many years later I heard how Nobby Stiles had been taken as a young boy to the house of a relative of Delaney's in Manchester, and Nobby's father had asked if his son could wear briefly the United shirt that had belonged to the great man and was now hanging on a wall of the little house in the back street. The shirt was taken down and placed on the shoulders of the little guy who would play so famously for United and England, and later Nobby would say that it was like some rite of passage.

When I heard that story I was reminded all over again of how it was when you were very young and football meant almost everything to you. How hard it is to relate those days to today. You wonder how it could possibly be that Jock Stein gathered together a team from a radius of thirty miles of Glasgow city centre and managed not only to beat but utterly outplay Internazionale of Milan, with all their wealth and power. Back then, when I was a boy, it could be explained so easily. Talent was all round you. You could see someone like a young Jimmy Johnstone weaving fantastic spells on some local field and if you were uncertain about your own ability, if sometimes you felt you were just another hopeful kid terribly unsure about whether you had enough talent to make something of yourself, you never doubted that there was passion and desire enough.

Football was so much more than a game, and for as long as I can remember it was at the centre of all my thoughts. I had a good and loving family, but life was very hard – in the early days I shared a bed with my brother and my sister – and always there was that drive inside me to fulfil my dream of playing the game that I loved. I became a footballer because I had the nagging belief that I had something that might just enable me to break away beyond the old mine workings and low hills that skirted Cleland. I might not be another Jimmy Delaney or Denis Law or Ian St John, who went to Liverpool from my local arena in Fir Park, Motherwell, I might not get to know all of the peaks they visited, but maybe I could do something worthwhile. Maybe I could win my chance and hang on to it, finally beat the odds that sometimes I felt were stacking up against me, hard as I tried. Maybe I could take a step further than Georgie 'Purdie' Kane.

Purdie was a year or two older than me and it was plain he had a real chance. He was a classic Scottish footballer, small and quick, and he took one big stride away from the village when he signed for Middlesbrough. He had caught the eye of a scout with his lively running and clever skill and he was away in England for a few years. Once I was with a group of kids standing outside the fish and chip shop at the Cross when Purdie came up from the train station on a visit home. He gave us a wave as he walked by, calling, 'Hello boys,' and I thought, 'Lucky guy.' He looked so alive. The briefest appraisal told you this was a kid who had moved up. I don't know why he didn't make it, why you can see him now in Kelly's Bar having a drink with the guys and talking about the old days.

There's no question he had the talent, but maybe it was enough for Purdie that he had a taste of another world. Perhaps somewhere deep in his nature he never really wanted much more than that, a brief flavour, a glimpse of something wider and then a return to all that was familiar. When it was clear to us that Purdie hadn't made it in England, I wondered if he had given it enough application, enough passion. Purdie had his life and I had my mine, and we were quite different people. I knew that well enough. Purdie was short and garrulous, a firefly in the Scottish dusk when the drinks were bought and the conversation flowed. I was a little taller and, I guess, a bit solemn and I tended to nurse a beer, if I was ever persuaded to have one. But we were Scottish footballers, no doubt, and I would certainly never forget what he gave me when he strode so briskly past the gathering of boys at the Cross. Like Jimmy Delaney at the bus-stop, he told me of other possibilities. He showed me I could achieve my dream of playing professional football.

That was the message, and not just to me, of Father Isaac McLaren of St Mary's, who had studied at a seminary in Rome and been beguiled by the style and the technique of Italian football. Father McLaren never made a lot of progress in the church, ending his days as he started, as a curate, but he will always be remembered fondly by generations of Cleland boys.

Father McLaren loved football, having been enchanted by the beauty of the game he had seen in Italy, and he grasped fully its value to the young boys in Cleland. He had a good eye for potential – and for the details of our lives. He noticed that Purdie was operating in time-expired boots. He saw his feet after he had played for the St Mary's Boys Guild team, and one day he produced, magically it seemed to Purdie, a new pair. Even today, when Purdie is fondly recalling his football days over a glass of stout, there will be a mention of the boots. 'European cutaways, the first in the village,' says Purdie, his eyes shining.

Father McLaren guided us in many ways. Once, at the end of a successful season, when he took the team away for a game, we were surprised when he had all of us trooping into a hotel that seemed impossibly grand. We thought it might be for a presentation but he sat us down in the restaurant, and for all of us it was the first time we ate amid such finery. During the course of our dinner, he quietly advised us on our table manners, and the proper use of a knife and fork.

Once a year he brought an orphanage team to the Corn Patch, and saw in the occasion an opportunity that went beyond the touchlines. The orphans were boarded out with families in the village, which was good for them Father McLaren reckoned, and also for their hosts. It was a reminder to us that if our own advantages at times seemed sparse enough, they surely seemed considerable to lads who didn't have even the basic security of family life.

So Father McLaren gave us some good grounding in the game of football, and in life. He tried to get us to lift up our heads a little bit and I always felt that this came from his own experience of going away from Scotland and seeing something of the world. He seemed to grasp more fully than anyone else around that the odds were stacked up against us, that the chances were that for many of us the outside world would forever lie far away over those low hills and be represented most strongly by the big, tough city of

Glasgow, less than twenty miles away. No one really needed to tell me there was another life going on outside the village and Father McLaren's greatest contribution to my cause was his genuine knowledge of football, and his feeling for the game. He was an enthusiast but his passion was informed by a knowing eye. He had been something of a player himself before he followed his vocation to be a priest and, although he did like a glass of whisky, he kept himself fit.

He was also a great organiser and very sound on the tactics of the game. He organised the Boys Guild team very thoroughly. There were games on Saturday morning and training two nights a week, and five-a-side in the church hall when the weather was at its worst. In that hall we worked on our skills and our fitness. Father McLaren wasn't giving us fantastic coaching in any technical sense, but he knew the fundamentals of good play well enough. As the snow piled up outside, you were taking on a Jimmy Johnstone or a Bobby Murdoch, you were learning the game and developing your skills and taking knocks. We had an extra education. Father McLaren took time with us individually, realising our differing needs and potential. Wherever he could, he would smarten us up, prepare us a little better for the world. It was warm and sweaty in the hall, and we felt at home.

Football in Scotland these days has a great bureaucracy, but you wonder what is happening to all the money that is invested, where it is draining away. You see so many of the Scottish league teams populated by foreign players, some of them of very questionable ability, and you can't help but wonder whether the Father McLarens and the Peter Caseys – he was my teacher at St Aidan's secondary school – might just make some difference today. Certainly, many Scottish players of my day and earlier could point to a schoolmaster or a clergyman and say, 'That man encouraged me when it was most important, he believed in me and pointed the way.' Would the jinking Johnstone or Murdoch or Gary McAllister, who came from just a few miles down the road in Newarthill, have made it into the light without the help of people willing to give their time and interest without any reward other than the satisfaction of making a difference in young people's lives? I know that my own prospects would have been doubtful without the help of Father McLaren and Peter Casey.

Father McLaren was the first to show his faith. He had me in the Guild team two or three years ahead of my time, playing alongside Purdie Kane, despite the fact that I was well behind the rest of the boys physically. Then, I was a left-sided midfield player. He played me partly as a warning to older boys, a statement that their places in the team were not assured and also, I think, because he saw something in me beyond the sum of the talent I was displaying. I knew I was far from the pick of the village crop. One boy, Michael Comfort, undoubtedly had superior natural skill but perhaps it didn't matter so much to him. Football wasn't quite the focus of his life. Michael liked a beer on Friday nights, even when he was quite a young lad. I stayed in. That may sound a little precious but I didn't take any great pride in staying in or not drinking. It didn't make me feel particularly worthy. I suppose I just totted up the odds against any fulfilment of my ambitions and decided that I had to create for myself any edge I could. Michael Comfort was just one of a crowd of talented boys and if he chose to handicap himself, that was my good luck. Even if I was very dedicated, and found it easier to turn my back on the pub than most of my friends, it scarcely put me on top of the pile. I knew I had something, and I knew I had the discipline and will to bring it out, but it was always going to be a case of my coming to it slowly but surely, and only then as a result of flat-out hard work.

Within the Boys Guild team I had a few special friends apart from Joe and John Delaney, including Jim Goligey and Terry O'Brien, both of whom could play a bit. I envied John quite a lot because he passed his eleven-plus and made it to Our Lady's Grammar School in Motherwell. The attraction was not the good education but the excellent football team. In retrospect, the odds against making a life for myself in football – and the hazards – seem even more daunting. So many times the fate of a young team-mate and friend turned bad for one reason or another and forced me to consider my own good fortune, not least in later years when Terry O'Brien died young, of cancer.

One breakthrough for me came against our powerful local rivals, Stevenson. They scored with some ease, which left me enraged. I got hold of the ball at the re-start and raced through the Stevenson lines. I was a boy possessed as I put the ball into the net. Father McLaren didn't say anything at the time, didn't suggest by his manner that I had done anything exceptional. I certainly expected a little more recognition; it was unquestionably the best goal of my youth, and maybe my life because, looking back, I had summoned up all my feelings for the game and my need to make a success of it.

As I was going into Mass the following morning, Father McLaren looked up from greeting the faithful at the church door and saw me slipping by. He stepped into my path, gave me the broadest wink and shook my hand, very firmly. I had a strong sense of achievement then. It was a moment that would always serve my self-confidence well, something to fall back on in times of doubt.

Mr Casey had a similar effect when he picked me out of the football intake at the new, big Catholic secondary school in Wishaw, and ushered me straight into the school team. Although I was still thin and bony, Mr Casey said that he liked my approach to the game. In fact, he said rather more than that after one good performance. He said I was the best thing since sliced bread. Nobody had said anything like that to me before and the feeling was quite heady. In Cleland, praise was hard won. It didn't gush, but I did have my supporters. My cousin Joe was a great source of strength in my youth. He was both a team-mate and a friend, and he was at my side to commiserate and celebrate at all the different turns in my march to a professional career. Joe had plenty of talent and eventually played for Hong Kong Rangers, the irony of which was mentioned more than once in our Celtic stronghold.

On the touchline, too, I had committed allies in my father and my Uncle Joe. Uncle Joe's liking for football was rivalled only by his enthusiasm for a glass of banana rum.

In Cleland, you took your pleasures when and where you could and, as I look back on an upbringing that was never marked by luxury of any kind, I know that I have plenty of reasons to be grateful. There was always enough food on the table, even in the most difficult of times, and if sometimes I moaned about the lack of two or three pence for entry to the swimming baths, there was never any shortfall of kindness or values.

I was born on 15 December 1951 at the hospital in Carluke to Francis and Mary Jordan. My sister Elizabeth had arrived a few years earlier, and my brother John would follow me two years later. When I was born my father was running the village shop. He had been trained as a quartermaster in the Army and the job, though modestly rewarded, was to his liking. He was a quiet but popular man, and this was partly because he organised the bus trips up to Parkhead for the Celtic Supporters Club. In fact, he was more than the organiser; he was the shepherd. He gathered in the wayward sheep when they lingered too long in the pubs, and when, as was often the case, the money for return tickets had been spent in the bars, he reached into his pocket and paid the fares.

When the Co-operative Society bought out the shop, my father was made redundant. That meant we lost our house but if this was a full-scale family crisis, Liz, John and I didn't feel any of the tension. There was still enough wholesome food on the table and if the loss of his job was a jarring blow to the gentle rhythm of his life, my father, like so many other Scotsmen down the years, accepted that he had no alternative but to forage for work beyond the village. The quest took him to the Ravenscraig steelworks, which is now flattened from the Lanarkshire landscape, and after that he worked in an ice-cream factory.

My mother worked the twilight shift at the McFarlane and Lyons factory, which was hard for her after tending the house all day and preparing for our return from school. She made our evening meals before going to the bus-stop for the ride to the factory. There was a solitary bonus. She would come home laden with chocolate biscuits, the one consistent luxury of our lives.

There was never any sense of hardship because it was simply the way it had always been; you took what you could and were glad of it. My father's mother, another Mary Jordan, had to look after seven children when my grandfather was killed in a colliery accident. That, too, was commonplace. When the collieries that honeycombed Lanarkshire – there were so many of them they were listed by number, my grandfather dying in a place that was never dignified with a name – were worked out, they brought in great machines to gouge out the surface of our earth for open-cast mining. Families grew strong where they had been most broken. My mother's father was disabled in the pit, losing half of his hand, but unlike so many others who gave way to despair, he didn't drink away his compensation. He bought one truck, then another, and built a haulage business that eked out a decent living.

In my own house, there was an especially strong urge to head over the hills and find something new. My big sister was a bright girl, and she became a nurse. While working in Leeds, she met and married a doctor. My brother John, who was a useful footballer, also felt the pull away. To most people's mystification, including my own, he went into the pop business where he worked for, among others, Bryan Ferry and various heavy metal groups whose names now clatter at the back of my memory. John was full of life and fun, and although I loved him deeply I knew I could never share his view of life. He doubtless said the same of me, but that would never limit my pleasure when he trailed into any town where I happened to be, taking a pause, healing a bruise, facing up to life again.

Meantime, we scuffled our way through the Cleland days, and

for me that mostly involved playing football as the life of the village flowed on down its predictable course. The drinking was ferocious on Saturday night, and so was the fighting. Almost invariably, the combatants would be raging drunk, with some of the animosities formed during the intense gambling by a group of men who found a quiet corner on the outskirts of the village, away from the gaze of vengeful wives and the law, and threw coins in the air in fiercely backed games of two up. The fall of the coins often saw off the last of the wages. Mass on Sunday morning was crowded and prayerful and in the congregation there were many sore heads filled with regrets.

Through all of this I mostly picked my way carefully, for I was merely passing through. Although my father and mother knew the value of discipline, it was softly imparted and I was never smacked at home. At St Aidan's I received my first taste of corporal punishment on my second day, the crime having been committed on the first afternoon of freedom when the school gates were thrown open. Mr Casey always swore that the only two things to come out of Cleland were the numbers 43 and 44 buses and I was on one of them when I got into a rare piece of trouble. Two or three of us were seen jumping on and off the platform and swinging on the bar as the bus groaned up the hill away from the school. We were reported and called to the headmaster, who administered the strap. Much later, I would acquire something of a reputation for throwing myself around a football field but until then that solitary strapping, and the values given to me by my family, kept me out of any serious trouble.

My parents also implanted in me the belief that you always had to give 100 per cent. Anything less simply wouldn't do. I watched my father go to his various jobs, burying his concerns about what lay in the future, and I saw my mother working at every opportunity to support him. Hardship was negotiable because it was in their blood. There were tough times on both sides of the family. My father's mother had various jobs supporting those seven children after my grandfather died in the pit, but at no time in my life did I hear the language of complaint. You might see the odd grimace but it was followed by a shrug of the shoulders. If you asked somebody how they were doing, they would say, however tough their circumstances, 'nae bad' – not bad. It was, I have always believed, the kind of upbringing that gave you the foundation to go on, absorbing the blows and finding something that you believed was worthwhile.

When I left Cleland, I knew in my bones that I would never return, not permanently, but as I was walking down to the station, past the war memorial and the bus-stop where I had seen Jimmy Delaney and first thought seriously about the meaning of his great career and his subsequent life, I knew the place would always be with me. I also knew that wherever I finished up, I would always have all of it – the smell of incense in the church, the racket in the hall when we yelled for the ball and made our tackles, the cries of glee and anguish when the two up coins landed, the fighters on Saturday night – and it would always be a source of strength.

Of all the memories, the one that is most vivid is the time I first played football. It was in Goreshall Street, on the new council estate, where we moved when we lost our house after the Co-op took over the village shop. People had been moved there from all over the district, out of run-down terraced houses and old, leaky tenements. A few kids, including me, were kicking a ball around in the street. First some fathers came out, introducing themselves quite shyly, and then the womenfolk emerged from their spanking new houses, talking over the fences. It was a bright blowy day and while the women, breaking from their chores, talked and laughed, the men and the boys played football.

When I think of Scotland, my Scotland, that is the image that leaps into my mind. There were shouts and laughter and the zing of the ball. It was a perfect, happy time and I know I will remember it until the day I die.

2

THE ROAD OF PURDIE KANE

FOR so long I visualised the walk that would take me away from Cleland. It would be the Purdie walk, one fine morning going down to the station with my bag over my shoulder. Sometimes it was so easy to imagine it, step by jaunty step. I could see it all so clearly, getting off the train in Glasgow, making my way to the great brick fortress of Parkhead – flashbulbs popping, blood racing and Jock Stein laying a hand on my shoulder, as he had done for so many of my heroes, and saying, 'Away you go, son. It's all there before you.'

That was the fantasy, and it was as insistent as an itch. Reality took shape much more slowly. First, there were some years of considerable doubt, and that shouldn't have been so surprising because for all the encouragement of Father McLaren, Mr Casey and cousin Joe, a wider world hadn't rushed to acclaim another Johnstone, Dalglish or Murdoch when I came charging over the brow of the hill. Not only had I not represented Scotland at any level, the Lanarkshire selectors had also failed to pick me out, although when I considered the range of their choice in those days, I was bound to accept that it didn't add up to a prima facie case of negligence. This, after all, wasn't so much a county as a republic of the game – and quite the opposite of a lone-star state. In Lanarkshire, everyone was obliged to play football, and the other requirement was that you did it well, with a confidence and panache that was deemed a birthright.

14

If I wasn't summoned by Jock Stein or Matt Busby, I did learn later that Celtic had invited me to train with them. A scout had called at the house and told my parents that there was some interest. There had also been an invitation for a trial with Leicester City, who were managed by the Scot Matt Gillies. No doubt if I had been fully aware of these overtures, I would have been more inflamed than ever with hope and ambition, but my mother, particularly, was reluctant to see me rush into the great chorus line of auditioning young Scottish footballers. She wanted something solid, something you could bank at the end of the week. Football would have been fine if it came with guarantees, but of course she knew – as I did – that it didn't. She said to my father, 'Look how many youngsters go away to play football with all their hopes, and giving no attention to an education and the chances of a decent job. Look how they are when their dreams are broken. What is there for them to fall back on?' Some time later, she said to me, 'What if you get an injury, or they don't think you're good enough. What are you left with, son?'

She carried the day because in the house, laying down her priorities, she could be quite forceful. My dad was different. He had his own strengths and opinions but he was quieter. After he was gone, it came to me strongly that he had never been vocal in his desires, or fears, for me as a footballer. He loved the game, I had no doubt about that, and he was proud that I had shown such determination and a certain degree of aptitude. He would never tell me if he thought I had played badly. He would say something like, 'That was great, Joe.' In his eyes, I was always the best player on the field.

He waited for me to decide what I wanted to do and when the decision was made he gave me all his support. It was only later that I understood how lucky I had been to have such a man for my father, as I could also see clearly my mother's view. She was a mother, fiercely protective, and she didn't want to see her first-born son separated from his boyish hopes and condemned to a lifetime of scuffling for a living. She didn't want to see me suffer the fate of Purdie Kane.

Deep down, though, I knew that however hard I worked, I would struggle to get anywhere academically. When I was eighteen I used to travel up to a draughtsman's cubicle in an office in Glasgow, taking the first of the train rides of a day that would stretch on to near midnight. I'd return home after football training and collapse on to my bed, and one day I finally reached the point of decision. I remember saying to myself with tremendous conviction, 'Oh God, I really have to pile up all my eggs in one basket. I have to settle for one thing or the other. I have to be a draughtsman in my collar and tie and my commuter's routine – or I have to be a footballer. The choice has to be made. I have to live my own life.'

Maybe it would have been different if Celtic had offered any kind of commitment but there had been no talk of an apprenticeship. They just wanted to take a look to see if I had anything other than a lot of determination. I knew that my physique was against me. I was scraggy and late in my physical maturity.

This view was confirmed when, at sixteen, I signed for the Blantyre Vics, a well-respected club that offered the cross-roads of Scottish junior league football. The league was populated by old pros and young prospects and those who would never be quite one thing or the other. As a young fellow, Jock Stein had played for the Vics, and Jimmy Johnstone had turned out for Blantyre Celtic. You could make your mark with a team like the Vics – or you could disappear. It was quickly apparent that I was in danger of the second fate; Blantyre would not be my proving ground. I played with tremendous passion and hope for three games, but I knew I wasn't making it. I simply wasn't strong enough. Old pros were running by me; younger guys were knocking me off the ball. It was not as I had ever imagined it on the Corn Patch. After the third game, a club official said to me, 'You're not ready, son, you're not making an impact. We'll keep your registration, but we'll farm you out to North Motherwell in the amateur league. You can go at your own pace there. We'll keep an eye on you.'

I thanked the man but inside I was crushed. At that age every set-back is a blow to your heart, but I knew the Vics were right. As a boy against older boys, I had been able to make my mark; my spirit had got me through. At Blantyre, I realised I had moved too quickly into a men's league. They were bigger, stronger and they were not interested in giving some wee boy a helping hand. He had to make it on his own. It was the football of the coal and steel zones and if the skills of a Johnstone had twinkled in this mining village, the first requirement was to prove that you could take all the hammering that would inevitably come your way. In fact, the decision of the Vics worked strongly in my favour.

In just a dozen games with North Motherwell, my football found new life and confidence. The manager Pat McCourt, a former professional, didn't make any fuss but I sensed that I was making a good impression. It was confirmed quickly when a scout of Greenock Morton, the Scottish first-division team, arranged a friendly game at North Motherwell. It appeared that a few of our players had been attracting some attention, and it may have been that I was one of them. Certainly, I was conscious that it might well be important for me to play as well as I could against a Morton team that had been drawn from reserve and good youth players. I knew I had a decent game, tackling hard and using the ball well, and afterwards McCourt asked me if I would like to go for a trial at Morton. This was one of the rare occasions when my father couldn't attend one of my games, but Uncle Joe had come along and, as the senior family representative, he took charge of the negotiations. He said to McCourt, 'Yes, we'll think about this. I'll talk to his father and we'll get back to you.' In my mind's eye, I was already announcing my ability in the colours of Morton.

Of course, I had to go up to Glasgow to show what I could do. I played for Morton reserves against Partick Thistle against a back-cloth of shipyard cranes and swirling seagulls, and I did well enough for the club to offer me part-time terms. Something even more astonishing happened after the game. A young boy came up to me as I was leaving the ground. I was already walking on air, but then this wee boy was pushing an autograph book at me and asking me for my signature. Suddenly, the euphoria was broken. It struck me all over again how much I had to do to make it into the company of my heroes. I scribbled my name and marched off, embarrassed.

Signing for Morton wasn't my pass out of Cleland – or the offices of McMenam and Brown – but it was a start, a small piece of the professional action and it was exhilarating that I had been handed it so soon after being threatened with oblivion at Blantyre. The trick now was to placate my mother as I nourished the dream, get myself the means of earning a decent living in a good job from which I could come home with clean hands and a face unimpregnated with the grit and the dust of heavy industry, while at the same time announcing my potential as a professional player. My father was delighted that I had got in at the ground floor of Scottish league football, and if it meant some disturbance to his unflagging support of Celtic, well, it was a matter of the blood. He was as gratified that I had received some recognition as a footballer as my mother had been when I came back from Glasgow and announced that I had been taken on by the small firm of architects, McMenan and Brown. She brushed aside my complaint that I would be earning peanuts – just £3.50 a week – and declared, 'When you have nothing in life, the first thing you must do is get yourself some qualifications. That separates you from so many of the rest. That gives you a chance.'

That was all very well for my mother's idea of respectability and security but I worried that I should be training full time rather than sitting in an office from nine to five, and then I panicked when I realised I hadn't checked that I would be free to play on Saturdays and go training in the evenings. I went to a neighbour's house to use the phone to call the boss of the firm, Mr McMenan. He was amused by my concerns. 'We will not be interfering with your football, laddie,' he said. He assured me that I would be able to leave the office at the stroke of 5 p.m. and he was always as good as his word. He never came up with a piece of work that would delay my arrival at training. In Scotland then, you had the feeling that it might just have been seen as a small sacrilege.

The regime was tough for a sixteen-year-old. I was out of bed before seven and some days seemed to stretch out interminably. There was no hanging out with the boys at the Cross, no courtships. There was just the office and Morton, the football club beside the Clyde. I played for the reserves in mostly empty stadiums, but some empty grounds can still bring up the hairs on the back of your neck. Celtic Park and Ibrox are two of them and I played in those places amid the echoes of greater days. It was good training on the ground floor of the game and when later I looked back to those days, I saw it was the time when I first grasped the difference between boyhood fancies about how it was to be a footballer and the reality of it, as the kids pushed to find a way through and the old pros hung on, battling, sometimes unscrupulously, to retain an edge.

Morton was a two-man band comprising Hal Stewart, chief executive and part-owner, and Eric Smith, the coach, a hardened former professional who had been cut down by injury but not before service with Celtic and Leeds United. Stewart was part shrewd football man, part entrepreneur. In some ways, he was decades ahead of his time. If he was alive today, I suspect his mouth would be permanently watering over the money-making potential around every corner. Back in the seventies, he didn't do so badly. One piece of wheeler-dealing was the marketing of Celtic cigarettes, a brand that he calculated would have big appeal in at least half of Scotland. Perhaps he imagined that just as the family that prays together stays together, Celtic fans, while light-ing up in the pubs and the bars, would make a similar pledge to die together. The Celtic brand went less ferociously than a house on fire but Stewart was undaunted. He kept Morton alight by buying players cheap and selling them at decent profits, and in this he successfully raided the untapped Scandinavian market, one notable success being the goalkeeper Erik Sorensen, whom he moved on to Rangers. Per Bartram, who went to Crystal Palace, was another. It was obvious that anyone who signed for Morton would not lack the backing of some good supporting salesmanship if he showed the potential to move into a higher sphere of the game.

Smith was a pure old football man, flinty in his attitude to the game but with a generous spirit. He survived the free-wheeling regime of Stewart better than most. Stewart saw Morton as both his plaything and his cash-cow. When the mood took him, he would march into the dressing room with the team-list he had drawn up exclusively on the basis of his own judgement. Smith shrugged his shoulders and got on with his job as best he could.

On midweek match nights I went straight from the office to Smith's house, where he would give me a bite to eat and then take me to the game. He was good to all the young lads and he was badly missed when he moved to the sunshine of Cyprus, thankfully with a few bob, to coach a local team. Sadly, Eric didn't get too long in the sun. He died shortly afterwards after suffering a heart-attack.

It was Smith who saw that as I began to put some more flesh on my bones I also showed the potential to do some damage up front and in the air, and several times he asked me if I had thought about going full time. Each time my replay was the same. I said I thought about it all the time but there was the problem back in Cleland, that pressure to give myself an option in life if the football failed. Smith frowned at my response; in so many words, he said I couldn't indefinitely perform my balancing act of a full day at work, and night school when I wasn't training, and then the draining effort to make some impact on the professional football field. I knew he was right. I was in danger of hurtling between two stools.

The possibility of fatally mixed priorities gnawed at me through all those days until that night I fell on my bed and realised that the past was gone and all the worrying baggage my mother had brought from her days of hardship had to be put down. I had done the best I could to soothe her anxieties but I had my life to lead; I had to seize the chance that had come to me – or spend the rest of my days growling my regrets over a drink at Kelly's. I had to go down the road trod so briefly by Purdie Kane.

Until then I had timed my two-week summer break from McMenan and Brown so that I could join in pre-season training with the full-time professionals. It was a taste of the complete football life and although it was hard, I never envied those lads who took holidays by the sea or scraped up enough money for a cut-price trip to the Costa Brava. But it wasn't enough, I knew that well enough, and the subtle promptings of Eric Smith and some of the professionals had nudged me to the point of decision. My mother wasn't pleased but I told her I knew what I was doing, and when I informed the club of my decision a contract was immediately produced. A few years ago a Scottish museum wrote to me for permission to exhibit my first pay slip. I sent it off, agreeing that in these days of the £50,000 a week young foot-baller it had a certain curiosity value. I was paid a basic wage of £7 with £5 extra if I made the first team. It was a modest enough investment in my talent but I knew the deal. Morton would pay me the money of the factory floor and I would shoot for the stars.

Sooner than I could have hoped in my most outrageous moods of optimism, both parties were entirely satisfied. With the full training, I could feel myself getting stronger and more confident in my ability to make progress out on the field and then, as so often happens in football, one player's mishap was the opportunity for another. In the pre-season there was a friendly game in Halifax. I came on for the last half of that game and fitted in well, so that when Stan Rankin, our big centre-half, failed a fitness test on an injured knee before an Anglo-Scottish Cup-tie at West Bromwich Albion, I was picked to replace him. I pointed out to Smith that I had never played centre-half in my life but he assured me I would be fine. I could tackle, I could read the game and hadn't I spent most of my life dreaming about such an opportunity?

It was all true enough, but perhaps I wouldn't have chosen to start off against a man as good and as experienced as the England international Jeff Astle. He was still at the top of the game, having been included in Sir Alf Ramsey's squad for the 1970 World Cup in Mexico, and a raw young Scot, playing out of position in his first outing at the senior level, was not likely to put him off a strong and functional game that was particularly effective in the air. However, I had already shown a bit of aptitude for the aerial game and the match went better than I could have hoped. We kept a clean sheet and Astle inflicted few terrors that night.

It was by far the most important game I had ever played, a fact of which I was totally unaware in the heat of the action, no doubt to my great benefit. Another thing I didn't know was that I had already been recommended to the manager of the team that had begun to be grudgingly acknowledged as the best in England. Don Revie, manager of Leeds United, was sitting in the stands at the Hawthorns ground, and he was watching every move I made. He had been told to do so by one of the greatest of Scottish footballers, Bobby Collins.

The powerful little man, who had been such an influence on the development of Leeds, was in his last days as a player with Morton. He had played first for Celtic and then Everton before being picked out by Revie as a foundation stone of a team that would become one of the best in Europe, and Revie was still in awe of his instincts for the game. Collins was living with his parents in Glasgow and travelling back to see his family in Leeds whenever he could. From time to time he trained with his old team-mates and one morning Revie asked him if he had seen any likely lads north of the border.

'Aye,' said Collins in a sentence that would change my life, 'there's a boy called Joe Jordan who's got a real chance – he's only a kid but he plays like a man.'

Leeds United! That spring cousin Joe and I had gone along to Parkhead to see Leeds play our beloved Celtic in the second leg of a European Cup semi-final. We had peered over a great sea of heads to watch two great teams in tremendous action. Leeds had been on a treadmill in England; they were the victims of their own success. They had suffered a fixture pile-up that makes the complaints of Sir Alex Ferguson and Arsene Wenger seem almost petty, and they had the additional problem of losing goalkeeper Gary Sprake. He was taken off on a stretcher. Celtic, a team that represented the last flowering of the work of Stein, narrowly won an epic game. Leeds, with John Giles and Billy Bremner playing with slavish brilliance in the middle of the field, never accepted that they were beaten. Billy scored a great goal, knocking the ball into the top corner, but Celtic had a lead from the first leg through George Connelly and, with a much less demanding schedule in their Scottish first-division season, they had the stronger legs and came out on top – but only by the finest of margins. It had been a phenomenal contest and Joe Brennan and I left the ground with our heads spinning. We had seen football at its competitive best, and my admiration for what I had seen came flooding back with a thrill that made the hairs on the back of my neck stand up when, in the dressing room at Morton before training, Bobby Collins said to me, 'They've put in a bid for you, you know.'

Leeds had made a bid for me – that phrase kept rolling around my head. I felt seven feet tall. There had been nothing in the press, not a whisper. I had played just twelve games for Morton. Part of me wanted to run into the street and yell to the world, 'Leeds have put in a bid for me, you know.' I was eighteen, I hadn't had a sniff of recognition from Scotland at any level, but one of the great managers, on the word of a great player, had looked me over and put a value on my talent – £15,000 for Morton with a bonus of £5,000 if I played twenty games for the Leeds first team.

I didn't say anything to anyone except my parents. I didn't

want to break the spell. I waited for the word, counted the seconds, and then Hal Stewart pulled me to one side after training and said, 'A top English club has made an offer for you. We don't know if we're going to accept but we'll let you know Sunday night. Get yourself prepared to go on Monday morning.' That was all he said. Prepare to go on Monday; prepare to make the Purdie walk, take a step along his road and maybe a little further, maybe to find the ground once occupied by Jimmy Delaney.

Sunday crawled along; I listened to the ticking of the clock. I'd given the club the neighbour's phone number and all I could do was wait for the call. It was supposed to come at five. I would never know why Hal Stewart chose not to tell me it was Leeds who were in for me. Maybe he had some other possibilities that would have been more profitable for the club, or perhaps, knowing my nature and my ambition, he guessed that I would be on fire to join Leeds and thought that might limit his scope to make the best possible deal for Morton. I was pretty sure Stewart was operating some business tactics but it didn't really concern me. All I wanted was to make the move and if someone gained some kind of extra benefit, well, that didn't matter to me. Until the phone call came I wouldn't breathe a word of anything to anyone beyond my own house. I hadn't even told cousin Joe or John Delaney. It was naive of me not to ask Stewart for any more information. He was probably surprised that I wasn't more inquisitive, but looking back I think it illustrated well enough my state of mind and my overwhelming priority. I wanted to be away to Leeds. Nothing else mattered.

The clock ticked past five and then half past and I was getting more anxious by the minute. I asked myself how much difference one phone call could make to your life. All the difference in the world was the answer. The call came at 5.45. I charged into the neighbour's house. Hal Stewart said simply, 'Bring your bag up on Monday morning, Joe. You're going on a train ride.' There was no more, but there didn't need to be.

I burst back into my house and told my parents. Concern registered on my mother's face. My father didn't say a lot but I could see he was absolutely delighted. I might have wanted more of a reaction, more acknowledgement of my sense that my world had changed forever, but looking back, I think I have a better idea of my father's feelings. He had always made it plain how much pleasure he had drawn from watching John and me play the game. He had made the long journey to Greenock to watch me play mostly reserve football, and on a day that previously he had reserved for watching his beloved Celtic. So when he heard that I had progressed to this new, extraordinary level, his feelings and his demeanour were consistent. Inside, there was no question he was glowing.

I had to tell Joe and John Delaney. I rounded them up and we went down to a steelworkers' club near Motherwell. It got busy there on a Sunday night but I wanted to get out of Cleland for a few hours. I told the boys my news and at first they were speechless. Leeds United! Over the beer I nursed, as always, I told them of how Bobby Collins had broken the news, how he had mentioned it almost as an aside as he walked away after getting changed in the dressing room, and how the long days had dragged since I first heard the word. We talked a little of the past and the possibilities that lay before me. I said that I would miss them but they would always be with me. The boys toasted my future before we got the 43 bus back to Cleland.

It was hard to sleep because so much was racing through my mind. How would I fare, still a mere boy, among the big men of Leeds United? I thought of the past, too. I thought of the fleeting time at Morton, and how, amid all the frustrations and anxiety about making it, there had been some great days. I'd played against Celtic, coming on as a substitute at Parkhead. We lost but I would never forget the thunder of the crowd and the sheer thrill of treading the holy ground in a big match. Most satisfyingly, there was the time we beat Rangers 2–0 at Ibrox. I started the game and although I didn't score, I got involved in a move that resulted in a goal for Collins, my hero and, as it would soon turn out, the man who put in the word that carried me to where I had always wanted to be, at the top of the professional game. Collins lashed in the ball from close range, and in his body language at that moment of triumph you could see that, even at that late stage of his career, all his passion for football and the hard edge of competitiveness were in full working order. Collins played Sunday football into his sixties. Only age could interfere with his rage to play – and to win.

Morton, I reflected, was a happy club even though it was involved in a permanent struggle to exist. I thought of the time I had waited in the corridor outside the office to receive my wages, and then been given half of them and told to come back in a few days to collect the rest. I thought of the anxiety about whether the dyeing of the first-team strip to a garish lemon would take properly. There would be no such problems at Leeds United but it came to me as I tossed and turned, perhaps there would be others. Would I be strong enough to exert my presence among those great players and self-confident characters? Would I be strong enough, and not too gauche? Could I earn some respect?

Such worries mingled with excitement as I walked down to the bus-stop, past the old brick works and the war monument display-ing the names of those scores of men who went to France with the well-founded fear that they would never see the village again. I was taking the bus to a meeting point with some of the Morton players. We drove up to the club and after training, Hal Stewart took me to Glasgow and put me on the train to England. Finally, he told me I was going to Leeds. He said I should be proud I was going to a great team and I said, yes, I was. I didn't need to add that I believed I was embarking on the journey of my life.

3

NO EASY RITES OF PASSAGE

IN the bag I lifted on to the rack in the second-class carriage of the train to Leeds I had two prized possessions. One was an oilskin coat I had worn to the architect's office. I was rather proud of it. My mother thought it gave me an air of distinction. 'It makes you look like a young professional man,' she said with an approving nod when I brought it home, and on the train up to Glasgow more than once I fancied it had helped earn me an admiring glance from a pretty commuter heading for her office.

The other much-valued item was a sweater of the finest Arran wool knitted by my mother. It was the kind of garment – as was soon pointed out to me with some force – you might see on the front of a women's magazine or a romantic novel. The coat and the sweater, I suppose, were part of the way I wanted to see myself – a young man keen to achieve something in life and own a few fine things – but I would go to Leeds United's Elland Road ground wearing my oilskin coat just a few times. The sweater also made the briefest of appearances, a single airing at one of the club's golf days. The fate of my fancy coat and sweater was swift and inevitable. They were dumped in the rubbish bin, along with a few of my illusions about making an instant impact on one of the great football teams of England.

When Billy Bremner, who had once told a football writer that his teeth looked like a row of condemned houses, first saw the sweater his mouth opened wide, and then a great scowl came to his pale features. He said, 'Jesus Christ, where did you find that?' Peter Lorimer and Eddie Gray were similarly dismissive of the coat, as were the rest of my new team-mates, when I reported for caddie duties at Moor Allerton golf course. Billy said the jumper made me look like Val Doonican, the folksy Irish singer who filled our television screens with an endless array of brightly coloured woollies. I didn't take it as a compliment. Even Peter and Eddie, the two Scottish players I had been placed between in the dressing room – natural allies, I thought – could only roll their eyes and mutter their disbelief.

At Leeds United, I discovered there were no easy rites of passage. First you had to be stripped bare. Whoever you were, and whatever you had done, was put under a new and fierce scrutiny. You were tested as strenuously off the field as on it. The reaction to the oilskin coat and sweater had nothing to do with anybody's idea of taste. They might have been some artifacts in some ancient ritual of survival and if you couldn't handle the process, well, it was a quick sign that you weren't going to make it.

No doubt it was painful. A lot of needling and baiting went on just about constantly, but it was the making of you in a strange way. You had to make some quick decisions about whether you were going to give some of it back, get a little tactical, or take another course. I knew myself well enough. I didn't want to duel verbally with Bremner or Giles. My decision was to keep my head down and get on with it. This was a team, I reflected later, that didn't just happen upon the means of competing harder and more ruthlessly than any of their rivals. It was a way of playing and living born of ferocious attitudes.

My four front teeth, of which I was also quite proud, were early victims of my immersion in the culture of Don Revie's team. Two of them were kicked out of my head, and another two loosened and subsequently lost, in one of my first appearances for Leeds, a reserve game against Coventry City.

There was hardly anyone on the terraces of Highfield Road stadium, but that did nothing to lessen my sense that I was already playing for my football life. A ball was hooked into the box low and hard and so naturally I dived for it. Already I was imbued with the need to compete a little more intensely than anyone who might stand in my path, but my reward on this occasion was to collide with the boot of a Coventry defender.

I played on until half-time but I was losing quite a bit of blood and felt groggy. Syd Owen, the former England international centre-half who was in charge of the reserve team, said that I should get dressed, which I did, carefully placing the lost teeth in an inside pocket of my jacket. In those less sophisticated days, however, it was a forlorn gesture. When I got back to Leeds I called the club dentist in some panic after looking at myself in the mirror, and when I went round to his surgery he said that I would have to wait for a few weeks before getting the denture that would repair the extremely serious damage to my smile. In a new city, where I so wanted to make my mark, it was a nightmare. When I called home and spoke to cousin Joe, he was eager to know how things were going.

'Aye, things are great, Joe,' I said through still wounded gums and lips. It wouldn't have been right to weep down the phone.

As I talked to Joe I recalled ruefully a phrase that had pounded in my head on the first day I travelled down from Scotland heading, officially at last, to Elland Road. 'Oh God,' I said to the rhythm of the wheels passing over the rails, 'don't let anything go wrong now.' Another thought that had been running through my head ever since that morning when I joined my team-mates on the road to Morton one last time, was the sheer fortitude of the club I was about to join.

In the spring cousin Joe and I had seen them battle so memorably with Celtic, and then, after that heart-breaking defeat so near to the great prize of European football, and finishing second to Everton in the first-division title race – a brilliant

Everton served so well by the midfield axis of Alan Ball, Howard Kendall and Colin Harvey – they lost the FA Cup final, in a replay, to Chelsea. I thought of how superbly they had played in the first game at Wembley, how Eddie Gray had slaughtered Dave Webb at right-back, and how victory would surely have come had Gary Sprake not made two critical errors in goal. My new team-mates had simply run out of their legs and finished with nothing, but in all that disappointment you could see the greatness of them. Don Revie, who was such a massive name in the game and had assembled all this competitive character, had also picked out me.

The Morton lads, the captain Billy Gray, Tommy Coakley and Gerry Sweeney, were delighted for me. They had plenty of experience – Tommy had been at Arsenal and Sweeney had played for Celtic – and they all said that I had fought hard for my chance. On the drive to training all three of them gave me advice about how I should meet the challenge. They also said that I deserved to get some cash bonus out of the deal. Morton, after all, were getting £15,000 from Leeds, with the possibility of £5,000 more if I made it through to the first team, and they had paid Blantyre Vics a mere £250. The boys said I should ask Stewart for a grand, but when I plucked up the courage he shook his head and said brusquely, 'No chance, son.' I protested, but quite feebly, because the truth was that really I was ready to walk to Leeds and Stewart, man of the world that he was, knew it well enough.

Bobby Collins, who would later become a godfather to one of my children, had warned me that I was going to a tough school, but he knew I wanted to make it to the top of the game, and he couldn't think of a better place to learn how to do that. Even so, the early going was tougher than I could have imagined, and this was quite apart from the loss of my teeth and the enforced retirement of key parts of my wardrobe.

Collins, I learned quickly enough, had been the cornerstone of the team that, while never loved beyond the borders of their own city, had come to command respect in every corner of the game. In those first days at Leeds I learned much about the legacy of my sponsor Collins. It was in so many ways a ferocious one.

Maurice Lindley, the assistant manager, met me at the station in Leeds when I first arrived from Glasgow and drove me to the Faversham Hotel in the university district. It wasn't a luxurious place; there were no airs and graces. In fact, it was hardly a step up from the modest establishments in which I'd stayed on the road with Morton, but it was clean and informal and guaranteed not to intimidate a kid from Cleland. It had also, I learned, been good enough for the likes of Giles, Bremner and Allan Clarke. Lindley said I should get a good night's sleep because I faced a busy day. I had to have a medical, complete the signing and be introduced to my team-mates. I didn't get much sleep as I thought about the pressure that lay ahead of me. As I watched the first streaks of dawn appear in the sky, I tried to visualise how it would be up at Elland Road, how much different from the Cappielow ground beside the shipyards, with its faded paint and seagull droppings. Never before had I felt so alone.

Lindley was right. It was a busy day. It was also devastating. I failed the medical. There was something odd about the rhythm of my heart. The club doctor – Doc Adams – said he would have to make another check the following day. Revie was at home, sick, on that first day but when I saw him briefly later in the week he welcomed me and said I shouldn't worry about the medical. Maybe I was a little too excited about joining a big club. Things would settle down.

Looking back, I can see why my heart might have been racing. The reality of the challenge I faced as a boy among professionals hardened by years of campaigning at the top of the game in England, in Europe and on the international stage had struck home as I walked through the car park. There I saw the World Cup cars of Jack Charlton, Terry Cooper, Allan Clarke and trainer Les Cocker. They were brightly painted Ford Cortina Es but they might as well have been war chariots. I saw Bremner and Johnny Giles, the field generals, the England strikers Clarke and Mick Jones, and the brilliant younger guns, Paul Madeley, Eddie Gray and Peter Lorimer, and suddenly the Corn Patch seemed a long way away indeed.

I went back to the Faversham in a fever of concern that the great adventure might be over before it had truly begun. At least Purdie Kane had a season or two south of the border. He had walked the stage without a skittering heart. Was Leeds a jump too far, too soon? I thought again of the tumult of that game at Parkhead, when cousin Joe and I strained on tiptoes to watch the roaring action, and into all the excitement, the sheer thrill of coming down to this place of heroes, came for the first time a touch of dread. It was unthinkable that the years of effort, and dreaming, should end in something so ignominious as a failed medical. What could I say if I had to trail back to Morton, and take my bag home to Cleland? Again I watched the dawn coming up over Leeds, and this time with as much foreboding as hope and curiosity.

When the doctor said, 'You're OK, lad, that must have been some kind of blip yesterday,' I thought I might collapse with relief. I was given a peg in the dressing room and the address of some digs. I was Joe Jordan, Leeds United, and the dream had been made real.

My new salary, £35 a week basic, was less than expected. I'd imagined I would be on something like £100 a week, but I was told there would be bonuses and, above all, the great opportunity I craved. I would eventually pick up £500 in signing bonuses from Morton, but not before going to Revie to tell him that a second payment of £250 was due. It came through quickly enough after that but as a player in those days it always seemed that you had to argue over everything, including those things that had already been agreed. My contract was for eighteen months, which meant the best part of two seasons.

It may sound bizarre today, when schoolboy players are guaranteed professional contracts worth hundreds of thousands of pounds at the age of seventeen, but I wasn't at Leeds for the money. I was chasing down glory. I would have chance enough to make my mark, said Revie.

Unexpected hazards had to be faced, beyond the need to strip down my wardrobe. One of the most troubling was the risk of being awarded a yellow bib, which was given to the worst player in training. To receive it was to invite terrible scorn. In one of my first training sessions, the shame fell on the great, World Cup-winning Jack Charlton. He was incensed and drawled out his bitter complaints. Jack always felt he was the subject of wind-up conspiracies and, I learned quickly, not entirely without cause. Once, he had returned to his new car to find a melting snowman sitting in the passenger seat, and on numerous occasions a bucket of water was emptied on him over the partition of the lavatory cubicle where he sat inelegantly reading the *Racing Post*. Jack would burst through the door, screaming for revenge. During card games he would convince himself that he was the victim of a conspiracy and on one occasion he gathered up the deck and threw it out of the window of the team bus. However childish they might have appeared on the surface, I realised quickly enough that those pranks and training rituals were all part of a wider game. They had a hard purpose, which was to feel out the strengths and weaknesses of each individual as they melded into a team driven in a way I could never have imagined in my first fleeting exposure to the demands of the professional game at Morton.

History has been harsh on the team I joined as it moved towards the peak of its powers. Some of the critical judgement is easy enough to understand – Leeds did always look for an edge, often by unscrupulously putting pressure on match officials, and were willing to intimidate any opponents in whom they scented a particular weakness – but it was often accompanied by a failure to grasp the dimension of greatness. Even today, acceptance of some of that quality in the team of Giles and Bremner and the men who operated so fiercely around them is muted. As someone who felt the force of the club's ambition, and the unwillingness to be beaten down by the disappointments that are inevitable if you compete so hard on so many fronts, year in year out, you just have to shrug away the failure to win over the critics. The decade when Leeds were right up there was marked by a level of competition that is hard to grasp today when the pool of potential champions is reduced to no more than three clubs. To be at Leeds then was to experience something that would always be part of you for as long you sought to compete, properly and with everything you had.

The greatness of Revie's Leeds may have been flawed to a degree. Maybe it would have been better if he had concentrated more on the skill and creativity available, but the commitment to stretching the team's competitive limits was utterly remarkable. In no way had ambition been slaked by the astonishing speed with which they had established themselves among the élite of both English and European football. They had come so far so quickly, and in those first weeks of my time at the club it was clear enough to me why it was so. There was a special look in the eyes of my new team-mates. It was one that said defeat would always be an imposter, something simply not to be recognised for longer than the time it took to play your next match.

Revie's genius was to recognise and develop that competitive character, and soon I realised why it was that he had moved so quickly to sign me on such scant physical evidence of my potential. Collins had said that I played like a man, that I didn't hide from any of the action, and that I hated to lose. When Collins said that to Revie, almost all other credentials became superfluous. Collins had used the words guaranteed to open most doors at Elland Road. He said that I played like a man and when I looked around the Elland Road dressing room, I saw that this was something Revie prized quite as much as any natural ability. He looked you in the eyes and it was as though he was searching for clues about how you would perform under pressure. Whenever a player went on to the training field, he was aware that at some point Revie's gaze would be boring into him. It gave an edge to everything you did and encouraged good habits. You never wanted to waste the ball or have somebody run away from you with it unhindered, if by some mischance you happened to have allowed it out of your possession.

The demands did not end when you came into the dressing room and showered. At all times you had to be a professional. This didn't mean I had to turn myself into a choirboy. I just had to keep my eyes and ears open. The result was a dressing room that seethed with peculiar resentments, and seemed to spend much of its time inventing reasons for dissent, but then became utterly united at the first call to action. Never before or afterwards would I ever know such a force of separate wills and attitudes applied to the common purpose of winning a football match.

In fact, there were two dressing rooms. Revie liked the first teamers and the reserves to mingle, so he split both teams in half and put one group in the home dressing room while the others used the one reserved for the away team on match days. In one way I was lucky in those early days to be assigned to the away room, away from the players who were most dominant in shaping the attitudes of the first team – Giles, Bremner and Charlton. I wasn't sure why Revie placed me between Gray and Lorimer. Maybe it was because we were all Scots, or perhaps it was out of the manager's conviction that Eddie and Peter had made such sure progress in their careers, the chances were that some of their already huge accumulated experience would rub off on me. They certainly helped me settle in after contributing so fully to that first assault on my dress sense.

Lorimer was a happy-go-lucky character, but a ferocious performer on the field. Gray was a little more intense, partly perhaps because he had such a rough time with injuries. He was a great team-mate and a wonderful performer with the ball at his feet. Many years later, Eddie was a superb first-team coach when Leeds United marched to the semi-finals of the European Cup under the managership of David O'Leary. I was terribly saddened when he was pushed aside in favour of Brian Kidd. Eddie was gutted, you could see that in his eyes, and whatever the talent of Kidd, you have to say it was a bad move. Eddie had earned the trust of the players, and they associated him with some of their best days. Now that regret can only be deepened by the relegation from the Premiership of an impoverished Leeds and the disappearance of Gray from a club he cared about so passionately.

Such a change of direction in a crucial role at a time when the club was already besieged by the problems that came with the trial of Lee Bowyer and Jonathan Woodgate would have been unthinkable in the regime of Revie. Cocker, Lindley and Owen were the bulwarks of a tight-knit family. Revie set the tone of everything, hand-picking his players and his coaches, and bedding them down in a zone of concentrated effort that was always jealously guarded. He wrestled with the smallest details in order to gain an edge. A cultured player in his own days for Leicester City, Manchester City and England, he had seen Collins up close on the field and, in the classic way of football management, it was a case of being drawn to an opposite. Revie could see in the little man qualities that he lacked himself – ferocity in the tackle and a mean sense of turning everything that happened on the pitch to his team's advantage.

Once, I sat in the dressing room and listened to Charlton talking about his admiration for Collins. Jack had not been the most committed of professionals at one point in his career, and Revie had felt it necessary to give him a hard talk about what he needed to do to be part of Leeds' future. It was, Revie said, really quite basic. He had to follow the lead of the barrel-chested little Scotsman, who was handed the job of laying down his team's values.

Charlton was distraught when Collins suffered a badly broken leg in a Fairs Cup tie in Turin, which drew a savage line under the best of his career. Collins didn't whine about his fate. He had been ruthless in his time and in the end he paid the price. When the bill was delivered, he took it philosophically. It was plainly a lesson that had gone to the very core of the Leeds thinking.

Revie, of course, knew that Collins had limited time as the general of Leeds. He was already in his thirties when he arrived at Elland Road, and his years in the game had been remorselessly hard. So Revie took great care in ensuring that the baton was passed into safe hands. He had made John Giles Collins' lieutenant and natural successor. It was an almost seamless transition as Giles moved inside from the wing, where he had so distinguished himself in Manchester United's 1963 FA Cup victory over Leicester City.

Here again, we saw the durability of a key Leeds performer. Giles had been deeply disappointed at Old Trafford, the club he had joined as a boy after dreaming, as I would later, of emulating heroes Jimmy Delaney and his great compatriot Johnny Carey while playing street football beside the Dublin quays. Giles' face didn't fit at Old Trafford and, despite a match-winning performance at Wembley and clear evidence that he was a player of great craft and outstanding potential, he was allowed to drift to second division Leeds. Busby said later that it was his great mistake. His rejected protégé arrived at Elland Road a driven man, and part of the force came from his desire to haunt his old club, which he did with great effect for more than a decade.

Giles was, like Revie, a skilful player but he realised more quickly than most that he was operating in a time when the niceties of your game could easily be swept aside if you weren't tough enough, both physically and mentally, to take pre-emptive action sometimes. He made it clear that he wasn't going to be anyone's target and the result was the quiet but menacing authority of a gunfighter. Having one such midfielder was a tremendous asset, having two was a gift from the football heavens. Giles and Bremner complemented each other superbly. Giles was the cool field-general figure while Bremner built his reputation with his energy and tremendous skill and imagination while going forward.

Sometimes I would sit beside Giles on the team coach and, like all the younger players, I came to value the experience hugely. John wasn't a cards player. On trips he would take a good book and spend quite a bit of time reading, as would I, but sometimes he was in the mood to talk. He was at his most fascinating when the chosen subject was the game and I began to understand how it was that he was so clinical on the field, how he always knew where to pass the ball and was never caught in possession. Small and compact, he had tremendous balance and, more than any other quality, fantastic vision.

When he described his view of the game, there was always one priority – simplicity. It was, he said, using one great example, the essence of Pele's brilliance, the reason why he would probably always be the greatest player the world had ever known. In the normal course of a game, you wouldn't see any extravagance from Pele. He would call upon his extraordinary natural gifts only when they were required to get him out of trouble or inflict some dramatic, vital hurt on the opposition. If there was a simple ball to play, he would play it. It was never an issue of a long ball or a short ball, just the right ball.

Giles never preached but said that all of us had to look out for the best examples in the game. He particularly admired the artistry and timing of Johnny Haynes' passing. He recalled how, as a young Manchester United player, he had gone along to Maine Road to see Haynes play for Fulham against Manchester City. He was stunned by the brilliance of Haynes' masterclass, and he told us that when he walked away from City's ground he formed an unshakeable ambition. He wanted to run a game in the way Johnny Haynes did it.

Giles had a few sayings you couldn't forget. One of them that has always lingered particularly strongly in my mind is that football is a simple game but a hell of a lot of work has to go into making it so. He led by example. He looked after himself. After training, he went home, or to his hotel room. Billy Bremner was quite different in many ways. He was more volatile, you could never be quite sure of his moods, but when the big games came you knew that he would be on the balls of his feet. He had a genius for making an impact when it mattered most. Billy loved nothing more than to score a spectacular goal in a big European game. On those occasions he was puffed up like a fighting cock, hungry for the action and the glory. Revie, I was told, had once ordered him on to his knees to thank God for all the benefits football had brought him. There must have been many times when Revie offered a more specific prayer of thanks of his own. It was that Bremner had not slipped through the Leeds net.

Giles played every game the same, he was relentless about detail. In their different ways, Giles and Bremner were second to none. They were the leaders, the men I had to follow, but the standards that had been set at the club were accepted implicitly by everyone. Norman Hunter was astonishing in his single-mindedness. Around much of the game he had a reputation as one of the ultimate hard men, and that was a standing no doubt well earned, but there was so much more to him than that. He had a wonderful temperament and excellent skills. Before a game his concentration was perfect. We could see him sizing up the opposition and it filled us with confidence, perhaps quite as much as it chilled the blood of our opponents. Paul Madeley was another phenomenal talent. He was known as the Rolls-Royce and the reason was self-evident when he moved imperiously on to the ball.

You did everything you could to meet these standards, or you were obliged to walk away. It was arduous work and, for a little while, when I realised how much I had to do to build up the necessary strength, particularly physically, the challenge was daunting. At moments of crisis, though, I received vital encouragement from Revie. Maybe he saw in my eyes a little fear that the challenge might be too great, but whatever the reason, he said to me on several occasions, 'Keep at it, Joe. You're doing well. You have the right attitude.'

I stayed in the Faversham for a week before moving into my first digs in a semi-detached house a short walk from Elland Road. Like everything else to do with the football club, the digs were carefully vetted by Revie. I stayed there for a little while with Lee Boyd, a young Geordie lad who was trying to make it at centre-half, in the footsteps of his fellow north-easterner big Jack. He was good and he shared all of my dreams but football can accommodate only so many and sadly Lee didn't make it. He joined the great legion of talented youngsters who were obliged to take as their one consolation the fact that they had tried and given it everything they could.

Soon I moved into new digs with two other young professionals, Terry Yorath and Brian Stuart. Yorath would have a fine career with Leeds, Coventry and Spurs, and moved to North America for a spell under the coaching of Giles at Vancouver Whitecaps. In a wide-ranging football career, 'Taffy' also coached his Welsh national team.

Stuart, a Yorkshire lad, was eventually given a free transfer by Leeds. His career was wrecked by a car accident, one of those random twists of fate that have ended so many hopeful journeys in football. The odds against the mishap that destroyed his prospects were sickeningly high. His car was misfiring and he pulled on to the hard shoulder of the motorway. When a breakdown truck arrived, Brian got out of his car and was standing between the two vehicles. At that moment, someone fell asleep at the wheel and ploughed into Stuart's car. He was caught in the crush and his legs were terribly mangled. He was a tough lad, ambitious as anyone, and he refused to quit. He had always looked after himself but the blow was too heavy. He had lost his chance in the big-time.

When I think of him now, I recall the good times we had in Mrs Gledhill's big house, where I was fitted into the attic. There were three sons in the house and we all got on well together. We had a great time in the digs, and ate ferociously well, with appetites primed by all the training. At lunch-times we augmented our diets with visits to Sheila's Café across the road from the club. It was run by Yorath's future mother-in-law and was a place where the younger players could rub shoulders, very respectfully of course, with the great men of the team as they ate their bacon and sausage sandwiches and, in many cases, discussed the form at Catterick, Wetherby and Doncaster.

Looking back now, I see it as one of the sweetest times of my life. Everything was so fresh and so much was before me. I was getting stronger and my fears of feeling that tap on the shoulder and hearing the awful news that I was not going to make it, as Lee Boyd had done, were beginning to dwindle. I had new teeth and a refurbished smile and I had no reason to believe someone would slump over a steering wheel and wreck the dream that I was now living. I could call cousin Joe and tell him that things were indeed going as well as I had hoped that night, which now seemed so long ago, when I shared a few beers with him and John Delaney in the steelworkers' club in Motherwell.

Already I had done a few things and seen a few places, including the big old, passionate stadium in Turin where, just a year after I had watched them with cousin Joe on tippy toes at Hampden Park, Leeds United successfully played the first leg of the last Fairs Cup final against the great club Juventus – the competition was to be superseded by a new one for the Uefa Cup. I didn't play but I was a member of the first-team squad and this time I got an excellent view of the action. There was the additional satisfaction that I had played a part in the triumph, admittedly a small one, but significant in terms of the development of my career. I had been on the bench at Anfield for the first leg of the semi-final against Liverpool, when Billy Bremner scored one of his patented big-game goals. In the second game at Elland Road I came off the bench when Jack Charlton was injured.

It was a good measure of my progress. Revie had taken me to one side to tell me that I was a little way off the mark in terms of strength. I had to work hard to get into the position where I could truly challenge for a first-team place. It was a critical moment, but again I had told myself that I would fight my way through. Now I could tell myself the effort had been worthwhile. Not only did I eat bacon sandwiches with the gods, I went on to the field with them. I was just nineteen years and few months old and, as they say in Mafia circles, I felt as though I was a made man.

4

THE MOST PAINFUL BUSINESS

F OR a long stretch of your life it is easy to believe that everything is in order. You have figured everything out, you know all the moves, and the rest of your existence is simply going to fall into place. It is the prettiest of thoughts but the lesson of time is that one day life is going to step up and crack you in the mouth, or somewhere even more vulnerable.

There was, anyway, just one speck of cloud in the bright blue skies of that spring of 1971. It confirmed a suspicion that whatever happened to me in the wider world beyond Cleland, I would always be linked to the village by something more than the mere iron chains of memory. The roots of the place ran wider and deeper than I could have imagined when I stepped on to the train at Queen Street station for the first leg of my journey into exile. I could leave Cleland, I had already learned, but I couldn't shake it off. The concern was nagging and specific. It was to do with the fact that of the three little Jordans who once shared a bed, only one of them looked into a future that hadn't been mapped. For me, that represented a terror of uncertainty. I didn't want loose ends. I wanted for my family what I wanted for myself. I wanted us to be all of a piece, all sure about where we were going.

As my football life began to fall into place and I received the affirming nod of the great Don Revie with the growing sense that soon I would be fulfilling my ambitions in the great stadiums of

England and Europe, my big sister Elizabeth was about to qualify as a nurse from a training hospital in Glasgow. She, too, would come to England, first to York – a city she loved for the grace of the period buildings, the charm of the narrow cobbled streets so different from the industrial moonscape of Lanarkshire – then to Leeds, where she would meet her doctor husband, Alan Sager, before going off with him to live in Lincolnshire. Liz was set and, it seemed to me, so was I. The problem that loomed so large in my mind – and seemed quite insoluble until I found the courage to talk to Revie about it – was our kid brother, John.

Liz and I had always known what we wanted to do with our lives. We had dreams but, more importantly, we had plans of campaign. Liz worked at her books. I played football with ferocious intent. Our lives were on course. For John, it was enough for him just to live the one he had been given. Right from the start, he did it in a clatter of high jinks. His laughter filled our little house. While Liz and I sought to escape Cleland, John embraced it in a way I never could. He was always happy in his own skin and his own environment.

John had a view of life that was different from mine, but I understood it perfectly. I wanted things he didn't and vice versa, and although we were brothers I suppose we couldn't have been more different in our demands on life and ourselves. My ambitions wouldn't make much sense in the world he wanted to create for himself, but then nor did his in mine. It meant that down the years we would collide always with the same pleasure. We stepped out of our separate worlds and were brothers as close and as different in our natures as we had been growing up in Cleland.

John was like the wind. He blew this way and that but he always reappeared in my life, sometimes with money in his pocket, sometimes not, but never ever asking for a penny, never dreaming of putting the bite on a brother who had always put much greater store on working towards a goal and then enjoying its rewards. He was as warm as he was free and there was never a time of night or morning so ungodly that, after reaching out for the phone, I didn't welcome the sound of his voice.

In common with 99 per cent of Cleland boys he loved to play football, and he did it well. He followed me into the St Mary's Guild team, then St Aidan's. He was good, certainly good enough to put into practice my belief that if you wanted something enough, you could go out and get it if you had the will and the energy. John never wanted to put that theory to the test. Yes, he liked to play football but no more than listening to some music, or larking around with his pals at the Cross. When I looked at Cleland I saw a dead-end, a slow immersion into a life of defeat. For me, football was a means of expression and a passport to another life. For John, football was fun, an enjoyable part of life, but it was not something to sweat over or drive yourself against. He saw the football field as a place of some challenge, but also a distraction – no more, no less. He couldn't dedicate himself to football. There were other things to do.

When he was old enough to go into a pub, he did it with relish. At the same age I would have been travelling up to Glasgow for football and, just maybe, the respectability that would have been so pleasing to my mother. John, essentially, wanted good companionship and a good time.

Parents always insist they don't have favourites and ours were no exception, but Liz and I were under no illusions. John was the baby and, as is so often the case, he was the spoiled one, the jovial one, the loud one who was always the life and soul of any gathering. I tended to sit in the corner. I was quieter. I worried about my future – and his. I worried so much that finally I got up the nerve to go to see Revie in his office and tell him of my concerns for my brother's future. I told him about the bleak prospects in Lanarkshire, how there were a dozen applicants for every decent job, how the mines had gone and the big steelworks had closed down.

Revie nodded his understanding. He came from a poor background and he knew how it was when your family had to battle for a living. Later, I heard the theory that it was those hard early days that had shaped so much of Revie's football thinking. It made him a little pessimistic, and very conservative. The glass was always half empty and not a drop could be spilled. He said he would do what he could and within a day or two he told me that he had talked to somebody at Leeds City Council and there was a job for John. It was not a great job but it would be a start. It would pay him a few quid and get him going in life. It would get him out of Cleland.

John came down to Leeds and I got him a place at my latest digs, Mrs Gledhill having had to give up her business in order to look after her sick mother. He came to the big city with an entirely open mind, naturally, and soon enough it was for him a spectacularly larger version of Cleland, with a social agenda to match. He made friends easily, especially girlfriends.

By now Gordon McQueen had signed for Leeds from St Mirren and he joined us in the digs. It meant that before I met and married my wife Judith, we were young men about the city and John enjoyed every minute of it. Gordon and I were subject to the discipline imposed by Revie, but John found Leeds to be something of a recreational treasure house after Cleland. It was a new world of clubs and a wide choice of pubs. You could get prawn cocktails and exotic drinks and there were always plenty of girls around anyone who had a touch of celebrity. So John, the young companion of two rising footballers, could enjoy himself without having to sweat it out in the morning. One Christmas Eve, when Gordon and I were off the leash – we didn't have a game over the holiday period – we had a few drinks in a pub before being invited to a party in a fancy restaurant. Eventually, we left for home well bevvied and in possession of a cold, cooked duck. It provided us with a fine, late supper and when went to our beds we left a carcass and some well-stripped bones. On Christmas morning we awakened to cries of alarm from our Scottish landlady, Mrs Jones. For some anguished moments she thought we had demolished the Christmas dinner.

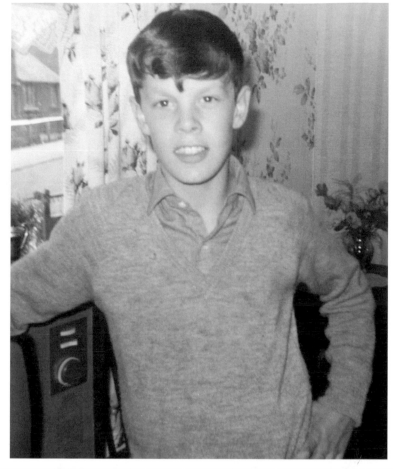

Right: The face of ambition, at ten years old.

Below: My first professional environment – Greenock Morton, circa 1970, and the men who shaped my future. *Front row, extreme right*: the great player Bobby Collins. *Second row, extreme right*: Hal Stewart, the manager-entrepreneur.

Two great captains, Billy Bremner of Leeds and Billy McNeill of Celtic, prepare for one of their greatest battles – Hampden Park in 1970 in the semi-finals of the European Cup. Celtic won an unforgettable match. I was in the crowd, on tippy toes.

The man who picked me out, Leeds United manager Don Revie, analyses the action, ramrod trainer Les Cocker at his shoulder.

My first match for Leeds – 23 October 1971 at Elland Road against Everton – and a moment of anxiety. Terry Cooper challenges John Hurst as Paul Reaney (2) stands guard and (*left to right*) myself, Jack Charlton and Norman Hunter look on.

Jack Charlton waits at the near post.

The FA Cup semi-final against Wolves at Maine Road, 1973. My father joined the post-game celebrations.

Wembley bound, Leeds United salute their fans. *Left to right*: Billy Bremner, David Harvey, Paul Reaney, Terry Yorath, Trevor Cherry, Peter Lorimer, me, Jack Charlton and Allan Clarke.

Job done, the 1973–74 league title is gathered in. Billy Bremner raises the trophy, Peter Lorimer offers Gordon McQueen champagne, and Paul Reaney, lost in his thoughts, puts his hand over my shoulder.

The call from Scotland. Team-mates (*left to right*) Billy Bremner, Gordon McQueen, David Harvey, Peter Lorimer and Eddie Gray share my pleasure. My sweater appears to have been forgiven, but then maybe Eddie Gray had no option.

My headed goal against Czechoslovakia sent Scotland to the World Cup finals in 1974 – the first time in sixteen years.

A word in the ear of genius. I consult with Jimmy Johnstone during the 1974 home international with England at Hampden Park.

Raiding against Zaire – World Cup baptism.

Billy Bremner's World Cup agony. His shot goes just the wrong side of the Brazilian post – a moment that might have changed Scottish football history.

Billy Bremner's classic Jack-in-the-box embrace after my equaliser against Yugoslavia in the decisive World Cup group game – a flash of hope that came too late.

The Jordan clan. *Left to right*: brother John, sister Elizabeth and me.

The great Jimmy Delaney, with my parents, heads the welcome committee in Cleland when I return from my first World Cup.

John had a feel for the music business, and through contacts made in the clubs he found employment working for a number of bands, including Bryan Ferry's and Black Sabbath. He sold T-shirts and records, sometimes officially, sometimes not. He wasn't building a career but simply living the way he wanted, dealing with today rather than some point in the future. John hit the road running, and then I saw him, as did my parents back in Cleland, only when he decided it was time to rest up a little and re-charge his batteries.

He would return to Cleland and, after seeing our parents, head straight for Kelly's. He would stand the drinks and tell the boys about how it was travelling across Europe, doing the gigs, moving the show, but always having time for a few drinks and a little fun. It wasn't always possible, he suggested, to fight off the girls. He was painting a vivid new world for the boys in Kelly's.

After Judith and I were married and started to have our children, John would come bursting into our house, wherever it happened to be, laden with presents. He spent his money in great, generous bursts and when it was gone, he would live within his means. Once he showed up in Oslo when I was playing for Scotland in a World Cup qualifying game. He had driven halfway across Europe to say hello and cheer me on. Whatever success I had, he always conveyed a sense of joy about it. Never once did I feel a breath of resentment that I had achieved some success while he scuffled for a living. He made it clear it was the way he had chosen, and the way he enjoyed living his life.

When I was playing for Manchester United and living in the well-heeled Cheshire village of Prestbury, our son Thomas was born and we asked John to be a godfather. He was delighted but, unfortunately, he didn't make it in time for the baptism. He slept in and Bobby Collins, my football godfather, stepped into the vacancy. John showed up later, bedraggled and apologetic. He had fallen out of bed in Leeds, he said, and run into the street and hailed a taxi. He ordered it to Prestbury and the bill was £90. I was obliged to shake my head in disbelief, and a little wonderment, as I was some years later when I was playing for AC Milan and received a call at 5.30 a.m. He was at Monza railway station. On this occasion he didn't have the price of a taxi, but he was bundled up with presents for the kids.

By then I had stopped hoping that John would settle down and build himself a little security. He liked it so much precisely the way it was. He could range across Europe, living from day to day. He had his base camp in Lanarkshire, where our parents kept his room and his friends were always ready to receive him with the old warmth. He could seek out my family and me wherever we were, and that was a touch of the permanence he was not inclined to fashion for himself.

Before I was married, John joined Brian Stuart, Gordon and me on a trip to Majorca and somewhere along the coast from Palma we met up with the young Kenny Dalglish and some of his friends. We drank quite modest amounts of beer and wine, but we were filled with the excitement of young men who knew what they wanted from life and were in the process of getting it. Later, when I was playing for Southampton, John rolled up after a Saturday match and I took him out with some of my new team-mates. Kevin Bond, whose father John had played for West Ham and managed Norwich City and Manchester City, and Jimmy Case, the former Liverpool player who was such a good, hard, clinical professional, were in the company. John listened to the football talk, made some entertaining contributions of his own, and in the morning was away on his travels.

That was one of his shorter visits but it lingers in my mind more vividly than any of the others because it marked the end of one of the happiest cycles in my family's life. It had been the last time John would come bursting into our house. A little later, on a Saturday night, I received a phone call from Sweden. A colleague of John's was calling to say, haltingly, that my brother had been in an accident and he had to tell me that it was bad.

In fact, John had died when the car he was travelling in as a passenger from one gig to the next had skidded into another car after hitting a patch of black ice. Nothing in my life had prepared me for such a shock. There were family tales of tragedy, the death of my grandfather in the pit, babies lost at birth, illness from the dust and the grind of the pits, but these were stories of old wounds that had had time to heal. The news that John was dead was shocking and unbelievable and numbing all at the same time. It hit me hard. Nothing before had even begun to touch me quite like this. It was a terrible intrusion into all the certainties I had built into my life, the most powerful one being that if you did your work, if you were dedicated enough to your ambition, things would always work out fine in the end. You could proof yourself against ambush, I insisted. Of course, you couldn't and now I knew. John's card was marked no matter what he did, I concluded bitterly when the first shock abated a little. The realisation was so harsh and sudden. John had never been ill, each of his days following the last one quite seamlessly. He never asked anyone for anything. You might think it would have been the most natural thing for him to ask for a little loan, £300 of walking-around money maybe, but there was never a question of that. He enjoyed a respite in our house, he amused and played with the kids, and then he needed to be off. He could never be in one place, however agreeable, for too long.

I packed a bag for Sweden and as I flew out, so many thoughts raced through my head. John was like so many of the lads with whom he had grown up in Cleland, boys who were happy to wile away their days in the village, doing the same thing, seeing the same faces. Most of those lads had no passion to see the world and escape the village, but they were alive now. They would have their drinks in Kelly's and go to their football matches, and John was in a mortuary beside a big, glassy Swedish lake. It was the emptiest feeling to think that he would never stand the drinks again at Kelly's as the boys crowded round to hear his stories, and he would never stride into my house, slumping into a chair with the presents tumbling down and my children crying with delight.

I was in Sweden for a week before I could take John's body back to Scotland. There had to be a post-mortem and an accident inquiry. Two people had died in the other car. The local police were kind and they took me to the hospital when I told them I needed the answers to some questions. Some of my questions no doubt came out a little strange. They were about everything and nothing. I wanted to know what he was wearing when he died, what were his last words before the crash. What had they been talking about as the miles flicked by? Was he wearing a sweatshirt? If some of the questions were indeed strange, stupid even, none of them received satisfactory answers. I suppose I was hooked on just one basic question, the big one – why? Why John, why at this time, in this remote place?

The boy who was driving the car happened to come from Southampton and I told him I was living there and I wanted him to come to see me when he was out of hospital. I understood that he might be in shock now, and no doubt that was also true of me. I had gone to the ward straight from the mortuary, where I had identified my brother's body. It was the most painful business. John had been thrown from the car and his body was found quite a distance from the point of impact. The boy in the hospital bed should call me when he felt up to recalling the details of what had happened. We could have a talk and maybe I could fill in some of the empty spaces. I was obsessed with the need to know what John's last words had been. I also wanted to know if he had been wearing a seat belt. There was no suggestion of drink driving, the accident had happened in the morning, but then it is also true that, in and around the music business, the margin between night and day can be quite slim.

The boy never called me and that gnawed at me for a long time. My brother had died violently and there was so much about his death I didn't know. I just had these bare images of a grey morning, a big lake, a squeal of rubber, and then, well, just the paperwork of death. I flew home to Scotland with John's body, and I knew that back in Cleland the lives of my parents had largely been destroyed.

In my own life, the black and white imperatives of the football man had finally been invaded. Football had shaped my life, provided all the drama that I had needed, but none of its highs and lows had prepared me for this kind of devastation. It was a new and terrible level of shock and it threw into doubt all my old certainties. I looked into my father's face and for the first time I saw that he was old. I had always thought that he would live forever. I knew, too, that my mother would never be the same.

The funeral in Cleland provided overwhelming evidence of the closeness of the community. St Mary's was overflowing with friends and relatives and quite a number of girlfriends. Indeed, that would have been hilarious on an occasion less sad. John's girlfriends made their way to Lanarkshire from places as far afield as Denmark, Manchester and London. One of them, Kathy Dwyer, was the mother of John's daughter, Vicky. We had heard about Vicky's existence just a year or so before John's death. Marriage had never been a serious prospect for John but it was good to know that he and Kathy had remained good friends after their parting, and it was a great satisfaction to my mother, particularly, as she grew old with the sadness of loss, to know that Kathy was such a good, natural mother. Vicky is a successful young businesswoman in Manchester now, holding down a responsible job with great efficiency. No doubt that aspect of her character came from her mother.

Unfortunately, my mother was obliged to suffer one more great sadness before she died of cancer in her eighties. She saw my father die, in great pain, after he had been taken into hospital and then, in a way that my sister Liz, with all her knowledge of medical practice, swore was diabolical, discharged. My father had been a smoker and it was a habit that my strong disapproval could never dislodge. Although he made it to the age of eighty-four, his last days were terrible. He had circulation problems and when they brought him back to hospital they decided they had to take away one of his legs. It was a terrible blow, and it was only then that I realised his life was coming to an end. When he died, Liz was incensed and made a series of official protests. Nothing came of it but she fought hard to register her complaints. She felt she owed our father that kind of protest. My mother slipped away quickly after that.

Although there were still plenty of reasons to return to Cleland from time to time, including seeing cousin Joe and his family, the Delaneys and all my friends, and to give Uncle Joe, as he sipped his banana rum, the latest progress report on my football career, there was no doubt a part of my life had ended.

Liz and I would always have the strongest memories of all that had shaped us in Cleland, but we had made our lives in new places and there was inevitably a heavy sadness as we returned to our separate homes after Mother's funeral. It was the pain of a final separation, the knowledge that so many of the promptings of our childhood and youth, which had been so fundamental to who and what we were, had been assigned to the past. My sister and I had broken away from the life that so many of our contemporaries had accepted as their lot, but we knew more strongly than ever before that it would never be too far from our hearts and our minds.

5

PASSING THE TESTS

YOU couldn't just bust your way into the Leeds first team, make a big show somewhere some raw night or Saturday afternoon and settle into the glory. You made a stride forward and then took one back. You came off the bench and tried to make an impact. You always worked to put that little bit extra in on the training field. You hated the idea of that yellow bib, or any hint that you had missed a stride. At Leeds, you grafted because if you didn't, you simply faced a full stop. At times it seemed you had to chip your reputation out of rock.

Sometimes it went better than on other occasions, but among the many tricks you had to acquire, the most important one was never to lose your head and get carried away with yourself. In the Leeds dressing room, under the gaze of Giles and Bremner, that would have been pretty much professional suicide. No, what you did was make sure you didn't run ahead of yourself. You kept your head down, did your work and made sure you were ready for when the call came.

Finally, it came for me in Leeds United's great season when Don Revie, driven to the wall, and public tears, by the criticism, even derision, directed at the team of which he was so proud, finally released the reins that he had always held so tightly, and said, 'Go out lads, go and play your game. You are better than I ever thought you could be. It would be wrong to hold you back.'

The declaration came after a shocking defeat by second division Sunderland in the 1973 FA Cup final. Revie spent the summer pondering the meaning of that defeat, and when we returned for the next season, all the caution fell away. Soon enough, no one could any longer dispute that Leeds United, with whom I had learned my trade, were truly a great team. Where the tendency had been to win an edge and then defend it in any practical and roughly legal way, now it was to express rich talent. After the hard insistence on winning, and then winning some more, now there were wonderful flights of imagination, great passing sequences. Once, Revie had taken the talented Terry Cooper on one side after he had played his way out of trouble down the line, and said that, yes, he had shown beautiful skill, but in future, when the game was tight, he should forget all that grace under pressure and boot the ball into the stand.

Of course, whatever Leeds did would be governed by that old sense of professionalism. There were still professional imperatives. Expression might be the air, but not self-indulgence or negligence. All the ground still had to be covered, which was fine by me because I would never forget that a key part of my game was a willingness to work. The great bonus for me was that I should graduate at Leeds at a time when the players were freed to explore all of their ability.

Before that, however, one more season for me was based mainly on that old, vital mixture of dedication and patience. In 1972–73 I played twenty-six times for the first team in various competitions, nineteen times as a starter. I played in a pre-season friendly game at Bradford and scored a goal, which is vital for a striker's confidence, at whatever level he finds himself operating. My first league game was against Everton, who provided a little sterner opposition. I didn't score but we won 3–2 and I made a decent contribution, running, fighting for the ball, holding it up when necessary, and Don Revie gave me a pat on the back. 'Well done, Joe,' he said. 'You didn't let us down.' It was another small rite of passage, something you could store away for the challenges of the future.

There was also a night of fantasy in 1971, a leap into the future that I hoped so fervently would take me on to the great battle-fields of football. Revie told me that I would be playing in the Nou Camp in Barcelona. Leeds, as the last winners of the Fairs Cup, would play Barcelona, who had been the first team to land the trophy. It wouldn't be the most important game the club had ever played, more a money-raiser for Uefa, but the manager thought it would be good encouragement for some of the young players.

The terraces of the vast and beautiful stadium were not packed but on a soft, warm night there was more than enough atmo-sphere for a nineteen-year-old still feeling his way into big-time football. Barcelona took the lead in the second half but we went right back at them with a goal. I scored it. Chris Galvin, a young Yorkshire lad, had lined up beside me and afterwards we could tell ourselves that we had battled well, and this was true even though Barca had produced a winner near the end.

Naturally, I flew back to Leeds with a little more self-belief, and this was enhanced when I picked up a copy of the *Yorkshire Post* and read, 'Leeds' younger players acquitted themselves well, and especially the goalscorer, Joe Jordan.' That was guaranteed to put some more spring into my step but, of course, it didn't push away the central problem of marching past the men who stood in my way – Allan 'Sniffer' Clarke and Mick Jones.

These two were, in their radically different ways, great England international strikers. My style was more Jones than Clarke. Mick was strong in the air, fought for every situation and was always available to hold up the ball as he led the line. He was everybody's idea of a traditional British centre-forward, brave and committed to the last seconds of the game. His departure was much mourned when he left Sheffield United, where he was seen as a front player worthy of representing the old steel town.

Allan Clarke wielded a stiletto. He was like so many of the great goalscorers, a loner, prickly and self-absorbed, but, as all the Leeds players had been, he was hand-picked by Revie. The manager had suffered a rebuff when he tried to sign Clarke after his free-scoring emergence at Fulham. 'Sniffer' turned a deaf ear then, choosing to go to the much more modestly placed Leicester City. Some managers might have taken the rebuff badly and scratched the player off their list of contenders for all time, but Revie was a lot more pragmatic than that. He knew that the goalscorer he coveted could be an awkward, indeed quite a cussed, character but that was no doubt part of his appeal.

Great strikers went their own way. They were obsessed with that most vital and difficult task, getting the ball into the back of the net, and this didn't always make for the easiest of dispositions. It would, have taken a lot more than that, though, to discourage Don Revie. He didn't mind if Clarke brooded on the edge of the team, fretful about his rights and recognition. Revie just ran back through his mind all the goals that Clarke had been scoring since he moved from third division Walsall as a stubbornly ambitious kid from the Black Country.

It was also true that the Elland Road dressing room could never be mistaken for either a charm school or a military academy. The humour was tough and so was the discipline in the areas of personal conduct and adherence to the match plan, but it didn't breed a roomful of conformists. Strong but differing characters brought their own slant to the common purpose of winning football matches.

The unifying factor was that the players did everything they could to protect their positions, which meant they generally performed so well, so consistently that Revie could fill his team – and his substitutes' bench and a few seats in the stands – with current international players. Clarke, distant and often quirky, would bring a final cutting edge, and Revie had bombarded Leicester with telephone calls. As was usually the case, the manager got his man, and he was so good at his job, and so consistent, it would take me a little while longer to mount a sustained challenge for his place. Most importantly, I was learning my business, moving closer to that point when I would force my way into arguably the most consistently competitive team in England and possibly all of Europe.

Season '72–73 was the time of my most significant push forward, so much so that it came as a disappointment when I didn't even make the bench for the Cup final with Sunderland, the game that burned itself so deeply into the psyche of Leeds United. My hopes had been raised because in the semi-final against a good Wolves side at Maine Road, I had enjoyed the greatest day of my football life. My father had come to watch, taking a bus down from Scotland and then almost skipping back to it for the ride home after I had helped the team fight their way to Wembley.

I hadn't played a lot for the first team that season but a few more milestones had been passed. I scored my first league goals, two of them in a 3–3 home draw with Ipswich Town. On another great day, at home against Arsenal, we won 6–1 and I scored two more goals. I felt that I was gathering a little pace.

At Maine Road I came on when Jack Charlton was injured early in the game. Jack no doubt remembers that day with a certain sadness. For him it marked the beginning of the end of his time as a cornerstone of Revie's Leeds and the extraordinary spell of personal success that had followed the early crisis meeting with the manager. Jack missed the final and that crushing humiliation against a second division team, and then headed off to make his name as a manager at Middlesbrough.

Jack pulled a hamstring as Wolves made it clear they were going to take a serious run at getting to Wembley. They had the means to do it with some outstanding players – John Richards, a quick and direct striker, the old head of Derek Dougan, and Mike Bailey, a big, barrel-chested driving midfielder. They also had the trickery of David Wagstaffe on the left flank. They were like so many first-division teams of the day, dangerous in any match they decided was theirs for the taking.

Billy Bremner scored another of his big-game goals and that proved to be enough as we battled through to the final whistle. I played well, really got stuck in, and at the end I was on a tremendous high. A big reason was the presence of my father. He waited outside the dressing room to speak to me before returning home but when Revie saw him in the corridor, he pulled him in to join the riot of our celebrations. Water and champagne were being splashed about but my father, dressed in his smartest clothes, didn't take any evasive action. I could see the pride in his face. I could see how much it meant to him and how he could relate it to the great day when he went down to Old Trafford to see his friend Jimmy Delaney play for Manchester United. Now he had come to Manchester for another big game, and this time he had watched his son play a part in an important victory. As he left me that Saturday afternoon, I had a picture of him holding court in Kelly's, and it was an extremely warming thought. He told me how well I had played and how happy he was.

On the way back to Leeds we called in at the Midland Hotel to collect some more champagne before driving back over the moors. Our first stop was at the hospital where Terry Cooper was being treated for a broken leg – a typical Revie touch, emphasising that Leeds were a team, a concept that stretched way beyond the men who fought out any particular battle.

On the drive, Gordon McQueen got a little carried away, which produced another insight into the way the Revie command system worked. Gordon got up from his seat and called down the bus, 'What do you want to drink, lads, what's it for you?' Revie got up quickly and said with some force, 'You sit down. I'll tell you what you're drinking. You just sit down there.' I was happy to take what I was given because, at that point, I held the heady conviction that I had played my way into a Cup final.

In fact, I had, but not the one with Sunderland. Gordon and I would take our greatest stride in the game a few days after that terrible defeat, when a lasting image for all football fans was of the Sunderland manager Bob Stokoe running across the field to embrace his goalkeeper Jim Montgomery.

Revie was shattered by that scene. There were tears in his eyes when he got up to speak at the after-game banquet and later, when he encountered Gordon and me as we huddled in a corner, sipping beers and sharing in the general gloom, he said, 'Now you young lads better look after yourselves. You are the future so get yourself ready for next year.'

However, with Charlton still injured, and Clarke and Bremner suspended at the end of another gruelling season, our first big challenge would come much sooner than that. We were both selected for the team to play AC Milan in the final of the Cup-winners' Cup in Salonika, and although both of us did well, we had, with all of our team-mates, the toughest of hurdles – the Greek referee who, we heard much later, would never again officiate at a big match. Several outrageous decisions, all of them favouring the Italians, meant they edged home for a narrow and extremely controversial victory. Revie, so soon after the Sunderland disaster, was once again devastated.

At that time, Leeds' situation could have formed an interesting study on the pressures that come to the driven football manager who has laid down so relentlessly his demand for competitive excellence. Revie was already deeply drained by the Sunderland defeat, which had come about largely because their goalkeeper had played the game of his life and we had missed a stream of chances, and some of the lads were concerned that the defeat by Milan might plunge him into some great and perhaps unshakeable depression. He railed against the injustice of both defeats but it was the Sunderland game that left him particularly distressed.

He pointed out that his team had proved immeasurably stronger and more professional over the years than the one that had carried off the FA Cup and was receiving such acclaim. Sunderland helped make Revie's point when they again failed to gain promotion from the second division. While Sunderland were surrendering their most basic ambition, Leeds, the team who were so mocked at Wembley, were building up a record of twenty-nine games without defeat in one season, a run that would be bettered only by the outstanding champions Arsenal thirty-one years later.

I find it a little awe-inspiring when I look back at Leeds United's capacity to take the blows and keep returning to the centre of the battle for honours. Right from the start of their intrusion into the top flight of the English game in 1964–65, when I was a boy dashing across the Corn Patch, they performed astonishingly well without the rewards to crown outstanding effort. In that first season back in the top division – under the old system of two points for a win – they became the only team to amass more than sixty points without taking the title. They finished level on sixty-one with the Manchester United team of Bobby Charlton, Denis Law and the young George Best, and lost on goal average. In the Cup final, with Jim Storrie and Alan Peacock injured, and Albert Johanneson overawed by the splendour and pressure of Wembley, they took Bill Shankly's great team of Ian St John, Roger Hunt, Ian Callaghan, Peter Thompson and Ron Yeats into extra time. A headline in the *Daily Express* announced a verdict more generous than the team would receive in future years. 'Nothing – but the best' said the *Express* banner.

In the ten years between 1965 and 1975, Leeds would reach ten Cup finals, winning four of them, take two titles, finish runners-up five times and never place below fourth. That is something to reflect on now, surely, when a manager such as Gerard Houllier of Liverpool was able to spend more than £120 million in five years and still have success defined as finishing fourth in the Premiership – until last spring, when his luck finally ran out.

The year before the blows at Wembley and Salonika, Leeds had beaten Arsenal, who had been defending the double, in the FA Cup final and forty-eight hours later were obliged to play their last league game of the season at Wolverhampton. A draw would have clinched the title but Leeds were exhausted and they lost 2–1. Derby County, who won the championship by a point, heard the news of their triumph while taking an end-of-season break in Majorca. There was a certain heavy irony here, we decided, when we considered how the authorities had so brusquely dismissed Revie's plea for a little breathing space.

Still, some time later a little light did shine on the battle-grimed Leeds banner, but if there was any celebration it was necessarily of a subdued kind. After that final league game, a Sunday newspaper published a sensational account of how Billy Bremner had tried to bribe a Wolves player into throwing the game. The allegation was made by Danny Hegen, who did not, it has to be said, enjoy an outstanding record as a professional. He alleged that Bremner had said to him during the course of the game, 'Give us a penalty and I'll pay you a grand.' It was a preposterous suggestion, made, we all felt, for the sake of some lucrative newspaper serialisation, and Bremner had a curt message for Hegen. He said he would see him in court and the result was a damages award of more than £140,000 for Billy – a record at the time.

John Giles went to court to support Bremner, and so did Derek Dougan, Hegen's own team-mate. Leeds were used to riding hostile comment and in one sense Billy's success in court was a rare bonus. However, it was part of a pattern in which Leeds were invariably cast as the villains. That could nag at your subconscious to some degree, and a few years later there was another outbreak of allegations when Revie defected from the managership of England and faced a final barrage of criticism before slipping out of football and into the long and painful illness that took his life.

Looking back over the years, it is maybe not so hard to understand why Revie and his team, and especially the first wave of it, attracted such dogged criticism. There is no doubt Don Revie had a ruthless streak, and if his ability to develop a team and mould the character of true competitors was phenomenal, there were times when he also lapsed into a much more negative – and cynical – approach. When he first arrived at Elland Road he didn't have much money to spend on the team and before he could achieve anything, he had to fight off the prospect of relegation. Perhaps that gave him the siege mentality that he was never able to shake off despite all the years of great success and the growing sense that he was gathering together a team to compete with any opposition on any terms.

If he could have let his team off the leash a little earlier, if he had allowed great players to express themselves more freely, no doubt the perception of a wider public would have been more positive. A lot of demons would have stayed in their cages.

All I can say is that Revie never demanded any judgement from me because he never compromised me or, to my knowledge, any of my team-mates. Never in my career did anyone I had come to trust try to compromise my integrity as a footballer. Some years later in Italy, I discovered the widespread damaging effects of the bribery scandal that had brought down players and officials, including the great World Cup hero Paolo Rossi, but again, I was never touched by any hint of skulduggery. At the time of the Bremner–Hegen affair, allegations of corruption were flying around in English football, no doubt partly due to the atmosphere of suspicion that inevitably followed the successful prosecution of three Sheffield Wednesday players, Peter Swan, Tony Kay and David Layne, for match-fixing in the sixties. If anything more did go on, it never brushed against me in the slightest way. I would certainly have been outraged had it done so. I hadn't spent all those years chasing a dream to throw it away for any amount of money. How, I wondered when I heard some of the rumours, did you fix a game? How did you arrange the scoring? How did you go about telling a professional that he should sell himself, his team, his family, and all the fans who paid their money at the gate, thinking they were investing in a common dream? I remember thinking, 'God, you'd have to be in some state to do something like that.'

At Leeds, I took things at their face value and what I saw was a culture that was geared to that single priority of winning, ruthlessly at times, no doubt, but always with an understanding that the moment you lost the edge of that appetite to finish on top, you would be drawn back into the pack. It was a prospect Don Revie could scarcely bear to think about, and you could see it so clearly on his face when he stood up in that bleak room in a London hotel and fought to keep the tears of defeat out of his eyes. When he gathered us together before the start of the new season, he swore that the humiliation against Sunderland could not, and would not, be the last entry on Leeds United's record of competing for the game's great trophies. He said how much he had hated to read and hear all the criticisms of the team after the Cup final defeat. It enraged him that people had been so quick to write off his team, saying that Giles and Bremner had gone galloping over the hill and the entire team had lost its cutting edge. He said that there could only be one proper response – to win the league title, and with some style.

'You lads,' Revie told Billy, 'are good enough to ram the criticism back down the throats of all those who have denied you the respect you deserve. You must go out to show them all what you can do, what good footballers you are. I want the title – I think you more than good enough to do that. I also think you could go through the season without losing.'

We couldn't know as we went flying into the new season that we were representing Don Revie's last statement as one of the great club managers. It gives me immense satisfaction that we were able to do it so well, and that not only did we break the record run for undefeated games, we finished five points clear of a new Liverpool, building up to their European triumphs, and fourteen points ahead of Derby County, the team who two years earlier had profited from the absurd demand that Leeds play two huge games in a little over forty-eight hours.

We fell in the thirtieth game, at Stoke City. How it happened will always be a mystery to those of us who played at the Victoria Ground that Saturday afternoon in late winter. We went into the game oozing the confidence that had been growing game by game, and it seemed that the pattern was unbroken as we moved easily into a 2–0 lead. We had no reason to fear an ambush because we had simply been rolling through the season.

I remember vividly a win at Stamford Bridge. We always had tremendous battles with Chelsea. It was a tradition that stretched back beyond those epic FA Cup finals of 1970, and now as we led the first division, and the possibility of an unbeaten season was being widely discussed through football, Dave Sexton's team came at us with tremendous force. They were a team of formidable skill and experience, with the touch of Alan Hudson, the thoroughbred class of Peter Osgood and the tricky running of Charlie Cooke, complemented by the hard physical challenge of Ron 'Chopper' Harris, Eddie McCreadie and the big tough central defender John Dempsey. But Chelsea were no match for us that day.

Bremner and Yorath ran the midfield and I scored a goal in the 2–1 win. The scoreline skimmed the surface of our superiority, and there was a strange additional satisfaction in the appreciation of the crowd. You have to remember that Chelsea fans, like so many others around the country, had never been keener to see the defeat of Leeds. The previous spring, the nation had risen up to acclaim our giant-killing conquerors Sunderland and now everyone outside Leeds wanted to see the ending of our unbeaten run, but there were ripples of admiration from the Stamford Bridge terraces as Bremner, in classic fashion, dropped deep to receive the ball and set in motion a flowing move. Bremner made his waspish attacks, his inspired aggressive flourishes and when we walked off at the end it was to a burst of what seemed like unqualified applause.

That sense was underlined when one of the Chelsea directors, the actor Sir Richard Attenborough, came into the mobile-home dressing room that was in use during the renovation of Stamford Bridge, to congratulate us. He said, 'Well done boys, that was a great performance' – a rare tribute indeed but such recognition was beginning to form a pattern. Wherever we went, crowds were feverish to see us beaten, but when we stood firm and got a result – and sometimes away from home it was a case of grabbing a goal and then shutting down the opposition – you could feel waves of respect. There was a huge crowd at St Andrew's, Birmingham, when we went there to defend our record, and again there was generous recognition from more than 50,000 fans. We might still be the team they most loved to hate, but we were achieving something remarkable. At St James' Park another vast crowd was stunned, then respectful, when Paul Madeley rifled home the winner from twenty-five yards.

So the match at Stoke seemed just part of what was turning into a triumphal parade. We cruised into the lead, and really we were making it look ridiculously easy against a team of considerable talent. Stoke had been kept in the top flight by their manager Tony Waddington's skilful use of older players of great achievement combined with younger stars of his own. He had signed Denis Smith and Alan Bloor, two big central defenders, Terry Conroy, a thin, brilliant Irish winger, and Mike Pejic, a tough little full-back who was good enough to play for England. We had them firmly on the ropes at 2–0 and then I burst through to score a third. Unfortunately, the linesman flagged for offside. Had the decision gone the other way, we would surely have reached thirty games undefeated. Instead, Conroy produced a couple of runs and somehow the momentum shifted. We were numb at the end of the game, which we lost 3–2, and Don Revie was, briefly, inconsolable.

It later emerged that after the Cup final defeat, he had thought long and hard about the future of the team. He wondered, as Jack Charlton went off to Middlesbrough trailing glory, if he had seen the best of his key players. Could Giles and Bremner continue to operate with such sharpness and vision in midfield? They had been at it for nearly ten years now, and might it just be true that their batteries were running terminally low? Charlton was gone. Might some of the other stalwarts be developing metal fatigue? Those were the questions Revie mulled over during that anxious summer. Then he came to us in the build-up to the new season with his battle cry, and although the Stoke result left all of us stunned and gutted for a few days, there was no doubt Revie had reached the right decision. There was still a lot of running left in his great side, and despite hitting the odd trough, which is inevitable over a gruelling season, even now, on playing surfaces infinitely kinder than the ones we had to endure back then, we cruised home to the title.

For me, it had been the season of the great breakthrough. I had been strong and eager for the challenge, and I won the confidence of the manager. Some of the time I benefited from Mick Jones's increasing injury problems, which by the end of the season brought his great career to an end. However, by then I was definitely a contender in my own right, having earned selection over a fit Allan Clarke for a Cup-tie at Bristol City. It was a typical Cup game, finishing in a draw, and I played well. We lost the replay but for once it didn't seem such a catastrophe. We had set ourselves one great goal, the title, and this season of all seasons we were determined not to fall between the various targets that had so regularly presented themselves at the end of each season. That didn't involve running up the white flag in the Cup. Any idea of going into that competition in a half-baked way, as is so common today, would have been considered an outrage. No, we didn't plan to lose to Bristol City but when it happened, it was more a call to arms than a disabling blow.

We won the championship away from the field of action. The team agreed to meet in the Queen's Hotel in Leeds if Sheffield United avoided defeat against Liverpool, our nearest challengers, at Bramall Lane. Liverpool needed to win to stay in the race. Gordon McQueen, David Harvey and I decided that we would become Sheffield supporters for the night. We wanted to be around at the climactic moment if it came that night. It did and the three of us hugged each other in the sweetest moment of still young careers.

David was particularly delighted. He had finally fought his way into the team after years of playing understudy to the often brilliant but also erratic Gary Sprake. David was a fine goalkeeper, brave and technically sound, and very popular. He was a dry, Yorkshire lad, quite eccentric in his way, but his team-mates appreciated the fact that on the field he put aside his slightly wacky tendencies and became every inch a professional. This was some-thing of a relief to the veterans in the team. They had always admired the talent and the courage of Sprake but they had also from time to time been dismayed by his moments of failed concentration, notably in the Cup final against Chelsea and on a notorious occasion when a gaffe at Anfield provoked the half-time disc jockey to play 'Careless Hands'.

I saw David at a Leeds training session a few years ago. He was the same old, easygoing character, utterly untouched by his days as a football star. Now he farms pigs on an island off the Scottish coast.

Revie got his title and he got to say, 'Well done, lads. I told you you could do it – and you did me and yourselves proud.' There was a rare light in his eyes when he said that. He had come through some desperate times and he had gone away to heal his wounds. Next year he could claim the prize that he had long craved. He could get his hands on the European Cup, the trophy that he had been held aloft by two other British managers only, men whom he had always so greatly admired, Matt Busby and Jock Stein, both from Lanarkshire. That would surely bring a little more warmth to his summer and mine. First, though, I had a little business of my own. I had to play for Scotland in the World Cup.

6

JORDAN OF SCOTLAND

F I'd said it quickly, I might have half convinced myself it was
just another football assignment, another challenge along the
road from Cleland; but that didn't quite work because, I suppose,
as long as I was in football there would always still be inside me a
little bit of the kid who stood at the bus-stop in awe of Jimmy
Delaney. However confidently I thought about it, and measured
the progress I had made since those days, the prospect still took
my breath away. Just two years out of the office of McMenan and
Brown, and since I had stood on my toes on the terraces of
Parkhead with cousin Joe as a part-time professional for Morton
and a star-struck Celtic supporter, I had, indeed, to go to play for
Scotland in the World Cup.

One fantasy after another may have become reality, but there
had always been one that beckoned most brightly, and, for the
longest time, seemed unattainable. It was to be not just Joe
Jordan of Leeds United, but Joe Jordan of Leeds United and
Scotland. It was to wear that blue shirt in the company of Denis
Law, Jimmy Johnstone and Billy Bremner.

Wherever I looked at Elland Road, players had that double-
barrelled confirmation of their status in the game, and I marvelled
at the wonderful ring of it. Bremner, Leeds United and Scotland,
John Giles, Leeds United and Ireland, Jack Charlton, Leeds
United and England – these were men of great weight. Right

through the squad, playing for your country seemed to be a right. For Giles particularly, his first cap for Ireland wasn't so much a glory as a formality. He arrived at Manchester United as a fifteen-year-old with a £5 note and his address pinned inside his jacket. He had shone in the streets of Dublin, where they played late in the evening, and then on the fields as a schoolboy who could play beyond his years. An international career was already not a dream but an assumption.

Bobby Moore, Kenny Dalglish, Nobby Stiles and Terry Venables were other players whose graduations in their national teams were virtually rubber-stamped through the various stages, so that when they walked out at Wembley or Hampden Park in their country's shirt, whatever thrill they had – and I'm sure it was great because playing for your country is a privilege that can only be fully understood when it is granted to you – it had at least been somewhat conditioned by firm expectation.

Certainly, they cannot have been as surprised and thrilled by the first call as I was when I went into Elland Road, less than two years after I had reported for duty in my ridiculed oilskin coat and with so much ground to cover as a physically under-prepared eighteen-year-old, to be told that Tommy Docherty, the Scotland manager, had phoned to say he wanted me in the squad preparing for a World Cup qualifier against Denmark.

The Doc, who would shortly be whisked away to Old Trafford to replace the fallen Frank O'Farrell, made it clear that I was not in the running for the Denmark match. He had noted my progress with Leeds, had seen something in me, and wanted me to get some experience of the international atmosphere, have a little taste of what could well come to me soon enough. I wasn't yet quite Jordan of Scotland perhaps, but this was a huge stride. However, I realised when I travelled up to Glasgow with Bremner and Peter Lorimer that, exciting as it was, it was not about to overwhelm me. It might have done if I hadn't had the Leeds experience. When I walked into the hotel where the team had assembled, the sight of such big-name stars as Denis Law, George Graham and Jimmy Johnstone wasn't such a culture shock; I had been two years in the company of Bremner, Giles and Big Jack and I could tell myself that this now wasn't a lunge into a new dimension, it was simply a natural progression. I had already covered quite a bit of the ground, and I could feel this in a way that might not have been the case if Hal Stewart had told me that I was heading for somewhere less prestigious than Leeds United.

Playing for Scotland was never something I was asked about, or shouted about, but the possibility of it had always lurked in a corner of my mind, and because I hadn't been picked at any level before the big team, the sense of achieving something major was, I suppose, all the greater. I couldn't begin to take it for granted, and when Docherty got his call to Manchester United in early 1973, his successor, Willie Ormond, made sure that situation continued for at least a few more months. At one of his first press conferences, Ormond listed players in two categories – core players, including Bremner and Dalglish, who had already established themselves at the heart of the team, and contenders who still had to convince him. Joe Jordan, he told the journalists, wasn't quite ready, but he had plenty of time on his side. Denis Law, such a superb player for so long, was in a category of his own. At thirty-four, the possibility of World Cup football had come very late, and he made it clear by his demeanour that he regarded it as very precious indeed.

I knew that I still had a lot to do to match the physical resources of my club-mate Bremner. His ability to jump back into brilliant action after quite serious injury still astonished me, as it had done on one of my big milestones at Leeds. I sat on the bench in that Fairs Cup semi-final first leg at Anfield when Billy scored an amazing goal. He hadn't trained properly for six weeks but he played like a fiend that night. I remembered that Bremner performance, and the awe I felt while watching it, when I walked behind him into the room filling up with Scottish internationalists before the game with Denmark. Maybe I would never have quite that extraordinary capacity to make such an impact, but Scotland, if and when they called upon me, would always be able to count on similar passion. In me, like so many of my compatriots, it had lodged in the blood and been stored away. It was a reality that makes the sad plight of today's Scotland team so difficult to understand – and to accept. The call to action came just a few months after the first summons by Docherty. Ormond picked me for the squad against England at Wembley, along with Peter Lorimer. Peter hired a car and, with gathering excitement, we drove down to London, the home of the enemy.

International selection was my reward for a good run in the Leeds first team, particularly that two-goal blast against Arsenal and some strong performances on the road to the Cup-winners' Cup final against AC Milan in Greece. The opportunity to show that I could battle against heavy odds had come in the ferocious semi-final second leg in Split, where the Hajduk team battered us for ninety minutes. The Croatians, fiercely supported by the crowd, had come roaring at us after losing the first leg 1–0, the goal scored by Allan Clarke. In Split, I had to run ceaselessly, offering myself for the ball as hard-pressed team-mates sought to lift the pressure. The demand had been for a professional per-formance and I had been able to deliver it, to the satisfaction of both Revie and Ormond. Maybe Ormond now believed my time was closer that he had first thought.

I didn't start against England, but I came on and did well enough. We lost 1–0, but there was no gloom. We had played with some confidence and cohesion and we had pushed England, who were in the last days of the great Ramsey era, all the way.

It was the first time I had played with Kenny Dalglish, who although just a couple of years ahead of me, was well-established in the international team. He had been given his chance as the hope of Celtic, one of the last examples of Jock Stein's greatness in nurturing exceptional young players, and he had taken it with superb accomplishment. Later, Lou Macari told me about the young Dalglish. From his first days at Celtic Park it was clear that he was intent on becoming one of the top professionals. He was a quiet young man but the intensity he brought to his game was quite remarkable. It shows on his international record. You cannot play a hundred times for your country without, above everthing else, tremendous desire. It's not just that you have had the physical strength and conditioning to be around for so long, and that you have had the talent; it means you've always had the will and the determination to fight off the opposition, to prove that you are still the top man.

When Kevin Keegan eventually left Liverpool for Hamburg, the Anfield manager Bob Paisley got it perfectly right. He saw that Liverpool, with their great running and passing, and Dalglish, with his tremendous finishing poise, were made for each other. It is not often that a club manager, confronted with the loss of a great player, as Keegan had made himself over the years, is able to look around and discover someone who can make a seamless transition, who is not only an excellent replacement but who might also bring in new strengths and subtleties.

Kenny was very strong on the ball but he wasn't that quick. His pace was in his mind. He was never flustered. When he received the ball he always knew what he was going to do with it – and his positional sense was quite phenomenal. Most great players have exceptional pace; it is the most common distinguishing mark of their status. Dalglish's supreme gift was to be able to read everything so well. It was amazing to see the number of people who dived in on him around the box and were left floundering. It was really the last thing they should have done against Kenny. They were just playing to his strength. He would pick up so easily on their intentions and the ball would be by them as they hit their stride. Their movement created half a yard for him and his composure on the ball did the rest. Picture a Dalglish goal and the likelihood is that you see him placing it coolly into the net, not with great pace but an absolute mastery of what he is doing. If you looked then at the quality of such players as Dalglish and Bremner, and the greatness of veterans Law and Bobby Lennox, you just could not have imagined that thirty years on, the Celtic and Rangers teams would be almost entirely filled with foreign players and the national side would be desperately weak and run by a German, Berti Vogts.

In 1973 there were not even glimpses of such poverty and this, too, was part of the extraordinary pride I felt, running out on to the Wembley pitch. I didn't tear up the famous field but I did well enough to make the team for summer games against Switzerland and Brazil. The Brazilians were the reigning world champions but the magnifience they had displayed in Mexico in 1970 had plainly passed. Obsessed by the fact that they had been kicked out of the last World Cup in Europe, the 1966 tournament in England, by the brutal tackling of Portugal and Hungary, when Pele, his face racked with pain, had to be carried to the touchline, the Brazilians were heading for Germany and the 1974 World Cup armed to the teeth with physical players. Pele had retired from the international scene, no doubt too early but embittered by his experiences in Europe eight years earlier. The Brazilians also, critically, had lost three players through injury: Carlos Alberto, the great full-back, Clodoaldo, another key defender, and Tostao, who had played so brilliantly in Mexico. Coach Mario Zagallo believed that he had to pack his team with physical players to counter another assault from the Europeans but it wasn't the Brazilian way. It was a betrayal of their best instincts, and nothing about their play in our game gave a hint that they would be able to match such talented teams as Holland and Germany, and, just maybe, Scotland. That was a pretty thought of my own, well buried, but I did well enough against Brazil and Switzerland and when we came to the autumn and the decisive qualifying games with the powerful Czechoslovakia team, I was still very much in contention for a World Cup place.

Ormond had been left in a strong position by Docherty and although we had to play the Czechs twice, we were in the good situation of qualifying if we beat them in the first match at Hampden. Ormond had me on the bench on a night of incredible expectation and tension. The atmosphere in the dressing room was electric, and it was handled well by Willie. He was a shrewd old character and although he would face some huge and damaging controversy on the way to the finals, he was very much in control of himself when we faced the Czechs. Ormond's great quality was that he understood both the strengths and the weaknesses of his players. He knew the chemistry of a team and the rhythm of a game.

Ormond pointed out, quite firmly, that we were in a position to make it to the World Cup finals for the first time since, literally, Pele was a lad – the 1958 tournament in Sweden, when the phenomenal teenager had exploded on to the scene so brilliantly in the final against the host nation. It had been a long drought indeed for Scotland, a great scandal in the failure to exploit so much natural talent, and this was the time to put things right.

We did, and how it happened might just be the greatest of my football memories. The Czechs, playing neat, cool football, went into the lead through a mistake by our goalkeeper Ally Hunter, and it brought a terrible silence to the great stadium. We had to battle back. Jim Holton, the big Manchester United centre-half who would die so tragically young of a heart-attack, got up at a corner and headed us back into the game to a great thunderclap of a roar. In the second half, Ormond sent me on to replace Kenny Dalglish.

I played alongside Law and we were applying tremendous pressure without getting any breaks. Billy Bremner had gone very close with a powerful shot and the crowd had built themselves into a state of tremendous excitement. Here it was before us, the chance to get to the finals of the World Cup, a competition in which our greatest rivals England had distinguished themselves over the last eight years. We couldn't afford to miss. Billy was playing at the limits of his skin and his shot bounced off a post and ran wide for the winger Willie Morgan to pick up. Willie shaped to cross and I anticipated the flight of the ball just right, slipping away from my marker and diving to head the ball, as sweetly as I would ever see or feel, into the bottom corner.

There were just a few minutes left and, naturally, the Czechs, a strong, clever side who two years later would win the European Championship, came back at us strongly. We had to hang on with some desperation, but Law did get a chance to put the game away. Unfortunately, he missed. Fortunately, though, it did not haunt him as he approached the end of his international career because the blue line held and we were back on the front line of international football.

Up in the Hampden stands, another, smaller, drama was unfolding. Tunj Ozbay, who owned a nightclub in Leeds and was a great friend of the players, had driven Eddie Gray, who was injured, Peter Lorimer, who was suspended, and Gordon McQueen to see the game. When my goal went in they apparently went as wild as any of the fans, jumping up and down and hugging each other. In the process, Tunj lost his car keys. After the game they were delighted, congratulating Billy and me and saying what a great occassion it had been. They had to get back to Leeds for training and treatment the following day, so Tunj hired a taxi. The only one available was a smart limousine – grand in all respects except for the heater, which had packed up. It was an extremely cold night and I heard later that the boys had been obliged to cuddle up in the backseat to keep warm!

Back in Glasgow, I was meeting my parents in the happy, teeming chaos of the Queen's Hotel, and of all our post-game meetings, this one lingers powerfully and warmly in my memory. Once again, the pride of my father glowed, and for me it was the greatest of things to see – a reminder that he was the humblest of men, and when something good happened in his life, it never touched his wider view of the world, never created any big appetite for anything beyond his own existence. He was very contented in his family and in himself, and he took everything that came to him, the good and the bad, with the same quietly measured reaction. Later, he came to Italy while I was playing with Milan, and was interviewed by the big sports paper *La Gazetta dello Sport*. The reporter said the club were thinking about getting him a job in Italy because whenever he came to see a game his son always played well. The reporter wanted to know what he thought of that prospect. My father laughed and said no, he was heading back to Cleland where he had his life.

He had seen a little of the world with his Army service in Africa and he had had a spell in the Orkneys, and he was happy to track my career, wherever it took me, and then go home to tell about it, to share it with Uncle Joe and Jimmy Delaney and all his friends back in the village. He was always happy with what he had, and the longer I live the more I know that this is a great and rare view of life. Above everything else, he was generous, and especially in how he understood all the strengths and the weaknesses of everyone he knew.

After the win over Czechoslovakia he was the same as always. 'Well done, Joe,' he said. 'It was a great goal and you played well,' but you could see on his face how much it had meant to him, and maybe when he got back to Cleland he would say rather more. In my presence, he never went overboard, and that would always be his way.

Later on in the evening, when my parents had left for Cleland and I went out on the town for a little celebration with Billy, Denis and his brother, the significance of what had happened began to register. Over a few beers I could see what it meant to both of them as their careers began to draw in.

Many years later, I bumped into Paddy Crerand at Old Trafford as we prepared to do some broadcasting. He confirmed the extent of the impact of the victory over the Czechs on an earlier generation of players. Crerand would have his glory with Manchester United in the European Cup, but he was a passionate Scotsman and he made it clear how much it had pained Dave Mackay, Ian St John, John White, Jim Baxter and him that in their prime they had been denied the great stage of the World Cup. In qualifying action for the 1962 World Cup finals in Chile, Crerand believed that Scotland had the talent to make a real impression but they were beaten in a play-off game in Belgium by the Czechs, who went all the way to a final appearance against Brazil in Santiago. Crerand said he would always swear that the Czechs should have been defeated by a Scottish team that had a much greater sweep of ability. Our chat was quite wide-ranging until we came to the plight of Scotland these days and then the Czechoslovakia games, and you could see, even after all the years, the pain on Paddy's face.

I was twenty-one and I had no real sense of all that yearning and frustration felt by so many players I had idolised as a boy. Now, at a late hour in Glasgow, I could see on the faces of Law and Bremner that so much of the history of Scottish football, and their own lives, had gone into the game against the Czechs, which circumstances had given me the chance to influence. As the night wore on, the meaning of the victory, and the goal I had scored to create it, began to seep home.

We didn't make it a crazy, late night, we didn't get drunk, but nor was it one of those nights when you could just say, 'All right, we'll go to bed now.' You couldn't just walk away from each other because there was too much to reflect upon, too much to savour, and I recalled something the great old football man Joe Mercer had once said. 'Always celebrate your victories,' said Joe, 'because in football you never know if it's going to be your last.'

Something else I noted in Glasgow, and when I thought about it I could see that it was all to do with the pain caused by the long Scottish absence from the World Cup finals, was Billy's determination to get back to Elland Road as soon as possible. There was

The match of my life. Judith and me shortly before our marriage.

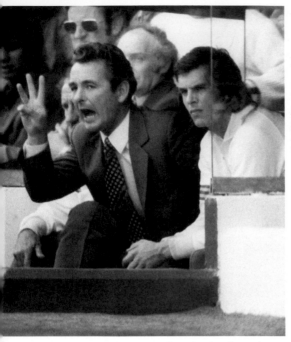

Sitting it out with Brian Clough, the flawed genius who devastated reigning champions Leeds United before going on to win two European Cups with Nottingham Forest.

The wages of the European Cup battle with Barcelona. My nose was broken and my face cut in the tough exchanges but we made it through. I knew my wounds would heal before Barcelona's.

The team that reached the European mountain top in 1975. *Back row, left to right*: Norman Hunter, Peter Lorimer, Paul Madeley, David Stewart, Gordon McQueen and me. *Front row, left to right*: Terry Yorath, Allan Clarke, Billy Bremner, Frankie Gray and Trevor Cherry.

Going for goal, I force my way between two defenders. We took the European Cup final to Bayern Munich in Paris and defeat was bitter. We felt the referee was against us.

Another source of bitterness – Peter Lorimer's brilliant shot is called offside.

At boiling point, Billy Bremner and I confront Bayern Munich's Gerd 'Der Bomber' Muller.

The pain of defeat. Leeds manager Jimmy Armfield attempts to console me at the end of the match. It was an impossible task and still would be today.

Wedding day in Leeds, happiness for Judith and me – and a spectacular hair day for best man Gordon McQueen.

Jimmy Nicholl of Manchester United and I chase down a ball in the 1977 FA Cup semi-final at Hillsborough. It was, along with the game, the one that got away.

The controversy that will never die. At Anfield, October 1977, the Welsh said I handled. I said I didn't. The referee gave Scotland a penalty and we made it to the World Cup of 1978.

The moment of victory – and before the storm. Team-mate Don Masson says, 'Well done, Joe.'

Heading for the World Cup – and the most painful days of his career – Scottish manager Ally MacLeod.

The end of a dream. Willie Johnston hears that his drug test after the game with Peru was positive. Johnston would soon be flying home. Team-mate Bobby Clark looks less devastated.

I walk away in disbelief after Peru make it three. Earlier in the game I had scored my first goal of this World Cup.

The brilliant goal that came too late. Archie Gemmill strikes against Holland in the final game in Argentina.

We're still alive – but not for long. Kenny Dalglish scores and I join the short-lived celebration.

no question of missing the first flight home to Leeds. The boys were already in training when we arrived, and Billy and I had a bath and a rub-down and we were waiting as they came in from their work. I could see how much Billy had wanted that moment, and how much pleasure and satisfaction he was gaining from it.

The English would not qualify – for the first time since 1958 – and although their critical match against Poland at Wembley, the game that effectively lost Ramsey his job, in which Norman Hunter would be so harshly blamed for a lost goal, had still to be played, Bremner wanted that morning to proclaim with his physical presence that at last the Scots had made it. An important part of world affairs had been put right.

We played our meaningless second game with the Czechs in Bratislava, lost 1–0 and then gathered to watch the English defeat on the hotel television. It would not be accurate to say the room was flooded with sympathy for England. Their success in 1966 and their impressive showing four years later in Mexico, when they were leading Germany in the quarter-finals before Ramsey withdrew Bobby Charlton, who had been controlling the game, had underlined the Scottish curse of football self-destruction – and Ramsey had never betrayed much sympathy in some of our hardest days. However, for the Leeds contingent – David Harvey, Peter Lorimer, Billy, Eddie Gray, Gordon McQueen and me – there were regrets for our English team-mates, Norman Hunter and Allan Clarke. Hunter was pilloried for missing the tackle that led to the decisive Polish goal, but the mistake happened on the halfway line and the Poles still had an awful lot to do to score. It was also true that although all of the criticism settled on Hunter, much to the anger of Don Revie, goalkeeper Peter Shilton made his contribution when he dived over the ball. Clarke's agony was that he missed a series of chances, a terrible fate for such a normally clinical finisher at such a vital time.

Still, this was football. Things can always go wrong, and any group of Scottish international players would have a better grasp of that than most. If we were in danger of losing any sense of this old reality, it came roaring back during the build-up to the finals in Germany. For a little while, it seemed that our chances of making any kind of success had, literally, floated down the Clyde.

We were in the middle of the home international series and had set up camp at the Queen's Hotel in Largs. I was sharing a big room with Billy and Peter Lorimer and, as the squad settled in, there was talk of a little relaxation in the town that evening. We had played the second of the home internationals the night before and had to meet England at Hampden on Saturday, and then there would be the pressure of the countdown to the World Cup. This was a chance to unwind a little, get to know my team-mates a bit better, but Peter, drawing on his greater experience, put me on my guard. He said he thought things might get a little noisy, and perhaps it would be a good idea if we had a beer and went to bed early.

Lorimer's warning did trigger a memory of one of my first trips with Scotland, when I was put in a room with the great Jimmy Johnstone. Talkative, endlessly sociable, the little man told a hundred stories and we had a stream of visitors to the room. The trouble was the talk, which was initially so enjoyable, went on way beyond the time I normally went to sleep and the following morning I arranged to swap rooms with Danny McGrain.

It just happened that Johnstone, a little unluckily it must be said, was about to become the central character in a drama that would dominate all of the back pages and some of the front ones, which we would carry to Germany as a great burden – a huge question mark against our ability to return successfully to the international stage. Jimmy wasn't an entirely innocent party but there was no doubt he was to a certain degree a spectacular victim of circumstances.

Peter and I went to bed early, which in the morning was a reason for the greatest relief as the various accounts of the night – and the morning – crackled through the hotel.

It appeared the boys had got themselves relatively merry before walking home along the pebbled beach. Jimmy, who was always so full of high spirits, saw a rowing boat and clambered into it, just for a little bit of passing fun. One of the lads – I was told it was the Rangers full-back Sandy Jardine – gave the boat a bit of a push and it slipped into the water. Unperturbed, Jimmy stood up in the boat and started to sing his version of 'Bonnie Scotland'. In mid-rendition, he realised he was drifting out towards the Irish Sea. Unfortunately, when he sat down to row his way back to the shore, he lost the oars, which slid into the Clyde. For a while the boys were not aware of the crisis and continued to sing 'Bonnie Scotland' before realising that Jimmy could do nothing about the fact that he was gathering speed and heading towards the horizon. Suddenly there was panic and the Coastguard was called. Before help arrived, Jimmy had gradually become a dot on the horizon, then disappeared.

By the time Peter and I got downstairs the drama was over but there was still plenty of evidence of the convulsion that had come to our World Cup planning. The big lounge of the hotel was filled with people – players, police, fire officers – and out in the car park you could see another crowd milling around. Jimmy sat in a corner, wrapped in a blanket and looking a little sorry for himself. He looked like a wee, wet spaniel. When Ormond came into the room you could see now furious he was. He stared at Jimmy with what would be recognised in Glasgow as a very hard one indeed. Jimmy's hurt expression said, 'What are you looking at me like that for?'

In the course of the next few days, Ormond explained this pretty thoroughly, and he made it clear to the entire squad that the mark had been overstepped to a disastrous degree. This was our return to the international stage. This was redemption time for Scottish football, and what did we have? A media circus. A thousand bleak jokes in bars and pubs across the country. It was not what anyone north of the border had in mind when my header had skimmed low into the Czechoslovakian net.

All kinds of indicators showed that our achievement in getting to the World Cup was guaranteed huge publicity, and that there was a real chance for the national game to put itself on a new footing, perhaps even draw a line under all the years of under-achievement. One such piece of evidence came when John Motson, who was just emerging as a leading BBC television commentator, took me to one side and asked if I could help him with personal background on some of the home-based Scottish players. John was already famous for his detailed research, and by coming to me he was admitting that the Scottish triumph had caught everyone by surprise. We were the only British team going to the World Cup – we had centre stage and massive attention from all the media. So what did we do? We took a boat ride down the Clyde and lost our oars.

Before the game with England we suffered, understandably enough, horrendous publicity. Well, I should say that most of us realised that the negative coverage was inevitable. The exception was the man at the centre of it. Jimmy was incensed by the level of criticism, and his fury increased when his wife was listed among his critics. What, the little man wondered, was all the fuss about? The boys had merely had a few drinks and a wee singsong, and things had gone slightly awry. These things occasionally happened in life.

Jimmy's anger was unabated right up to kick-off time at Hampden, where the atmosphere was as electric as anyone had known it. It had, of course, been fierce enough for the Czechs, but now it was the English coming among us at a time of pain and embarrassment. Johnstone's performance was volcanic. He had one mission and the beating of the English, for once, was quite incidental. What he had to do was vindicate himself in the eyes of all Scotsmen – and maybe one particular Scotswoman – and he did it gloriously. The little man had never been so mesmerising, running at the English and going by them as if they didn't exist.

We won 2–0, the goals coming from Kenny Dalglish and me – quite messy goals, but it didn't matter. They were the result of fierce pressure, and every time Johnstone touched the ball he seemed to spread panic in the English defence. For Dalglish and me, it was just a question of mopping up the rubble created by a player who, when he was on his game, played with a kind of manic genius.

At the end of the game Jimmy swapped jerseys with the English goalkeeper Peter Shilton, which was quite comical because the sleeves stretched way beyond his fingertips – a major problem for him when he put everything into his last ambition of the day, delivering a huge V sign to the Hampden press box. Some of the criticism from big-name Scottish writers, including John McKenzie and Jimmy Sanderson, had been particularly savage and Johnstone knew how to nurse a wound. Because of the length of the goalkeeper's sleeves, the V signs were not as explicit as he would have liked, but he kept making them. No one could say it was a failure of communication.

In a way, Johnstone was a symbol of all that was best and also most self-destructive about Scottish football. He had delivered quite magnificent goods against England, but at the same time he failed utterly to see why he was under pressure that day. Stories of Jock Stein's efforts to channel Johnstone's amazing talent had long since entered legend. It was said that the Celtic manager had spies in all of Jimmy's favourite bars and pubs and that whenever he entered one of them, sometimes when he should have been at home, calls went to Stein's office at Parkhead. Jimmy would shake his head in mystification, so it was alleged, when the barman lifted the phone within a minute or two and called out, 'It's for you, wee man – it's Big Jock.'

Jimmy's display restored his love-hate relationship with the media and gave us some desperately needed momentum for the approach to the World Cup, which included friendlies in Belgium and Norway before the first game with Zaire in Dortmund. Yes, it was true our campaign had drawn ridicule before it had officially begun, but the quality of the game against England had done much to restore the faith of our followers. It also put Willie Ormond in a better mood.

Discipline will always be a vital element in a successful team, as I had learned so comprehensively at Elland Road, but in football there is no redemption so powerful as a real performance, and that was what he had produced at Hampden. The defence had looked solid and the attack, lifted by the speed and the invention of Johnstone, had put England on the rack for ninety minutes. It was also true that despite their failure to qualify, and the demise of Ramsey, England could muster formidable strength. Although Scotland had celebrated the Polish success at Wembley, there could be no obscuring the fact that England had missed a lot of chances and Jan Tomaszewski, the big goalkeeper labelled a 'clown' by Brian Clough, had produced some phenomenal saves. The old enemy might be down, and out of the forthcoming action, but they were still able to provide one of world football's better form guides.

We lost in Belgium, won in Norway, and for me the greatest exhilaration was that, as far as Ormond was concerned, I had clearly moved beyond the status of a World Cup contender. I was a permanent presence in the team now, and the coach's first reservations that I still had quite a bit of ground to cover seemed to fade a little more with each passing game. I scored against Norway, and was pleased with the way I had linked with the midfield. It seemed certain that I would start against Zaire. I was full of running and growing confidence. I wished I could lock into this frame of mind, this sense that anything could be achieved, as long as I played the game.

I suppose this was an early start to the prime of my football life. I was twenty-two and a regular for the champions of England and World Cup-bound Scotland. I had never been so stretched as in this run of league, European and international games, and had never been on the road so regularly. There had been hardly any respite between the end of the season and the start of the long international campaign, but as we moved through Brussels and Oslo, there was not even a whiff of fatigue. I was riding on the purest flow of adrenaline I had ever known.

A big element of the excitement was the general sense of going into the unknown. It was new for me and fresh and thrilling ground for Law and Bremner, too, and Ormond was feeling his way into an unfamiliar world. It was quite touching that Bremner, with all his own heavy responsibilities as captain, took special care of me. He sat in on several press conferences in which I was involved, conscious that this was new and possibly difficult terrain for me. It emphasised that despite the reputations of the stars and all their experience at the top level of club football, this was a whole new dimension for the entire squad. Thus we were both delighted and relieved by the 2–0 victory over the Africans. It was only later that the overall strategic requirements of Group Two – Scotland, Zaire, Brazil and the almost invariably formidable Yugoslavia – became clear.

No one had said before the game that we had to pile up the goals because of the two tough games that would come later. The important thing was to win, to build on the restored confidence engendered by the victory over England, which had done so much to clear up the damage done on the Clyde. Zaire were a skilful team. There had been reports of dazzling talent emerging in Africa and certainly it was not unknown for teams to come from nowhere to cause major upsets in a World Cup. After our mishap in Largs, fears were expressed that the erratic side of our nature might emerge once more against a team who had nothing to lose.

Instead, Peter Lorimer fired home a glorious volley in twenty-eight minutes after I headed the ball down to him. It was our first World Cup goal in sixteen years and it seemed that a great bank of tension had been released. Six minutes later the Zaire cover broke down and I was able to meet a free kick from Bremner and send it past Kazadi, who was maybe not the greatest goalkeeper the World Cup had ever seen. We spent most of the rest of the game controlling the play, passing the ball around and feeling rather good about ourselves. We had got through the first challenge without finding any hazards, and we believed we were good enough to compete seriously with both Brazil and Yugoslavia.

In this we were proved quite correct. The Brazilians were clearly not the team that had soared to such brilliant levels in Mexico four years earlier. There was no Pele, Tostao, Gerson or Carlos Alberto and for a few thrilling minutes it seemed that we were about to score one of our greatest victories. By this point, it was clear that Denis Law's best days at the highest level were drawing to a close, and Ormond had put Dalglish in his place. I went near with a couple of headers and then, close in, I got up to knock the ball down against one of their players, from where it flew to Bremner, who had got into a great position just a yard and a half from the line. Unfortunately, the ball hit his shins and went past a post before he could react. Looking back, that was probably the moment we lost our chance of doing more than restore a little national honour on our return to World Cup football.

We finished ahead on points but with the game still locked at 0–0. Meanwhile, the Yugoslavs were putting immense pressure on us by running amok against Zaire, winning 9–0 after tearing into a 5–0 lead after half an hour. Dusan Bajevic, who had missed Yugoslavia's opening 0–0 draw with Brazil, led a charge that had been ordered by the team's famous coach Miljan Miljanic after he had studied the first-round performances of all the Group Two teams.

Scotland, and Ormond, were now once more under fierce pressure. The Yugoslav break-out meant that we almost certainly had to beat them in the final group game, which was an intimidating thought when you flicked over their team and saw the names of such outstanding players as Dragan Djazic and Vladislav Bogicevic. The Yugsolavs, like the Scots, had a reputation for virtuoso performers but a streak of inconsistency, which so often betrayed some of the best talent in the European game.

At least we knew what we had to do. To eliminate all doubt, we had to win because we had to accept that the chances of Brazil scoring a mere two goals against Zaire, now that the African team had had their morale shattered by the onslaught ordered by Miljanic, were quite remote. The match was as hard as we could have imagined. Tackles were flying in at various heights and the deadlock would be broken only by some outstanding play. This came from the remarkable Djazic, who wandered off to the right in search of a little time and space before cutting in at speed and crossing for Stanislav Karesi to open the scoring with just nine minutes to go. That had all the appearance of a killer blow, but somehow we got ourselves up again. Tommy Hutchison, who had come on for Dalglish after sixty-five minutes, broke down the left after beating his man, crossed to the far post and I knocked it in for my second goal of the tournament. There were two minutes left – two minutes to brush aside those powerful Slavs, or wait to see if Zaire could hold Brazil to less than two goals.

We couldn't score the vital goal, but Brazil could through Valdomiro. The details were heart-breaking for us. As we packed our bags, Denis Law went through all the possibilities that had slipped away down the years and Billy Bremner ached for the extra split-second he had needed to put away the Brazilians when their goal stood so exposed. Valdomiro's goal, the one that separated us now, came with just eleven minutes to go, the result of a tragi-comic mistake by my friend the goalkeeper, Kazadi. The Brazilian had the ball out on the right goalline with no chance of a shot on goal, but his cross came straight at Kazadi who tried to grab the ball against his chest but managed to fumble it into the net.

That was the end of our road. We were finally beaten by an aberration that was worthy of any of the legends of shaky Scottish goalkeeping, and it was far from the least of the ironies we had to suffer. In our distress, we were told that with banishment from the World Cup had come a forlorn and unique achievement – we were the first team to be ejected from football's greatest competition without losing a game. We had scored three goals and conceded one, and two of the matches had been against classically strong teams. Yes, maybe we had gone down the wrong road against Zaire in the opening match, but we were surely not without honour.

It was good to realise that most of Scotland saw it that way. We were given a tremendous reception back in Glasgow. Thousands came out to the airport, and the city and the country seemed to be saying that we had moved the national team back into the mainstream of international football. We had acquitted ourselves well against some major teams. We didn't have to hang our heads in shame; we had fought it out with some of the best, and this was surely the foundation for better days.

That was an encouraging thought, and my own spirits were further lifted when I went down to Cleland for a personal reception for the native son. The streets were filled with warmth and familiar faces. Cousin Joe and Uncle Joe were there, and John Delaney, and of course my father, wearing the expression that said everything was right with the world. Also present, in his best clothes and with his knapsack discarded, was Jimmy Delaney. In all the hubbub, I hoped I conveyed to him the part he had played in helping to shape this happy day for a Scottish footballer.

Much later, down all the years, the pleasure of that return to Scotland became a little clouded by some hard reflection. For all the welcoming cheers, we were really returning from a missed opportunity. The further I went in my career, the worse that sense of mislaid horizon became. There would be other opportunities, for both me and the Scottish team, but never, I concluded, such a good one. Billy Bremner was still operating around the best of his game, and if the tournament had come a little late for the great Denis Law, there was the power of Peter Lorimer and the unfolding promise of Kenny Dalglish. David Hay and John Blackley had come on to their game, David Harvey was an extremely solid goalkeeper – a rare treasure for a Scottish team

– and there weren't many better full-backs in the world than Celtic's Danny McGrain.

There was also the unexploited genius of the wee, wild Jimmy Johnstone. He disappeared from the equation after his extraordinary performance against England at Hampden, and only once did it seem possible that he might burst into the World Cup action with anything like that influence. He was on the bench for that vital game with Yugoslavia and, as the game seemed set in its deadlock, an intervention from Johnstone, some of us thought, might just work. Ormond was impassive as Johnstone fidgeted on the bench. No definitive reason emerged to account for why he was barred from the action. He wasn't injured. Inevitably, suspicion was aroused that he finally paid for his lack of discipline – first when he drifted down the Clyde, then, after picking up his chains and running so gloriously at Hampden, when there was a little bit of a scene on the university campus in Oslo, where we stayed before the friendly with Norway. The days had dragged in the far north and on one occasion a few drinks were taken. This led to a singsong and, naturally, Jim was one of the more enthusiastic, and louder, singers.

Maybe that was the reason he slipped beyond recall in Willie Ormond's calculations, maybe not. Perhaps angry officials of the Scottish Football Association brought their influence to bear. Willie Ormond never went on the record, so we are left with the mystery of why a brilliant Scottish footballer wasn't able to deliver all of his talent when it mattered most. One day we may get a thorough analysis of the problem, as it affected Jimmy Johnstone and so many of his compatriots. Maybe it will take less than a thousand years.

7

FROM REVIE TO ARMFIELD VIA CLOUGH

THE warmth of that reception in Glasgow, and my day of personal glory in Cleland, had the potential to linger for a lifetime. However, within days of my return a cold wind swept through Elland Road and consigned those good feelings to a place where they would have to be revisited in less stressful days, when a little of the anger and the disbelief had dispersed.

What happened at Leeds after the World Cup formed my first harsh lesson in how football can stalk and then pounce on contentment. You learn, sooner or later, not to trust that state of mind and that, when it touches you, the smart reaction is to get up on your toes.

That wasn't so easy for me because I was on the downside of tremendous exhilaration – and effort. Physically and emotionally, my resources were in a trough when Don Revie, my football godfather, suddenly announced that he was going off to manage England and, as far as a shocked and suddenly disorientated dressing room was concerned, in his place was a man who might have arrived from Mars or Venus.

By 1974, Leeds United was entirely Revie's creation. The club had been fashioned in his image of a perfectly ordered football operation and even his harshest critics had to concede that he had produced an extraordinary body of work, and that rarely before the last season had a team come to realise so completely its potential to produce outstanding football. Every one of those critics, that was, except our new boss, Brian Clough. Clough came into Elland Road wearing shorts and a T-shirt and holding his son Nigel by the hand. He didn't seem to be exuding much respect for the reigning champions of England, and this was a reinforcement of an earlier impression when, after agreeing with club chairman Manny Cussins to take the job, he immediately flew off with his family for a holiday in Majorca.

He made no attempt to meet the players as they prepared for the new season, making just one contact with the dressing room, a phone call to the captain Billy Bremner. Clough suggested Bremner fly out to see him in Spain. They could get to know each other a little and discuss prospects for the new season. Billy declined with thanks. He said that he would rather get stuck into pre-season training with his team-mates. That was, after all, the Leeds way. The Clough way, we would find out soon enough, was something that mocked everything that had happened in the days of Revie.

Revie's departure left the strangest feeling. The buildings were the same, and while Clough was sunning himself on a Spanish beach, so was the routine of the club. After more than a decade under the old manager, that routine had become as well-honed as some ancient ritual. His presence, though, had touched everything, given it a weight and a meaning that without him just disappeared before our eyes.

Gordon and I, the newest big boys on the first team, felt the wrench as much as the older players, who had had their careers and their lives shaped by the obsessive, often old-fashioned mixture of sentimental warmth and cold, calculated winning instinct that Revie had become. We always knew we would probably never quite get to the bottom of a man who one moment was as hard as nails and the next was talking mistily about his affection for the songs of the legendary music-hall star Gracie Fields; but we looked forward to the challenge of it as he extended and deepened our football education.

The important point for Gordon and me was that we had been picked out as key members of the next phase of Revie's empire. We had passed our first tests and viewed with growing confidence a future under a football man who, everyone sensed, had finally relaxed in the knowledge that he had indeed built a great team, and one that deserved to be released to their full potential. That was before the Football Association had come calling after Sir Alf Ramsey, following much encouragement from officials who had so quickly forgotten the vast contribution he had made to the development of the English game with his brilliant planning of the 1966 World Cup success, had departed for his modest retirement home in Ipswich.

Some of the veteran Leeds players, and notably John Giles, were convinced that it wouldn't have taken much persuasion by the directors to have kept Revie at Elland Road. Yes, he was flattered by the invitation to pick up the baton put down by Ramsey. Maybe he too could earn the knighthood that had come to Ramsey, who was, like him, a product of one of the least privileged sections of the working class, but he also knew what he was leaving behind at Elland Road. Even the all-conquering Ramsey had once said during a training session, 'One of my greatest regrets is that Johnny Giles wasn't born an Englishman.' Revie was conscious that he was separating himself from a host of internationalists and some of the greatest players of their generation – Giles, Bremner, Lorimer, Hunter and Gray were the brains, the hearts and the guts of his remarkable team, and of this key group only Hunter would be available to him in an English vintage that was looking rather thin.

According to Giles, the reason why this reality was not exploited by the club as Revie negotiated with the FA, was that there was sharp resentment of Revie in the boardroom. At one moment of triumph a director had asked, 'Why is it that the manager gets all the credit for what has happened here?' I would learn down the years that this is often the way in football.

Frequently, great accomplishment breeds a form of jealousy, even among those who have most benefited in terms of prestige, and the reality was that the Leeds board made no great effort to keep the man who had carried them to the top of the football world. Giles, drawing from all his instincts and experience, had clearly anticipated such a reaction in the board-room.

His theories were persuasive when you stopped for a moment and thought about the dynamics of a winning football club. When a manager turns around a team and builds real success, the role of the directors automatically diminishes. What do they have to do? Their opinions are no longer being constantly sought by the media. They no longer hold the destiny of the club in their hands. They do their most vital work when they appoint the right manager and give him the means to do his job. The rest is to rubber-stamp success and there's not a lot of personal glory in that.

When a club flounders in the wake of a successful, departed manager, the directors become crucial again. The headlines accumulate, the personal profiles increase. They are besieged for interviews and they are made to feel important in a way that wouldn't be possible in the businesses in which they had their success. It had been the same with Ramsey and the bigwigs of the Football Association. He had delivered incredible success, at the cost of power and influence for the committee men who had formerly picked the England team and treated the manager as some lightly regarded retainer.

At a club such as Leeds, the directors inevitably slide a little further from the spotlight the more the successful manager entrenches himself. As Giles made his points, and with the news that Revie was indeed leaving breaking across the dressing room like a shockwave, the great mystery of what was happening began to unravel. Quite a few things began to slip into place.

We recalled that the board had behaved in a similar fashion a year earlier when Everton had made a tempting offer for Revie to move. When the rumours began, as we travelled to Salonika for the Cup-winners' Cup final, we were anxious to dismiss the possibility that we might be losing the manager to Goodison Park. Giles flew to Salonika from Russia, where he had been playing for Ireland, and he had heard nothing.

'Well, is he leaving?' he demanded to know. We said we didn't know for sure, but the rumours were strong and there had been something in the press. 'Well, we'd better find out,' said Giles, who was senior professional in the absence of the suspended captain, Bremner. Giles went with Norman Hunter and Peter Lorimer to Revie's room.

'Is it true?' Giles asked. 'Are you leaving for Everton?'

'Yes, it looks as if I am, lads', Revie replied. 'Everton have made a great offer and it's something I've had to take seriously.'

It was clear that the Leeds directors had made no great move to dissuade him. Looking back, I suppose that should have put us on our guard, but the move fell through when Revie was seen in Liverpool talking to some Everton people, and the resulting publicity put him in the role of being party to an illegal approach. In those days, that was a much more serious matter than it is today, when Chelsea showed no qualms about trying to tempt away a current England coach.

The element of shock when Revie announced that he was leaving to take the England job was no doubt increased by the fact the team had performed so superbly the previous season. We were runaway champions of England. How could such momentum be hijacked in midair? Well, Giles explained it cogently enough. It was because a bunch of directors were too vain to see that without Revie Leeds United could very quickly become just another football club.

Everybody at Elland Road lost something when Revie collected his personal effects, including the rabbit's foot and other good-luck charms by which he placed such store, and drove away from the ground for the last time as manager. For Gordon and me it was the loss of a relentlessly attentive – and sometimes paranoid – mentor. That last aspect of his character had leapt out at us one day at Elland Road. Without any warning, he blurted out, 'I like my players in digs, I like them in that kind of atmosphere, but you two have got yourselves a flat.' He was saying that we had broken a part of the code at Leeds, we had gone our own way beyond his supervision. For flat he meant 'love nest'. There was no doubt that, like any normal young men, Gordon and I were not averse to letting our hair down a little. When we had done our work, and without compromising any of that, we liked to go out at the appropriate time and enjoy ourselves. We never created any scandal. We never wandered around the streets blind drunk, as a later generation of Leeds players would do at such devastating cost to the club's reputation. There was no love nest. Both Gordon and I were, apart from anything else, Scotsmen. The idea of paying for digs and at the same time renting a flat struck us as rather bizarre. We pleaded our innocence, but Revie was not totally convinced.

Later, we would laugh about the steps he had taken to monitor our lifestyle. They included calling up a local reporter, John Morgan, who lived near our digs in the Middleton suburb. 'What are they up to?' Revie would demand to know. 'What time are they coming home? Are they bringing girls back?' In fact, Revie had quite an elaborate network of spies. He considered it a fundamental part of his job. He had all these young, red-blooded lads shaping the destiny of the football club, and he hated the idea of anything going wrong. If Gordon or I had strayed too seriously off the path he considered to be proper, he would have been one of the first to know.

Once, he had made that demand of the young Bremner, who apparently wasn't always the most socially retiring of characters when he first came down from Scotland, to kneel down and give thanks for all his good fortune. He never touched that extreme with Gordon and me but he made it clear enough that we should never forget our responsibilities.

Much later in life, I found myself reflecting on how Revie might have reacted to the circus of the Beckhams. He would have seen it coming early and he would have had none of it. Of course, it was a different age, one much better suited to the Revie ideal. That could be summed up easily enough. He had his organisation, his culture of professionalism and a group of talented young players who had to be protected from both the world and themselves. He had his team and his results, a relentless stream of them, and he didn't want to leave anything to chance.

He wanted all his players to be married as early as possible to nice, sensible girls. He wanted them tucked away without problems that could deflect them from the most important thing of all, which was playing football of the highest possible standard. Now he was leaving, we had to wonder what would become of us, and all the passion he had generated. The best we could do was blink our disbelief and wish him well.

I had as big a reason as anyone to do that. In the few days between my return from the World Cup and the announcement of his move, he did some vital work on my behalf. He gave me a new two-year contract and it came with a substantial rise. I would be on £170 a week. That might not sound so much today, when the agents of unproven teenagers demand seven-figure signing-on bonuses and £50,000 a week, but then it was excellent money. It was also, by the standards of the time, a decent statement of thanks for what I had done and a display of confidence in my future.

I was pleased but not too surprised. All those boyish yearnings to make something of myself as a footballer had been replaced by some hard confidence. I had played against the Brazilians in the World Cup and I was part of the champion team of England. What had I to fear? John Giles, a man whom I respected hugely and I knew had a good opinion of my ability and my attitude, was the logical choice to replace Revie. Who better to protect and develop the legacy of the greater manager? Who knew more about the foundation of our success or had made a greater contribution to it out in the heat of battle? Giles surely was the man. It seemed so obvious. Only fools could take a different view, but then that may have been the problem.

Just as the dressing-room consensus had hardened into the belief that the job should go to the midfield general, the Leeds directors, beaming like cats who had gained possession of all the cream, went public with the triumphant news that they had signed the man who had for several years openly despised all that we had achieved.

John never made a case for himself, even when the chairman called him into his office to discuss the job, by which time, I learned later, Billy Bremner had made it clear that he wanted to be considered. Clough would later claim that Giles was the leader of the Leeds 'mafia' and had led the resistance to his appointment. That was complete fiction. Even though it was clear that John was entering that phase of his career when he had to think about the future, he had been as shocked as anyone else by the departure of Revie and he still thought of himself as a player, one who had just taken a crucial role in delivering a superb title win.

The case for his appointment was strong in several areas – and, interestingly, Bill Nicholson, the great manager of Tottenham Hotspur who delivered the double, had nominated him as his successor at White Hart Lane to work alongside the Spurs hero Danny Blanchflower – but, above all, he offered the chance of continuity. He knew the basis of Revie's success and he knew, more than any other possible candidate, the way the team thought and reacted to any challenge before them.

In another year he would be player-manager of West Bromwich Albion, leading them to promotion and a high place in the first division before deciding that the manager's life was not for him. He hated the necessity to defer to the views of directors who had little real knowledge of the game, and it depressed him that sometimes he couldn't get the rewards that he felt some players truly deserved. I was so sure he would have done the Leeds job well, and partly because he knew the kind of players he was dealing with. They had his respect.

From Clough we received something close to outright con-tempt. It was quite amazing when you stopped to think about it. Considering his style in those first days, you could reach only one conclusion. He was the wrong guy in the wrong place and whatever instincts he had for the game – which we learned later were quite brilliant when he led Nottingham Forest to two European Cup wins and proved that tactically and psychologically he was one of the great managers – were simply thrown away at that point in his career. Maybe he had to go through the Leeds experience to learn his limits after achieving so much success so quickly at Derby County, where his reign had ended in the tumult of players almost rioting against the board's decision to dismiss him.

There was no doubt some moves had to be made at Elland Road in the near future. Every team needs to be reshaped from time and time and, with Giles and Bremner pushing into their thirties, Leeds were no exception to the rule that preparing for change was a key part of the manager's job. The difference between how Giles would have viewed the challenge and how Clough met it could scarcely have been greater. The biggest problem for Clough was the baggage he brought. We all knew that in his days as Derby manager he had never had a good word to say about us. Indeed, he simply dismissed us as cheats. It did not encourage much trust.

He was the last man you would have thought would be given the job, even though he had undoubtedly produced a fine team at Derby, with Roy McFarland, a skilled England centre-half, and Colin Todd, another excellent defender. Alan Hinton gave them speed and width along the left, and John O'Hare was a strong centre-forward. Clough also recruited the vast experience of one of the greatest players ever to come out of Scotland, Dave Mackay. But we always had the measure of Derby, we always knew we could take them, and perhaps that was part of the problem when Clough arrived at Elland Road, suntanned from Majorca and carrying a squash racquet. He didn't make an introductory speech, he didn't even say, 'All right, lads, I'm your new manager, let's go.' When we finally had a full team meeting with him in his office, he made the notorious comment that if Eddie Gray had been a horse he would have been shot long ago. This was said to a brilliant, dedicated player who had suffered more than most with injuries. His words broke across us in a strange, disturbing rush. There was a deadly silence as we absorbed the meaning of what Clough had said, and then he announced that as far as he was concerned we could all throw our medals into the bin. We had not won them honestly.

It didn't seem to be a genius stroke of man-management, and this was especially so as it came from somebody who had already caused outrage among Leeds supporters when, as a guest speaker at a dinner thrown by Yorkshire TV that was supposed to be celebrating Peter Lorimer's award for being voted the local sportsman of the year, he sneered at the team's achievements, then announced, in mid-speech, that he was going for a 'piss'.

Clough displayed none of the thoroughness that was Revie's stock in trade. Our first game under his managership was a pre-season friendly with Aston Villa. We went for a pre-match meal at a hotel in West Bromwich, and the manager's team talk came in a brief, casual stroll around the car park. There was no formal announcement of the team or the way we would play.

It had been so different in Revie's regime. Before a Saturday game the ritual was unchanging. Before coming into the dressing room to deliver a team talk full of detail, Revie would send in a secretary to summon one of the players. You always knew what it meant when your name was called. You had been dropped and the manager would explain why. Invariably, he would soften the blow, maybe say that you needed a rest, but you were, he insisted, still right at the heart of his plans. He would then go into the dressing room to give a breakdown on the opposition, a general game plan and, finally, go through a list of specific demands on individual players. He listed the strengths of the opposition, warned us about where trouble lay and highlighted points of danger.

From that carefully structured routine, we had moved so suddenly to chaos. One of Clough's problems, and it had obviously not been considered by the board, was that he was simply without brownie points as far as both the players and the fans were concerned. As a rival manager, he had been too strident in his criticisms. At a time of fierce competition – in ten years, seven clubs had won the title, with Leeds, Liverpool and Manchester United all winning it twice, and Leeds finishing runners-up five times – he had given Revie and his men no credit, not even the concession that they had always been a factor, always had to be considered in the final equation of a title race.

For me, there was an additional problem. Although Clough played me in the early games, I sensed he didn't rate me too highly. I learned later that Norman Hunter and John Giles had formed a similar impression about Clough's view of them, as though he saw in the physical aspects of our play something he found unacceptable. In the cases of Giles and Hunter, however, he swallowed his reservations and they played throughout his rule of just forty-four days. Whether he came to the club with a negative view of my contribution, or was merely reacting to my form, I didn't know, but the unfortunate truth was that I wasn't doing myself a lot of justice. Maybe I was drained from the championship campaign and then the immediate immersion in Scotland's World Cup. That had been lot of new experience, and emotion, to deal with but, whatever the reason was, I was coming back into the dressing room knackered after a game.

Suddenly, it wasn't enough just to have won the battle for acceptance. Now I had to push on, enjoying the camaraderie in the team, but also making a mark in a way beyond mere battling. Everyone, including Clough, knew I could do that, but for all of us there was a sense that this was a new situation and perhaps we all had something to prove. That was what was so de-stabilising about the manner of Clough's arrival. It seemed that the old reality had been put into reverse; instead of seeking to build confidence, the new manager was working to break it down. It was hard to know what he expected to gain from this. He had inherited a team that had won the championship with some ease. At the very least, you would have thought he would have seen that this achievement had bought him plenty of time to make changes he might come to consider necessary.

My time ran out quickly enough under Clough. He went out and signed Duncan McKenzie, John O'Hare and John McGovern. McKenzie was a talented forward although perhaps not in the classic image of a Leeds player. He could perform marvellous tricks, but some of his best ones came off the field and included jumping over a Mini car. While O'Hare and McGovern were both hard workers, with the former showing that he had enough strength and nerve to do a good job as a target man, they didn't obviously strengthen a club that had been used to strikers such as Clarke and Jones and midfielders of the quality of Giles and Bremner. However, if I could blame Clough for a lot of things, they didn't include the loss of my first-team place. For one reason or another, I just hadn't played well enough in Clough's brief time at the club and I paid the inevitable price.

Fortunately, it could have been a lot heavier. Clough, it was plain to everyone including himself, was not the man to pick up the baton from Don Revie. His regime was broken and over in those few weeks of failure, and the directors had no option but to admit that they had completely misread the challenge of replacing

101

the manager who had so powerfully shaped the club over twelve years of relentless competitiveness.

For our part, we felt we had had a visit from a wrecking ball, and our regrets could only be intensified when he went on to such brilliant work at Nottingham Forest. It was a comfort, though, to learn that quite how he did it would always be a mystery, even to some of his key players. My Scottish team-mate Archie Gemmill said that he didn't think he was the only one who was never quite sure why he produced everything he had for Clough. 'You could never be sure of what he was going to do or say next, and maybe that was the trick,' said Gemmill. 'Maybe you played partly out of fear. He certainly kept you on your toes.'

Maybe Clough's greatest problem at Elland Road was that his new players had long been conditioned to operating in such a condition. No tricks of motivation were required; provocations, psychological sleights of hand, were superfluous to a pattern of intense competition. If you wanted to put an edge on a player's desire, hand him a yellow bib after training. Drive him back into the dressing room with derision. Get his blood flowing in a serious way.

The additional problem for Clough was that despite the brilliance of the drive for the championship, there was a certain fragility about the team. Mick Jones had come to the end of his career, finally giving way to the recurrent problem of a chronic knee injury. Giles and Bremner were another year older, and if Terry Yorath had put in some powerful performances when Giles had been injured in the title year, he too was one of those players who had failed to convince Clough that he represented an important part of the club's future.

Revie's departure in itself demanded a measured reaction and some understanding of the insecurities it would breed in a dressing room that had long been filled with certainties about what was expected of each individual. There was no coaxing, no reassurance from Mr Clough, and when he left the ground for the last time, Leeds were in the most unfamiliar of positions, near the bottom of the first division.

Champions do not go bad so quickly and when Jimmy Armfield, the amiable, pipe-smoking manager of Bolton Wanderers, arrived at Elland Road, he was smart enough to realise that. His style wasn't to the liking of some of the senior players, especially Giles, who had always favoured the direct approach. John often became impatient with the new manager's belief that compromise was a necessity to heal some of the wounds opened up in the brief, painful time when Brian Clough had attempted to kick dust over the regime of one of his greatest – and least respected – rivals.

On one occasion, Armfield left Giles out at Newcastle and put him on the bench. With ten minutes to go and Leeds trailing 3–0, Armfield told John to strip down for action. Giles' expression combined disbelief and defiance and the idea was shelved instantly. Nobody needed telling that we were a team fast approaching the end of our time, and this incident was another indicator that, if Revie had stayed on, or been succeeded by someone from within the club, the process might have been more gradual, and so much easier on the spirit and the confidence of players who had been operating so successfully together for so long. We are talking a matter of degree, though. There was still formidable talent in the squad, of course, and individually most of the players could look forward to a few more productive years on the field – but not as a group. As a unit, there was a strong sense that we didn't have much left.

Armfield, who had a lot of experience in the game, had to close down a whole era and start another with as much tact and timing as he could muster. At the same time, he had to nurse the team through a season that had started, by their own standards, quite catastrophically. There was also the quite significant matter of a run at the greatest prize in club football – the European Cup.

Elland Road was certainly not the right place to seek out a quiet life. Jimmy Armfield may have made a few mistakes in dealing

with individual players, but he faced a huge challenge in circumstances that had been made very tense. The old trust and certainty
had broken down, and overall I thought he did all right. For one
thing, he restored me to the team, and that was before Clough
came back to Elland Road to sign the two players with whom he
had struck up a rapport – his own men, O'Hare and McGovern.

For me, the challenge was quite basic – to re-entrench myself
and get a little stronger. As Revie settled into his new job as
England manager, one that would eventually cloud so much of his
achievement at Leeds, I counted myself lucky that I had known
both him and the team he had made when they were at the peak
of their powers. Overwhelmingly, I had a feeling of sadness and
disappointment that he had left Elland Road. I couldn't have
wished for a better grounding than the one he had given me.
When I arrived I had so much catching up to do, physically,
mentally, professionally, but he carried me through. I often
wondered what would have happened to me if I'd gone somewhere else, if when Hal Stewart finally opened the box, the name
on the paper was somewhere other than Leeds United. It might
have taken me longer to pass the tests, maybe circumstances
would have worked against me. I may not have got the same
foundation in those principles that served me well right to the end
of my career. I like to think I would have done it anyway, but I
wouldn't have had such a great start.

In the end, when the trauma of the Clough days had passed, I
could only be grateful that I had survived and prospered at Elland
Road. I had been schooled in the basic principles, made it into the
team and stayed there – and, finally, I was accepted as part of
something extraordinary, and perhaps unique, in football. Thirty
years on, my perspective on those days remains the same. Of
course, the game has changed dramatically and the players have so
many more rewards and freedoms, but some basic requirements
are still in place. Standards of commitment have to be accepted.
You still have to have good habits because without them, without

the spirit among team-mates, a fierce camaraderie, you just couldn't do it, not consistently. You wouldn't be able to win more than one championship, or to come back – and this was the key to Leeds United and will always mark out the great teams – after crushing disappointment.

All the major players and teams have been slapped down and then fought their way back. Why? Because the managers have set certain standards, created an atmosphere, a team spirit and durability. This cannot be built without the strongest leadership. You have to have a figurehead, such as Sir Alex Ferguson or Arsene Wenger, who picked out Bryan Robson, Roy Keane and Patrick Vieira. You have to have a sound transfer of the baton, and if that doesn't happen you have a major problem. For Leeds, the extent of it would emerge soon enough. They needed to replace Don Revie and, of course, it just happened that in his time and his place he was unique.

8

A STATE OF FLUX

JIMMY Armfield must have felt as though he was walking into a minefield when he moved from the relative calm of Bolton Wanderers to a taut and wary Elland Road. Everyone had been bruised and shaken by the last few weeks, and this was as true of the battle-hardened veterans as the youngest apprentices. The senior players were so used to the style and methods of Don Revie, and the space he had granted them to wield their influence in their different ways, it was inevitable there would be friction from time to time. There was pressure on everyone to rebuild the image of Leeds as a winning team and to do that we had to re-create some of that old sense of permanent values.

John Giles and Billy Bremner might say, as all of us probably did when we looked at ourselves in the mirror, that they were professionals who wanted the best for the team, and heaven knows they had done enough to make that claim, but, in the end, a bit of human nature comes into play.

Leeds United had been shaped by intense experience and what could an outsider, however well meaning, bring to this ferocious party at such a late hour? Jimmy was no doubt aware of that deep sense of separation from the rest of English football that Revie had developed down the years and one way he tried to counter it was by employing his folksy Lancashire approach to life as best he could.

Once, he infuriated Giles when, after dropping him because, he claimed, the pitch would be too heavy for him, he pointed out that his own grandfather had come from John's native Dublin. This was the manager's opening gambit after Giles had come striding into his office, his face thunderous, after hearing the announcement of the team. Giles said he didn't care where Jimmy's grandfather came from, all he wanted to say was that he had played more than five hundred games for Leeds and that quite a number of them had been played on pitches that looked as though they could have doubled as First World War battle-fields, and if the manager wanted to offer a reason for dropping someone he should come up with one that might make a little more sense.

In such fraught circumstances, reaching the final of the European Cup was a rather fine achievement. Perhaps not surprisingly, we didn't get a 'good luck' message from Brian Clough and nor did we get any sense that the referee was in a mood to do us even the basic favour of impartiality. Getting to the Parc des Princes in Paris for the big game, and seeing the concern on the face of the great Franz Beckenbauer as we stretched his Bayern Munich to their limits, was something to restore our pride if not, in the end, our spirits.

For Armfield, like everyone else, Leeds United had been a tough place to settle in to – all those little tests of nerve and confidence – and after the upheavals he had been required to smooth away, he too had every reason for satisfaction. As damage control goes, it was a formidable effort and said a lot for that Armfield instinct for compromise and, perhaps even more, the enduring ability of Leeds' players to dig down and find some fresh reserves of will and ambition.

My own contribution through the league season was mostly restricted to that will and ambition. Inspiration, for some time, had flown out of my football. Although Armfield made it clear that he thought a lot more of my ability than Clough had done, and proved it by putting me straight back into the team, I still couldn't snap back into that old stride. I fought, I hustled, but the more I tried the more elusive I found the confidence that is such a vital part of a striker's game. Indeed, whenever I tried to tell myself I was winning the battle, that I was just a stride away from getting it all back, another discouragement showed me I wasn't. The worst of it was a sound that I was hearing for the first time in my professional career. I was being barracked by a crowd that had always been welcoming, always shown their appreciation that here was a strong young player who knew what was required at Elland Road.

There is nothing more dispiriting in football than a harsh judgement from the terraces. No matter how unjust you may think it is, the booing gets into your bones. So maybe the fans don't understand all the intricacies and subtleties of the game; perhaps when someone else scores, they do not pick up on the value of the unselfish run you put in to split the defence, or the knocked-down ball that came from a brave intervention and resulted in a team-mate scoring a spectacular goal, but there is almost invariably an accurate sense of who is feeling good about himself and who isn't. Fans can sniff that out like hounds in pursuit of a fox.

Most players are at some time trapped in this vicious circle, and with so many old heads in the dressing room I was not short of an encouraging word. What you have to do, said the old sweats, is tell yourself that the fans can go and stuff it. You know what you can do, so you just have to get on with it.

I did that most effectively in the European campaign. I put in strong performances in Zurich and Budapest as we made confident progress to a quarter-final against Anderlecht and the big challenge of a semi-final with the Barcelona of Johan Cruyff and Johan Neeskens. Cruyff, the Golden Dutchman, was in imperious form. He had taken Spain by storm after his transfer from Ajax of Amsterdam, and we knew that to have any chance of making it to the final we had to hit Barcelona hard in the first leg at Elland Road. We had to do nothing less than resurrect the most stirring days of Leeds United.

In fact, we did it in a fashion that recalled some of the best work of the great years, and I was proud – and much relieved – to play a part. The goal that put Cruyff and his men on their heels flowed from one of Revie's most insistent demands of his players – when the ball goes dead, his team must burst into life.

Giles took a quick free kick with his usual probing precision and I was able to run free of the cover and knock it down sideways for the in-running Bremner. He hit it as sweetly as he had ever done anything on a football field, volleying into the top corner of the net. We hoped that might break the spirit of Barcelona, but they were too good to be swept to one side. They equalised and dug in to resist a second-half siege. That holding action might have succeeded against a less resolute team than this one, but we were fighting so hard to restate our place in the game, and near the end Allan Clarke gave us a precious edge for the second leg when he shot home from close in. I had got my head to the ball for another vital knock-down.

After the lean months, I was naturally delighted to have made an important contribution to such a big win, and the idea of returning to the great Nou Camp stadium, where I had taken those early, tentative steps as a Leeds player three years earlier, as a key player was tremendously exciting. It might have been less so, though, if I had known quite how the Barca defenders were preparing to receive me. Within twenty minutes of the start of the Nou Camp game, I had a busted nose and a fast-closing eye. Marinho, Barcelona's Brazilian World Cup player, was the man who did the damage. He whacked me off the ball on the blindside of the referee.

It was painful but also quite flattering and it certainly did not diminish my willingness to have a go. I got on the end of a long ball out of our defence and played it down to Peter Lorimer, who lashed it home. Barca were inflamed now, and although they equalised, they became increasingly desperate in pursuit of the second goal that would bring them level in the tie. There was a lot of cynical work, and when Gordon McQueen finally responded to some relentless needling, landing a big punch, he was sent off.

The last twenty minutes were incredibly tense. An extraordinary climax of noise emanated from the great terraces, one crescendo exceeding another. Prompted by the brilliant Cruyff, Barcelona streamed towards our goal, but the ten men of Leeds refused to break. This, I think we all sensed, might be the last of the team the football world had come to know for their winning instincts, and if we had to go, we would go hard. No blood or sweat would be withheld.

We received a great reception when we returned to Leeds, and it seemed that the work of redemption was well under way. Certainly, my own approval level had risen sharply on the terraces and in the media. This was also true, it appeared, in one of the great clubs of Europe, our final opponents, Bayern Munich.

A few days before the final, a spread in the *Sun* announced that I was high on Bayern's wish list. The German coach, Dietmar Cramer, was quoted at some length, saying that if he could buy anyone from Leeds it would be the big striker Jordan, a dangerous player who was strong in the air and would always trouble a defence. Sometimes you read things in the press that, even if they are flattering, have to be taken with a little caution, but this seemed to be a well-researched piece and emphasised the fact that I had been in good form throughout the drive to the European final. I had a sense that Cramer's comments carried more than a touch of authenticity, so I filed them away for future attention, to be reviewed, maybe, after I had made a significant impact on the big game.

Again, I played well, as did all my colleagues, but the run was over – and some of the old bitterness would return to our hearts. At the end of the game some Leeds fans rioted, wrecking seats and creating a notorious image of frustration in defeat. The truth was that the players felt equally angry. It was the worst refereeing we had encountered since the Cup-winners' Cup defeat by AC Milan in Salonika two years earlier. The fine Bayern team, so coolly marshalled by Beckenbauer and led up front by the predatory Gerd Muller, were under pressure from the start.

It was encouraging to look into the eyes of their players, including those of the Emperor, Beckenbauer. They looked uneasy. They liked to play at a controlled pace, but we were tearing at them. I knocked a ball down to Peter Lorimer twenty-two yards out and he produced one of his trademark thunder-bolts. It ripped into the back of the net but the referee waved away the goal – said that Bremner had strayed offside. It was a travesty of a decision, we felt, and another one came when Clarke wriggled his way into the box before being brought down by Beckenbauer. The referee pointed for a corner. It was hard to believe such a decision could happen at that level of the game. Clarke was between Beckenbauer and the ball. We continued to attack, but we had the numbing sense that whatever we did we would be thwarted. Bayern, against the run of play, scored two goals in the last fifteen minutes. To their credit, they seemed almost embarrassed to take the prize.

Memories of Salonika and the loss to Milan came flooding back. Then the rage was so great that coach Syd Owen had come on to the field to tell us not to swap shirts with the Milan players. The occasion was one, he said, not to be remembered. Indeed, the only question was whether we would ever be able to forget it. Later, when I went to Italy, that old raw anger returned when some of the Milan players recalled the game. They laughed at the memory of how we had so dominated, how their goalkeeper had made some miraculous saves, and how it was that they had collected the trophy after scarcely mustering a single shot. They said you could call it cynical, outrageous, anything you liked, but the game had been won and in the end that was all that mattered.

Anyway, these things tended to level off. Milan flew back to Italy for what was considered to be something of a formality, the victory over Verona that would bring the great prize of the league title, the fabled *scudetto*. They lost 5–3.

In Paris, I lost my Leeds shirt in the dressing room and searched for it desperately. Eventually, I tracked it down to the kit-man as he dragged the skip to the team-bus. I wanted the shirt to remember not a defeat but the last drive of a great team. We didn't get where we wanted, not right at the end, but we had made the journey; we had pulled out all we could and there was a certain honour in that. Sometimes you define yourself in defeat even more than in victory, and for anyone who wanted a study of a team that was always determined to fight as hard as they could, that effort in the Parc des Princes would do well enough. Some of the best of the team had gone, we all knew that, but not the cussed pride, the defiant belief that somehow we might just find a way to win.

Along with that badge of noble defeat, my front teeth also went missing. Normally, I would put the denture in my jacket pocket in the dressing room, but on this occasion I had believed that I might well be celebrating a moment of great triumph and I decided that I didn't want to be running around out there with my arms in the air but with no teeth. Nobby Stiles had done that after winning the World Cup at Wembley nine years earlier, and he said his wife had never forgiven him.

So I handed my teeth to Dave Harvey, which on reflection was not the safest thing to do. Dave was out of the game following a car crash and his place had been taken by David Stewart. When I got back into the dressing room, Dave had gone missing. There was no celebration, but I still needed my teeth. Eventually, someone handed me the denture on the team bus heading back to the hotel.

I shoved the teeth back into my mouth and grimaced. At least, if necessary, I could try to smile in the brave way that is sometimes expected amid the resignation of defeat. In the meantime, I would bury my head in my chest and try to remember that the important thing to know was that you had given your team everything you had. I looked around the bus and saw that all my team-mates were grappling with similar thoughts. No one quite put it into words, but there was an overwhelming sense that we had come to the end of something. So this, someone might have said if they could have mustered the energy, was how it was when a great team reached the end of the road.

Perhaps inevitably, as the bus rolled through the brightly lit streets of Paris, I thought of how it had been in those early days when everything was before me at Leeds. One memory that came back into focus when I thought of how far I had come with this team, now on the point of break-up, was a big game at West Ham during another title challenge. I came on as substitute in a match that was crackling fiercely, London clubs always saving their biggest performances for games against Leeds – at home, that was. I remembered taking the ball to the great Bobby Moore, imagining that I could go by him – yes, I was feeling good and strong that day – and he took it off me in the cleanest tackle. I was already cursing myself when he came through and took the ball. I knew I should have passed it, but only when it was too late. I had hesitated for a fatal moment and West Ham went downfield from my lost possession and scored. It cost us a vital point and when I went back into the dressing room a wash-bag flew past my head and splattered against the wall. It had been thrown by Revie's angry lieutenant Les Cocker. It was not so much that he had thrown it at me but what had happened. It troubled me a lot at the time and on the train back north Revie had come over to Gordon McQueen and said, 'You better look after your mate, he's feeling it quite badly tonight.' He knew that it was something I would never forget.

After losing the European Cup final, the first instinct was to seek the shadows where we could nurse our wounds, but Armfield, unlike Revie, was not averse to taking his players to the sunshine, even when duty didn't demand it. So instead of returning to our separate lives and wondering how many of us would re-assemble at Elland Road for the next campaign, we gathered a few days later for a 'winding down' session beside the swimming pool of a five-star hotel in Marbella. Jimmy meant it to be a relaxing, bonding trip but the unity of the team had already reached its zenith and the new manager was dealing with forces that had long been shaped.

One major eruption showed Armfield, if it was necessary at this point, that he was dealing with a team who sensed they were in a time of flux. As is usually the case when players get together off-duty, there were some high spirits and practical jokes and, on this occasion, evidence that in the wake of Revie's departure discipline had slipped. Wear and tear on some relationships was apparent when Armfield called a special meeting of the team late one afternoon. It seemed that, the night before, some of the high spirits had gone beyond the approval of the hotel management. Two of the players – it turned out to be Billy Bremner and Allan Clarke – had got a little carried away as they returned to their room and the result was a game of football involving a pair of shoes put out for cleaning by one of the guests. Armfield described it as 'some misbehaviour' and said if there was any repeat we would all have to fly home early. Nowadays, when players frequently appear on the front pages of the tabloids accused of the wildest behaviour at home and abroad, this may sound trivial, but it was serious enough back in 1975.

Revie had applied the fiercest discipline in the matter of off-field behaviour. He had monitored the nocturnal activities of Gordon McQueen and me. He had the young Bremner kneel down and give a prayer of thanks for all his good fortune in being a professional footballer. In the past, the players would have presented a solid front but on this occasion some raised the point that all shouldn't be punished for the misbehaviour of the few.

Eventually, a compromise was reached and our time in the sun stretched on for a few more days, but there was no question about it – Leeds United was changing before our eyes. For Armfield it was plainly time to bring in some new faces.

Did that include replacing mine? I had had some great years at Leeds but I knew that sometimes in football the best thing that can happen is moving on to a new challenge, a new environment. For the first time I had begun to muse on reports of impending transfers. I had established myself in the Scotland team and, judging by that report on the interest of Bayern Munich, there might just be a place for me beyond Elland Road – perhaps even beyond England.

As we whiled away the time, taking our drinks beside the pool, playing a little golf and cards and letting the tensions of that ultimately frustrating season drain away, my thoughts were increasingly drawn to what the future might bring. Of course, in the meantime, there were the usual diversions, not least the requirement of being on guard against the practical jokes so beloved of many of my team-mates. Even in that atmosphere, total relaxation was always out of the question.

On this occasion, one of the usual ringleaders, John Giles, was not so forthcoming. He had a room away from the crowd and, it would soon become known, moving business of his own to consider. West Bromwich wanted him to be their player-manager and he was spending a lot of time mulling over his future. Nevertheless, he was around and you had to be wary. This was my first thought as a bellboy appeared by the swimming pool with a board anouncing a phone call for me. The boy told me that the caller was waiting so I followed him, somewhat apprehensively. A Mr Dietmar Cramer, coach of Bayern Munich, was calling me from Germany. Of course, there had been that story in the *Sun*. Neither Bremner nor Giles had mentioned it to me but no doubt it was the kind of thing they might store away for future use, and when I looked around I saw that they were there, sipping their rum and cokes and, no doubt, waiting for the entertainment to begin. I whispered to Gordon McQueen, 'I think those tormenting bastards are at it again. Take the call for me.' When I heard what I took to be a phony German accent at the other end of the line, I handed the phone to Gordon and in a loud voice that carried across the pool, he said how much he would like to join the great Bayern Munich but added that the move would be possible only on one condition. The deal also had to include my great friend and brilliant team-mate, Gordon McQueen.

The conversation went on for some time, and there was no change in the tone of Gordon's voice. I also noticed, with some alarm, that Bremner and Giles were paying no attention. Suddenly, my blood ran cold. Here, maybe, was one of the top coaches in Europe, the holder of the European Cup, seeking my services just a few days after his greatest triumph. Finally, Gordon said, 'Yes, thank you, I'll certainly think about it – but only if you think about Gordon McQueen.'

McQueen said that maybe the call had been the real thing, maybe Bremner and Giles had worked their most deadly stroke without even trying. When Gordon kept hammering on about the need to sign McQueen, the voice at the other end was apparently very calm, and gave no sign of breaking into laughter, simply saying, quite patiently, 'Yes, I know McQueen is a good defender, but you know we do have Beckenbauer and George Schwarzen-beck [the German international centre-half] and I don't really think I need strengthening in those positions.' I could only shudder again when I recalled the detail of that story in the *Sun*, and my feeling that really it was something more than routine speculation. In my anxiety that I had ruined the chance of a great move, I thought of challenging Bremner and Giles, but that too would have been courting another kind of disaster. I just had to try to sleep with the idea that Cramer had put down the phone with the sad conviction that, however impressed he had been with my fighting displays across Europe, it probably wasn't a good idea to sign a raving Scottish lunatic.

Two days later, on our last morning in Marbella, the phone in the hotel room rang at a very early hour. It was, said the voice on the phone, Dietmar Cramer calling from Munich. Gordon, who was sharing the room, was still fast asleep and it seemed to me that it was far too early for Bremner or Giles to be on a wind-up mission.

'Have you thought any more about what I said the other day,' asked the voice, which I was now nearly certain belonged to the coach of Bayern Munich.

'Yes, I have,' I said very quickly. 'I shall be in my home tomorrow morning and here's my telephone number.' When he called the next day, he said that he was faxing Leeds United with an offer of a million marks, a record bid from a club who had produced some of the biggest names in European football.

Suddenly, the pain of the Parc des Princes and all the doubts of a long and ultimately frustrating season fell away. It was the football life, of course. One day it could pitch you in the dirt, the next it could carry you to the stars. I had a vision of riches in Germany, a big Mercedes and a life of luxury for my steady girlfriend Judith, but also – and I knew that this would never be a secondary concern as long as I played the game – I would have the chance to develop my football. The journey from Cleland was poised to move into a new dimension. First there was the Corn Patch, then Morton by the shipyard cranes, then Elland Road in glory and despair, and now, maybe, Munich's shining, futuristic Olympic stadium, the home of Beckenbauer and Muller, the Emperor and Der Bomber. First I had to persuade Jimmy Armfield and Leeds United that I had earned my right to move on.

I drove down to Elland Road in a mood of great excitement, perhaps as exhilarated as at any time since Bobby Collins whispered into my ear that Leeds had bid for me. However, Jimmy Armfield puffed on his pipe and was emphatic.

'Yes,' he said, 'there is a fax in the office. Bayern have bid a million marks but you can't go, and there's nothing I can do about it.'

There it was, no argument. I had less than a year left on my contract, but I was in the hands of the Leeds board. They had had my services for five years, and now they stood to make a profit of around £200,000 but it didn't suit them to sell, so there was nothing to do. I argued vehemently with Armfield. I asked him what kind of justice was there in this. How was it that in practically any other walk of life you could better yourself whenever you wanted, but here, so long after the George Eastham football 'slavery' case fifteen years earlier, a club could retain your registration and, in effect, own your life. Of course, Armfield had been a professional himself for many years. He had grown up at a time when great footballers, including his club-mate at Blackpool, Stanley Matthews, and down the road at Preston, the equally brilliant Tom Finney, players who had filled stadiums all across the country, could not officially be paid more than £20 a week. There was the terrible story of how Finney, after many years of superb service to Preston, was offered a new life in Italy with rewards that he found staggering, but after days of waiting in great suspense he received the flat word from the boardroom: 'No.'

Now, twenty years later on a morning in Leeds that had started so brightly, I was in the same frustrating position. I railed against the situation but Armfield just sucked on his pipe and said, 'I'm afraid it's just the way it is, lad.'

Apart from any money involved in a move to Munich, which I assumed would be much better than it was at Leeds, there was that sickening feeling of being imprisoned by somebody else's will. I wanted the experience of playing in another country and living for a while in a different culture. I wanted to see how they did it in Europe. I wanted to continue and widen my journey from Cleland. I had come from Lanarkshire, as Jimmy Delaney and so many other professional footballers had done, but although I loved the place I didn't want to go back. I didn't want to be one day standing at that bus-stop with a knapsack over my shoulder. Times, and expectations, had changed me, and it was extremely hard to come to terms with the fact that I too might be trapped in a time warp, where footballers lacked control over their working lives. I was proud to come from Cleland, the people there had always supported me, but I had my own life and I wanted to be able to keep taking my chances to deepen the experience of it.

Much later, I recalled John Giles saying how much he had admired the courage of Kevin Keegan when he shook away the hold of Liverpool a few years after I had been denied my move to Europe. Keegan was a superhero at Anfield, and some of his friends and team-mates were amazed that he would want to leave a place that had become his personal fortress. Keegan had the feelings that had so inflamed me after the phone call from Dietmar Cramer, but the difference was he insisted on his move. Giles lamented the fact that whole generations of players had been denied the chance to improve their careers and their lives, and he said that would always be a matter of resentment. It was amazing, when I thought about it, that players such as Giles and Bremner, who had given so much to one club, had to settle for any rewards that Leeds had been willing to offer. Today sometimes we look at football with shock and disbelief, and in recent times nowhere more so than Leeds, where a great club came so close to extinction because mediocre players were receiving more than £30,000 a week, but just twenty-odd years ago the situation was equally absurd in that quite different way.

Although I feared the worst, I didn't accept my fate immediately. The more I thought about it, the angrier I became.

'Listen, Jimmy,' I said. 'I don't care what you or anybody says, I will be back down here tomorrow and I'll still be demanding my move. I'm off.'

Maybe I just had to make noises like that. They no doubt came out of my bruised pride because, apart from anything else, for a grown man who had just accepted the responsibilities of family life, it was quite humiliating to learn that you could not do something that elsewhere would have been perfectly acceptable and legal.

At the time, some of the Leeds fans who had given me so much support down the years may have had the feeling that I was a 'selfish git', but from my viewpoint I had always given full value and here was a step I wanted to take. Bayern were the reigning European champions – the following year they would repeat their success – and I wanted to be part of something like that.

'I'm sorry,' I said to Armfield, 'I'm not being disloyal. If I'm playing next week, you'll get what you got last week. But this is something different, this is about my life, my future and everyone has the right to do the best they can for themselves and their families.'

I called Cramer in Munich in some despair. He said that he was sorry but he had done all he could. Leeds had received an official offer from Bayern and, yes, it was a club record, and he just couldn't go beyond that. Now he had to move on.

That was football. One moment life was fixed, you had a clear goal, and the next it was all a matter of chance. At another time, maybe Armfield would not have seen me as a valuable member of his team, and would have told the board they could sell me at that considerable profit and he could produce a satisfactory replacement at half the cost. Clough, presumably, would have snatched the German money. Time was running out for so many of the players who had made Leeds United what they were. The time simply wasn't right for me. As I walked out of the ground, resigned to spending at least another year in a place that until so recently had been the centre of my universe, I couldn't help remembering the first time I had been in that car park, or thinking how quickly the days, and the magic, had gone.

9

THE OLD TRAFFORD EXPERIENCE

AFTER the force of being part of an all-conquering Leeds, and the dousing of the flame that spurted when I thought I might be joining Franz Beckenbauer and the reigning champions of Europe, the football horizons crowded in for a while, at least as far as the staple of club football was concerned. There was still the chase for redemption with Scotland, but for a while a vital edge had gone from the daily challenge of my professional life.

Eventually, as I had hoped when I vowed to fight through these suddenly less promising days, my career would stretch out with new challenges again, and in places that were touched by fantasies established long before the rise of Don Revie's Leeds – Manchester United and AC Milan, where greatness was so tangible that, even when it desperately needed to be revived, you could breathe it and smell it.

First, two hard years had to be got through – one long battle to maintain and develop my reputation in a team that no longer spread fear among the opposition when they ran on to the field. In the year after that bleak bus ride through Paris, the brilliant creative force of Leeds had dispersed, and so had the heavy armour. Jimmy Armfield sold John Giles to West Bromwich Albion, Terry Cooper to Middlesbrough, Billy Bremner to Hull City, Terry Yorath to Coventry and, most surprisingly, the younger Norman Hunter to Bristol City. That was the heart of the team – one that Armfield

121

believed had grown too old and weary. In the cases of Giles and Hunter, particularly, that view provoked considerable disagreement in the dressing room. Giles no doubt had seen his best days but Hunter was still at the peak of his powers.

The fact was that for all my respect for the players who had driven the club to such success and set amazing standards of commitment and resilience, I had to accept that in some ways Armfield was right. Giles and Bremner might still be phenomenal midfield generals but they were growing older and a manager who doesn't recognise such realities is simply not doing his job.

This was a desperately difficult task for a new manager at Leeds – on reflection, perhaps it was one of the reasons Clough had behaved in such an erratic fashion when he arrived at Elland Road. Perhaps, quite apart from his own prejudices, he realised that a lot of pruning had to be done despite the success of the previous year. In football, there is no easy way of doing that. Jimmy's manner was not what the Leeds players were used to but he had had a long and distinguished career as a player and a certain amount of success as a manager at Bolton Wanderers. He was doing what he had to do in the best way he could and it should have been no surprise that it made quite a lot of people unhappy. However, the decision to part with Hunter, who had been such a huge factor in Leeds' defensive strength, was certainly made to look premature when he helped, superbly, to maintain Bristol City's fleeting life in the first division.

The transition was never going to be easy. Jimmy inherited the dilemmas that would, inevitably, have presented a new set of challenges to Revie, too. Jimmy obviously felt that he had to produce a reshaped Leeds, and no doubt there was a case for a serious review of the team's strength. The trouble was that you just couldn't go out and whistle up a new Giles or Bremner or Hunter.

Tony Currie was seen by Jimmy as the new Giles, but that was asking too much of even the highly talented player signed from Sheffield United. Currie, blond and with a lovely touch on the ball, made a mark in the game and won seventeen caps for England, but he couldn't begin to match the control and generalship that had for so long been the Giles trademarks. Armfield signed other good players, including the little Welsh craftsman Brian Flynn from Burnley, but the team refused to catch fire. The best we could do was reach an FA Cup semi-final in 1977 against Manchester United, which we lost 2–1 at Hillsborough.

In the circumstances, I could tell myself that I was doing well enough. The team might not be going places, at least not for a while, but that might not be my fate. I was holding my place in the Scottish team against the opposition of Derek Johnstone and Derek Parlane of Rangers and Andy Gray of Aston Villa. Johnstone was a particularly potent rival, the hero of Ibrox with a forty-goal scoring mark. I continued to do my work in the way that had served me well under Revie and in the World Cup campaign and had, I learned with a thrill that reminded me of that first time I saw myself bracketed with Bayern Munich, impressed another great European club, Ajax of Amsterdam. Yes, the Ajax who had given the world Cruyff, Neskeens and Krol, who had swept into the seventies with a brilliant hat-trick of European Cup victories over Panathinaikos, Inter Milan and Juventus, were the latest to apply for the services of the graduate of the Corn Patch. Naturally, I was delighted to sit down with Ajax officials and my lawyer, Ronnie Teeman, at a hotel near Leeds airport.

Ronnie and I had not discussed pay demands in any detail. We just assumed that a club of Ajax's stature, one that had been accommodating some of the world's most outstanding players for so long, would not be skimping on wages when it came to an important signing. However, when they did make their offer, after encouraging talk of the vital role I would play in Amsterdam, it was a crushing disappointment – just a few pounds more than I was on at Leeds.

Some people might say that I had my chance, that if I yearned for a wider football experience and the opportunity to experience the continental game, I should have gambled on my ability to make an impact in Holland and gain financially later. Some press reports even suggested I was trying to drive a hard bargain and turning down a 'fantastic' offer. It simply wasn't true. I was ambitious and, more than anything, I wanted to continue to develop as a footballer, but when Ronnie and I discussed the Ajax offer, and considered that Dutch tax levels were just as punishing as those in England, we decided that I had no option but to say no. It was another heavy disappointment, one to rank with the Munich affair, and it made me wonder if I would ever cross my new Rubicon of the North Sea or the English Channel. However, one of the other aspects of being a professional, apart from dedication and good discipline, is a determination never to allow yourself to be undervalued. Some critics said, 'Well, Joe Jordan had his choice,' and it was true. I chose to say, 'No, thank you.' I wasn't being shopped for by the great Ajax in football's bargain basement.

It meant that, in terms of my club career, the promise was of a bleak Christmas and, compared with the three or four that had gone before it, a grey New Year: Leeds remained locked in mediocrity and once again the doors of European football had first opened to me, then slammed shut. What could I do? Play hard and hope that something else turned up. It was a formula that had worked well enough in the past and this time, after the jarring experience with Ajax, I was rewarded more quickly than I could have hoped. Leeds' willingness to listen to Ajax's bid – the figure mentioned was £300,000 – had sent out the message that I was available. The result was spectacular. One late, dark afternoon Jimmy Armfield called me at home to say that Leeds had accepted a bid of £350,000 from Manchester United and United wanted to talk to me as soon as possible.

I met the United contingent in the Elland Road car park and they followed me to my home. I kept the big car in sight in my mirror, which was quite an act of concentration because my mind was racing – back, once again, to that bus-stop in Cleland where I had first weighed the great deeds of my co-villager, Jimmy Delaney of Manchester United and Scotland. Going to Leeds had been an immense experience. Now I felt that, as far as English football was concerned, I was entering into a final dimension. These might not have been the greatest days of Manchester United, but the very name of the club had a meaning that still flew beyond the latest column of wins and losses.

The sense of a huge club was still there, even though it was ten years since Sir Matt Busby had realised his dream of winning the European Cup, a decade after the Munich air tragedy, and the pickings had been thin since then. There had been a brief, traumatic visit to the second division, and the new manager Dave Sexton was in the first stages of repairing the damage caused by Tommy Docherty's dramatic exit following his hugely publicised affair with the wife of club physiotherapist Laurie Brown. The much-respected Sexton was clearly getting powerful backing. His offer for me was a British record, and it was not as though United were notably weak up front. They had the current England striker, Stuart Pearson, and beside him the gifted former Leeds star Jimmy Greenhoff.

The composition of the United signing team suggested they didn't want to leave anything to chance. It consisted of Sexton, Busby, club secretary Les Olive and the chairman, Louis Edwards. Plainly, there would be no obstacle to an instant deal; compromises and decisions could be reached on the spot. Leeds had said yes and in the lounge of my house, all the men who were needed to agree my terms and seal the contract were congregated. In one corner of the room an animated conversation was going on between Sir Matt and my father, who was visiting with my mother. They talked of Lanarkshire and the old days and, inevitably, Jimmy Delaney.

Sexton and I went into the kitchen to get down to the heart of the negotiations. I was on £270 a week with Leeds and, as a newly married man, I was hoping for a decent rise. The offer came swiftly and was entirely satisfactory.

'We're thinking of paying you £500 a week,' said Sexton.

That was in line with their top-paid players, my compatriots Lou Macari and Martin Buchan, and I said it would be fine. We agreed on a piece of business that by today's standards may seem slight indeed, but then it represented, at least in the mind of the public and some football directors, a quite dreamy level of reward for a leading player. I was due a signing bonus of £17,500, 5 per cent of the transfer fee, a hefty amount in 1978 but much less impressive when you worked out the tax due on the lump sum. The tax man would have claimed 82 per cent if I hadn't immediately paid it into a pension fund.

After the George Best years, the image of a leading footballer was one of designer clothes and fast cars, but the reality of it was that someone wanting to build a family was still some way from a life of financial ease. Back then, £500 a week sounded like a fortune, especially to someone such as my father, but the fact was that when the tax man had done his work you didn't get anything like that figure and you weren't going to earn that kind of money until you were sixty. I was just twenty-six when I sat in that pleasant but hardly extravagant house in Leeds and said yes to Manchester United's offer. I owed £15,000 on my mortgage and three and a half years later, when I left Old Trafford, I still had a mortgage for precisely the same amount.

I was twenty-nine by then and the father of three young children, and, given the way I played and the physical pressure that was involved, had a maximum of five or six years left as a player. This is not a complaint. It is simply a matter of historical record that the football dressing room was still a long way from a place of milk and honey nearly twenty years after Jimmy Hill led the Professional Footballers' Association in their successful drive against a maximum wage of £20 a week.

In football terms, I had been able to cover so much ground at Elland Road and had made it to a World Cup but, like all the top players of that period, my financial rewards had been quite modest.

For more than ten years, Elland Road had been filled to capacity and a virtually new ground had been built without any borrowing. The building had been done by one of the directors, Bob Roberts, a fact not without a certain irony. Roberts was one of the directors who least favoured granting testimonials to long-serving players. He said he didn't agree with them on principle; the players, after all, had been well rewarded for their services. It is amusing, in a grim sort of way, to imagine what that director might have thought of the £40 million-plus wage bill that would carry the club almost to the point of extinction twenty-five years later. As another matter of record, most of the Leeds players of the great era never received more than £250 a week as pillars of the club's success, and they derived much cynical amusement from the embarrassed confession of Don Revie that the reluctance of the board to grant their requests for improved win bonus offers was because there was every chance they would have to be paid out.

None of this, however, diluted the pleasure that came when I was able to walk back into the lounge with Sexton and tell my father that, just as he had been for his friend Jimmy Delaney, he was now obliged to return to Old Trafford to watch me play. Busby said he was delighted that his club had got hold of another good Lanarkshire boy, and Les Olive suggested I signed my contract there and then. I said I would rather wait until the following day to sign. I would come to Old Trafford, they had my word, but it had all come in a rush – the entire meeting, starting in the car park, had taken scarcely more than an hour. I wanted to talk a few things over with my wife and my parents.

Deep down, I was very excited. Sexton had a great name in the game. He was known to be a man of very high standards of behaviour, and we had developed a quick and easy rapport. He was determined to build a new phase of success at Old Trafford, and I was his first signing. I was confident of making the team, of course. There was no doubt that he would give me every opportunity, having just committed himself to the British record

transfer fee. Stuart Pearson was a fine player and Jimmy Greenhoff, though ageing, was still a formidable talent, but Sexton had
come for me and he was backing his judgement with an unprecedented valuation.

'There's just one detail,' Sexton said to me before I signed. 'Do
you mind if Stuart Pearson keeps the number nine jersey?' I said
that didn't bother me at all.

Slightly more thought-provoking was a meeting with Jimmy
Armfield the following morning when I went into Elland Road to
collect some of my gear before driving over to Manchester. As I
came out of the dressing room, Armfield was waiting. He asked
me what I was doing. I told him I had an offer and I was going
over to Old Trafford to sign. Jimmy handed me a piece of paper
with a telephone number written on it. He said Liverpool Football Club had called. Bob Paisley wanted to talk to me.

Here, for the boy at the bus-stop, was another astonishing
development. I was about to leave the recently great Leeds
United for Manchester United at a record fee, and now there
was a late intervention from the reigning European champions. In
the spring, Paisley's team had supplanted Bayern Munich with a
victory over Borussia Moechengladbach in Rome, a feat they
would repeat against Bruges at Wembley in a few months' time.
Paisley, the dry, brilliant heir to Bill Shankly, who would win
another European Cup – defeating Real Madrid in, of all places,
the Parc des Princes in Paris in 1981 – was already in the gym at
Melwood, Liverpool's training ground, when I called from the
phone in the physiotherapist's room. He said he wanted to invite
me to play for Liverpool. He knew I had been talking to
Manchester United, and that United were a great club, but he
wanted me to think about the past and probable future achievements of his club.

I learned a few days later he was at the same time negotiating
for Graeme Souness, who would take his place in the brilliant axis
formed with Alan Hansen, Kenny Dalglish and Ian Rush. For a

few moments the idea of Anfield, the throb of that stadium and the momentum of a brilliantly organised and talented team, was quite intoxicating. Paisley was offering me a chance to experience the kind of sure-fire glory I had known when I made my way into Don Revie's team. But what could I do? I had given United my word – and in the presence of my father.

I told Paisley how flattered I was, but also how I felt I couldn't go back on my word. The old pro, who had once roared into Rome in a British Army tank, was extremely gracious. He said, 'Well, lad, if that's your decision, I respect it and I wish you all the best.' This, I heard later, was a much more gentle reaction than the one Bob McNab, the England full-back, received when he told the great Shankly that he had decided to join Arsenal rather than Liverpool. When McNab had visited Anfield, Shankly had told him he was going to be one of the great full-backs, but when the player called a few days later to say he was signing for Arsenal, Shankly hurled down the phone after saying, 'That's fine, laddie, but I have to tell you, you cannie play.'

My conversation with Paisley put me in a rather pensive mood as I drove over the Pennines. Yes, Liverpool were a great team and there was every chance they would get even better, but I had given my word and United were United – still a name to make the hairs at the back of your neck stand up, still a massive club. Later, as United failed to make the great impact Sexton was looking for, and Liverpool sailed to another great European triumph, there may have been reasons for me to wonder about my decision, but they never really registered. It was enough that I was playing for United, and, eventually, playing some of the best football of my career.

I didn't score until my sixth game, at Newcastle, but I did score in the derby match against Manchester City, which was a big help in the battle to win over a crowd who had, actually, shown no signs of turning against me. Sexton was also patient and encouraging. He said I wasn't to worry, I was playing well, I had brought strength to the team and he was very happy with the way things were going – but a manager, especially one who had just laid out a record fee, would say that, and a striker, even one who was aware that he was making a wider contribution to the team, would fret that the goals weren't going in. Sexton's message was reinforced by the great Busby when we met in a corridor of Old Trafford on one of those early days. He asked after my father and how I was settling down in Manchester. I said I was anxious to score a goal but he said, 'Aye, laddie, but don't worry about that. The goals will come all right. You're playing fine. Just keep doing what you're doing and everything will be all right.'

I appreciated the sentiment coming from such a source but there was only so much even the Father of Old Trafford could do to reassure me. However well he plays, a striker has to score. It sets the mood of his week, his life, and I was lucky that the big crowd seemed to appreciate the value and the honesty of my work.

Right from the start the Old Trafford crowd were behind me, and when a few goals started to go in, and my confidence improved, I felt that I was playing as never before in my career. I didn't try anything fancy, didn't go into areas where I wasn't sure of myself, but there was no doubt my general game had improved. I had matured, physically and, as a player, mentally, and it was an exhilarating time to go out on to the field. When you are playing before a vast crowd who are plainly on your side, and you are producing the goods for them, you feel you've broken new ground and you think, 'Christ, I can do this and I can do that.' I hit that vein of confidence and it didn't come and go. It went on for more than two years. It wasn't just a good spell. I could look at myself in the mirror and say, yes, there's no doubt, you're a better player.

By now my playing personality was set. I had established the fact that an opponent might get the better of me in the initial stages, but he wasn't going to subdue me; I wasn't going to go away. The main objective was to impose myself on the defender, collect the ball, get it down, play and win the freedom to say,

'Look, whatever you do, I'm on my game.' If the defender couldn't disrupt that mood, if he couldn't impose himself, well, I was going to have a field day. OK, if he wanted to bully me, intimidate me, he was going to have to do it not just for a little spell, but for ninety minutes. He might get in a good tackle, read the game well, he might even win a ball in the air, but the trick was not to allow him to think it was going to set a pattern that couldn't be broken at any second. He knew I'd be thinking, 'How do I get round this?' and was going to come back. I never let a defender stop thinking along those lines.

The first requirement, and it was particularly so in those days, was to look after yourself. A defender could go through you, scythe you down, and the referee would say 'play on'. Diving, in any form, simply wasn't an option. I learned everything about physical survival on a football field at Leeds United.

Obviously, some defenders were tougher and more difficult to get the better of, but the overall standards of competition were such that you could never get on the plateau where you could say, 'I'm going to have an easy afternoon.' However, if someone was misguided enough to give me time and space, I was going to do some serious plundering. I built up a reputation as a hard, physically aggressive player who said, 'Put the ball in the box and, don't worry, I'll go for it.' I could never argue with being categorised a hard man, but I also played. I played with Leeds and Manchester United and right through to the end of my career. No, I wasn't an elegant centre-forward, but I could control the ball and I could read the game. I could hold it up until I had support, and pass it. I could be involved in the build-up and, if the centre-half gave me any time at all, I could do him damage, not only with aggression but also with play. Inevitably, there were confrontations with certain defenders, which defined the way I had come to play the game. This wasn't so much about what was right or wrong, but a code I had to develop for when the action was fierce and somebody was plainly trying to intimidate me.

The most serious incident I ever had was with John Wile, the big West Bromwich Albion centre-half, and it came in one of my early games for United – an FA Cup replay at the Hawthorns. Albion, who were now playing under Ron Atkinson, gave us plenty of trouble in my first game for United at Old Trafford and looked like going through until Steve Coppell nipped in to score a late equaliser. It was the same pattern in the replay, West Brom pressing hard with Bryan Robson, who a few years later would become such a dominant influence at Old Trafford, and the excellent goalscorer Tony Brown showing up prominently. It was clearly going to be one of those games that involved a battle every step of the way; the ferocity of the game was increased to maximum levels by our reluctance to surrender the old trophy. In the middle of this hard action, and with no build-up, no point of grievance on either side, Wile laid a punch on me off the ball. We were standing together in the middle of the field and he got away with it. You didn't have six or seven TV cameras covering every angle in those days.

It was completely out of order, uncalled for and unnecessary. I knew he was there; we had been battling hard, and although the play was intense, the referee had been doing a pretty good job. He'd let the game flow well enough but he wasn't missing any significant skulduggery.

I realised I was the victim of a piece of pure bullying. He was trying to intimidate me and I knew that I couldn't let it rest there. In the second half I found myself running down the line and presenting a great opportunity for Wile to damage me again. I could see him coming across and I thought he was going to take me with everything he had. Everything about his approach sounded warning bells and I took protective action, holding up my arm as a guard. He came crashing into me and was carried off the field. He was taken to hospital and it turned out that, sadly, he had a broken jaw. I don't even like to say that. It was not something that made me proud but I could rationalise my action.

If I hadn't protected myself, Wile could undoubtedly have broken my leg on the touchline, and it was also true that I could have had my jaw broken in that first incident. The point was that his punch had taken me past a point where it is right to go.

We would play many more times against each other, and there was no repeat of such extreme action. He did go on television to complain about the incident, which struck me as a little odd in view of what had happened, how he had started the train of events. There was a big controversy in the press about it, but no consequences other than Wile's broken jaw. I didn't even get booked. They were, no doubt, rather hard times out on the field.

The strangest collision I ever had was with Brian Kidd, when he was playing for Manchester City. We were together in the box, waiting for a corner kick, and suddenly he punched me in the face. I was as much dumbfounded as angered. We were both strikers and hadn't been involved in anything at all during the match. There had been no niggle, no frustration, no nastily placed elbows – just, bang, a punch out of the pale Manchester City blue. I didn't square up to him or make any fuss, but I let him know how I felt and left him with a general warning that he should behave himself – and be on his guard. At Leeds they didn't teach you to go around punching people but they were strict about one thing. If you were punched, you were obliged, for the sake of both yourself and the rest of your team, not to forget it.

By the end of that first season, I had gleaned a handful of goals only but I felt that I was establishing myself well enough. Before the spring I had been warmed by the arrival from Elland Road of my great friend Gordon McQueen. Like me, Gordon had a passion for United and he too had received some feelers from other clubs, including some contact from Liverpool, but when the question was asked, 'Do you want to join United?' he found it irresistible.

Tommy Docherty had earlier shown an interest in taking Gordon to Old Trafford, and when Sexton revived the move he was thrilled. We both agreed that, however hard we had to work for success, there was a feel to the Old Trafford experience that brought its own reward. We roomed together with United and Scotland, and now, so many years later, we still agree that those few years, which flew by so quickly, were among the most thrilling of our football lives. With such players as Lou Macari, Martin Buchan and Sammy McIlory, we went about the serious business of remaking the greatest club in the history of English football. If it didn't quite happen for us, if Alex Ferguson's run to the top of the game and a stream of trophies was still a decade and a half away, we were still part of something that we knew to be great. You only had to walk into the ground to sense that. Old Trafford had been the home of so many wonderful players. The feeling, and the smell, of the glory was all around you. The great satisfaction came with the knowledge that you could handle the place, that it didn't overwhelm you when you ran out on the field and felt the waves of expectation. It was a challenge in itself being in a massive club and coping with the fact well enough that it seemed natural to be there, and when this was established in your mind, you knew that you could shoot for the great prizes.

It also helped at Old Trafford to be playing for a man such as Dave Sexton. In my second season I suffered a bad injury, a pulled thigh muscle, which I may have aggravated by my eagerness to play. The manager was no party to that, he wanted me to be right and, eventually, it was agreed I should have an operation to clear up the problem. I got through the crisis with no sense that the manager was agonising over every medical bulletin. He knew when he had a committed player.

Sexton was desperate to succeed but it never affected his approach to his players when he believed they were giving him everything they had. He never passed on his pressures. Later, when time ran out on him – after coming so close to winning the FA Cup final against Arsenal in 1979 and, the following season, chasing the title to the last day of the season, only for Liverpool to win by just two points on their way to another European title – he never passed on a hint of reproach to the players.

Sexton, the son of a champion boxer, had already had a fine career when he arrived at Old Trafford, guiding a talented Chelsea team to the FA Cup, over those two tumultuous games with Leeds, and then going on to win the European Cup-winners' Cup. In the end, it was painful that we could not add to his roll of honour, but sometimes in football there are other ways of measuring a man's impact on a team.

You have to measure all the circumstances, including the strength of the opposition, and probably this is what Sexton did when we beat the great Liverpool team over two games in the FA Cup semi-final of 1979. The first match was at Maine Road, the scene of my triumph with Leeds six years earlier, when my father was swept up in the dressing-room celebration. Liverpool were bristling with good form, running away with the title again – their third in four years, and by eight points from Nottingham Forest – through the bite of Graeme Souness, the subtlety of Kenny Dalglish and tremendous organisation and balance. Dalglish gave them an early lead, scoring with typical panache, and we had to battle to contain them, but as the game wore on, our confidence grew and we began to believe that we could win. This suspicion was confirmed when I equalised, and Brian Greenhoff put us into the lead. Inevitably, they came at us strongly at the end and they managed to squeeze an equaliser. We had to go to Goodison Park for the replay but Sexton said that the journey to the shadow of Anfield should not disturb us. If we produced a similar performance there was every reason to believe that it would be us and not the mighty Liverpool heading for Wembley. Confidence was well founded; we held Liverpool comfortably enough in the first half and Micky Thomas came on in the second half to provide the cross for Jimmy Greenhoff's winner.

That Cup-tie defined our best work under Sexton. We fought Liverpool every inch of the way, and ultimately beat one of the greatest teams in the history of English and European football. The manager appreciated this so much that at a training session soon after the game he presented all the players involved with a watch paid for from his own pocket. He said he wanted to mark a great performance, something we could be proud of always.

The final against Arsenal was a different matter. Twenty-five years on I've still to see a scrap of film of the game. I don't think I could bear to look. Defeat is something you have to come to terms with in football; you have to learn how to cope with it, how to see it simply as the other side of victory, and if you can't get past that first crucial level of understanding, you are guaranteeing yourself more grief than you could possible handle. Even so, some defeats are so much harder to take than others. The Arsenal defeat, Gordon McQueen and I agreed recently when we looked back at those days, was one of the hardest.

We lost twice. Goals from John Talbot and Frank Stapleton put Arsenal into comfortable control, and that edge was developed by the fine play of Liam Brady. The Irishman, who was heading for a highly successful stint in Italy, was on top of his game, cool and evasive. His extremely refined left foot had rarely been put to more effective use. Then, somehow, we were back in the game. It was like a sudden storm on a humid day that had made you lifeless. I won the ball wide and sent it into the middle, where Gordon McQueen scuffed it past Pat Jennings. There had been prettier goals but the one McIlroy scored a few minutes later was, as far as we were concerned, something you might be inclined to hang in an art gallery. He did a little shimmy, broke past the cover and sent the ball into the corner of the net. We had picked up our beds and walked. Suddenly, we were full of life and the belief that we had Arsenal beaten now; they looked absolutely gutted when McIlroy put in the equaliser.

Unfortunately, we made the ultimate mistake in those circumstances. We stopped playing for a minute and Arsenal, who no doubt could not believe their luck, leapt back at us. Brady crossed to Alan Sunderland, who had found some space and put the ball past Gary Bailey. We committed the cardinal sin – we took our eyes off the ball and, speaking for myself, I have had what seems like a lifetime to regret it. It was the closest we got to delivering silver to Dave Sexton. In the following season, my best at Old Trafford, when I won the first of my Player of the Year awards from the fans, we chased Liverpool home. At one point I thought we had the great prize of the first division title, but the talent and the organisation of Paisley's men were, in the end, just too strong.

We didn't challenge in season 1980–81, and the patience of the boardroom began to fray. Sexton was a fine manager and he had everybody's respect but it was now fourteen years since United had won the title – thirteen since the great Busby climax of the European Cup at Wembley – and in the spring of '81 it was clear that the directors were thinking of change. A run of seven successive wins at the end of the season might have caused a little pause in the boardroom, but not enough. Sexton was sacked and big Ron Atkinson, who had built well on the foundations left to him by John Giles at West Bromwich Albion, was appointed. Sexton and I lived near to each other in Cheshire and he called me the morning he was sacked. He asked me to come to his house. He said that he had bought some prints by his friend, the great Manchester artist Harold Riley, and he was going to take them to the ground and hand them out to the lads. He wanted me to do that now.

The picture was of Old Trafford and a game between United and Spurs. It still has a prominent place in my house. When I look at it I think of a good, generous football man – and I deplore, all over again, the fact that we didn't deliver to him, and ourselves, the FA Cup that day at Wembley when we so briefly, but unforgettably and unforgivably, lost our heads.

10

LIFE BEYOND THE TOUCHLINE

MANY years after the cheers had died, when I had half-forgotten how it was to operate along the line separating the glory and the pain in the great stadiums across the world, I was reminded all over again of the debt I owed to the woman who had been at my side through all of it.

I was jolted into remembering how tough it can be to go to a new place in a new country and how, in another situation, I might just have found it too much when, at the age of twenty-nine, I finally made it into the big, sophisticated world of Italian football. That circumstance would have been not having a wife who knew all my fears and hopes and who, whatever the difficulties and changes involved, was always at my side. That simple, warming fact, made it possible for me to operate as both a top professional and a family man who could come home, however drained, to something more than the self-absorption of how he played and how he stood on ever-shifting ground. What made me think of this was the expression on the face of David Beckham on one of his worst nights in Madrid.

A face that is probably the most photographed in the history of football spoke of great strain and more than a little bewilderment. He was sent off for calling a linesman, in some of the very little Spanish he knew, 'son of a whore', and he was yelling and gesticulating wildly. In that breakdown of self-control he could no longer be anyone's idea of the young master of the football universe. He was angry, confused, didn't seem to quite know what was happening to him. He had been caught up in frustration and had snapped in a way that was surprising and shocking in such an experienced player, who was captain of England and had enjoyed so many of the astonishing rewards of today's game. Then, when you thought about it, it was only surprising if you ignored the growing pressures in his life off the field. It made me think, 'David boy, you have to get your life organised in a different way. If you don't, and for all your talent, you have no chance.'

Considering his plight made me recall those days when it first came to me that in all the tides and moods of football, those that sweep you to success and the others, the tricky ones that bring disappointment and anguish and sometimes terrible insecurity, you can never lose sight of one harsh reality – you are always potentially a step away from disaster.

Something can go wrong with your mind or your body in the time it takes to miss a goal or get involved in a bad tackle. What seemed so easy yesterday might suddenly be impossible today. The ambush of the body or the brain can come from nowhere. It can break your leg. You can wake up one morning and wonder where you have mislaid all your old confidence – and will you ever find it again? It means that off the field you need a point of focus, a sense of the wider life beyond the touchline. You need to go somewhere secure and get back some perspective.

The most valuable asset of all is the kind of anchor that can only be provided by someone who loves you enough to put up with the pressures and the mood swings, who understands why you are drawn to such an emotionally perilous business. Why would a woman put up with all of this? Because, if you're very lucky, she knows what this crazy life means to you, despite all its hazards and uncertainty and why, without it, something would go out of your life and leave you perhaps irreparably diminished – certainly not the guy she met when there was music and excitement in the air. This, I'm told, is not exactly the plot line of a garish television series entitled 'Footballers' Wives', which apparently revolves around celebrity, fast cars and fast lives. The kind of support that Beckham seemed to be so conspicuously missing as we saw the decline in his performance in the second half of his first season at Real Madrid, and read about the misadventures in his private life while his wife and sons remained in England, has been the underpinning of my life in football for more than thirty years now – ever since Gordon McQueen and I went to the Leeds disco Cinderella's in 1973 and I met a girl called Judith Smith.

Don Revie would probably have arranged that meeting if he could have done. It came at the time when he had asked a local reporter to keep the nocturnal activities of Gordon and me in his sights. Revie, in common with most managers, wanted contented and secure personal lives for his players for the practical rather than sentimental reason that a happy footballer is less likely to be caught up in destructive distractions. Revie had a clear picture of the ideal footballer's wife. She was respectable, good with children and money, and supportive of her husband's volatile career – as a bonus for a dutiful young player, she could also be attractive enough to knock your socks off.

The tall, dark girl I met on the way to a farewell party thrown by departing goalkeeper Gary Sprake scored resounding ticks in all of those boxes – and not least the last one. Down the years, Judith has met every challenge that my career has presented to her and if it is true that I played some of my best football at Old Trafford, there is no doubt that it was around that time that Judith's reaction to the demands of being both a mother and the wife of a professional footballer on the move was especially superb. Her handling of my response to every crisis – and triumph – had always been tremendous, but when my days in Manchester were drawing to a close, when as a footballer and a family man I faced the most important decisions of my life, Judith consistently rose to the occasion.

There were other times, I know more vividly than ever now after nearly twenty years in and out of coaching and managing jobs, living week by week from one result to another, that I would have struggled desperately to get through it without her. In terms of my professional state of mind, my happiness when things were going well on the field and my frustration at set-backs in the effort to produce successful teams, Judith has known the best and the worst of times, but never did she flinch at the pressure – or question whether or not I should seek out a more tranquil or predictable way of life. Basically, she agreed that however many uncertainties football heaped upon us and our young and fast expanding family, it also offered the chance of a good and exciting life.

This fine balance was something we discussed many times between our first meeting and the day we were married in 1977. There might be a certain consistency in this story of a dedicated professional if I said that I applied at least some of Revie's criteria to my assessment of the poised and lovely girl I met in Cinderella's and then proudly took to the nightclub of the players' friend Tunj, where Sprake was having his farewell bash, but that would be the purest fiction. I didn't appraise Judith Smith. I fell in love with her.

Such a development, frankly, was not at that point part of my career or life plan. I was still just twenty-two and establishing myself in the great Leeds team. I had made myself something of a hero in my homeland after the goal against Czechoslovakia and I had finally become comfortable with the denture I needed after that collision with a Coventry defender's foot. My smile, I believed, had become workable again. The old face had been put back together and it was hard to imagine that life could have been much more fun.

It was around this time that Revie had quizzed Gordon and me about the non-existent love-nest flat, but the fact was that while Gordon and I were young men like most other young men, we were both strongly aware that there always had to be a point of discipline, and this was no great trial. I had got out of Cleland at eighteen without becoming a heavy drinker and that was something of an achievement. I always liked a glass of beer, and later I developed a taste for good wine, but at no stage in my career as a footballer had I gone off the rails. I could go out with the lads, as I was doing when I met Judith, but I always knew when to call a halt.

It also helped our concentration on football that although we had a good lifestyle, better than most young men of comparative age, we were not rolling in money in the way of today's players. Champagne was never on our list and I never saw anyone use a £50 note to light a cigar. I never saw a £50 note. I never saw a player in a Bentley or a Maserati or a Ferrari. On the night I met Judith I was driving a Peugeot, a nice car but nothing flash – even less so when I took Judith out of the club and saw that somebody had driven into the back of it. However, I dressed well. After the painful shedding of the oilskin coat and the big sweater, that had always been something of a priority. Certainly I felt good about myself, but not so good that I would expect to bowl over a young woman who was clearly not going to be automatically impressed by an upwardly mobile young footballer dressed in a designer suit and with too much self-confidence.

Judith had returned to Yorkshire for her studies after moving with her family to Carlisle, where her father was a geologist with the water board. Our backgrounds were quite different, but that was never a problem. When I eventually met her family in Cumberland they couldn't have been more welcoming and if I had any worries about the impact Cleland would make on her when I took her home to see my parents and friends, they were unfounded. Judith might have belonged to the middle class but she had an easy, relaxed manner and found no terrors beyond the barriers of a tough, rock-hard Labour community. No one had reason to say that Joe Jordan had brought home some stuck-up English lassie.

When the time came she could assure Father McLaren, who had been such an influence on my football and my life, that our children would be brought up in the Catholic faith because that happened to be her own. Cleland might have been a million miles from anything she had experienced, but she moved among my people as though she had known them all her life. My mother and father, whose expectations no doubt ran at least as high as Don Revie's, were clearly impressed by my choice. The fact that we would marry became inevitable. It was simply a matter of finding the right time in the busy football calendar.

An indication of how hectic that schedule could be was the fact that my stag night, which I shared with Gordon McQueen, was organised in a hotel thousands of miles from the wedding site in Leeds – I had a 'wee' drink with my Scottish team-mates in Buenos Aires at the end of a summer tour a year before the World Cup in Argentina in which we hoped to be competing. Gordon, who was my best man – as I was for his wedding, soon after mine – was in charge of arrangements and, with Don Revie no longer around to tell him to sit down when the drinks were being produced, he was keen for it to be a memorable night.

The feature of the evening was a game called Captain's Bluff. I never quite learned the rules but they seemed to be loosely based on the need for the eventual winner to drink vast amounts of freely mixed and not always specified liquor. Gordon, Kenny Dalglish and I were among the front-runners, but I could no more give you the name of the eventual winner than I could the entire composition of the Argentinian cabinet. There was a great singsong. 'Bonnie Scotland' was sung in honour of Jimmy Johnstone but respect for the great little man didn't extend to taking a boat trip on the Rio Plate. We trailed home with throbbing heads, but, thankfully, no news of fresh disasters.

Although Judith's parents lived in Carlisle, it was decided that it would be most convenient to have the wedding in Leeds and so a packed bus duly rolled down from Cleland. Aunts, uncles and cousins joined my parents in the bus, along with my old friends, and the leader of the party was Father McLaren, who conducted the wedding. The reception was held in Tunj's club, a stylish, expensive-looking place, which was probably what prompted Uncle Joe to ask Gordon to go to a nearby off-licence and load up on extra booze. The bottles were put under the tables, quite furtively. Tunj knew what was going on but he brushed aside any apologies.

'Don't worry, Joe,' said Tunj. 'This is a great day in your life.'

Another one was when we moved into our first house in a stone-built terrace in the village of Bramham on the outskirts of Leeds. We paid £17,500 for the fine little house into which Sir Matt Busby and the rest of the Manchester United hierarchy would soon be marching with life-changing proposals. That was the first big decision of our marriage, but as Judith understood without any great pleading from me, it was something of a formality. The football life was nomadic, she knew, and the reality of it was evident six months into our marriage. At the start of one day she was pregnant and happily settled into the first of the many houses we would share and at the end of it she was reaching for the yellow pages for the telephone number of a removal firm.

Judith's greatest test as a wife and mother coincided with mine as a footballer. It took shape in the brief hiatus left by Dave Sexton's sacking, when the old dream of playing in Europe came back into my sights. The new Manchester United manager Ron Atkinson resumed the contract talks that had been opened some months earlier by Sexton asking me what it would take for me to re-sign. My answer was £1,000 a week. The manager was keen to do it. He didn't seem to think my demand was unreasonable but the negotiations stalled in the boardroom. Atkinson asked the same question and I gave him the same reply. Atkinson said that he didn't see £1,000 a week as a problem and he reported back quickly to say that the directors were agreeable. That was a rise of

100 per cent. Even with the crippling British tax it represented a significant leap in our lifestyle.

Under normal circumstances, it would have been a suitable time for Judith and me to take a glass of champagne. We already had a good house in a well-heeled village in the suburbs of Manchester, but by now we had three children and this extra income would make life much more comfortable. It was not a great time to move, especially for Judith. Lucy, our eldest child, was three years old. Our youngest, Thomas, was just six weeks. In the middle, Andrew had already acquired a formidable appetite.

On the face of it, the family conference should have rubber-stamped the decision to stay at Old Trafford, but a huge and exciting complication had arisen. Just a few days earlier, before Atkinson had made his offer, when I went to see Liverpool play Bayern Munich in a European Cup semi-final at Anfield, I had been approached by a journalist from the big Italian daily *Il Giornale* of Milan. He introduced himself as Tony Damascelli. Over the next few years Damascelli would become a great friend, but on this occasion he was quite businesslike. He asked me if I had ever thought of playing in Italian football, did I have any vision of that. If I did, there was definitely some strong interest in me. AC Milan and Bologna were two clubs likely to make a bid if it seemed that their interest might be rewarded.

Although Milan had only just returned to *Serie A*, they were still giants of the game. Their relegation had been imposed by the League after a great bribery scandal that had ripped through Italian football and now, after a year in the shadows but still playing before huge crowds in the San Siro stadium, they were retooling for a return to the peaks of the game. I was told that I was on a shortlist of foreign strikers, which also included the Belgian star Jan Ceulemans. Another target was the superbly gifted Brazilian Zico.

Atkinson was trying hard to keep me, but in the days that followed my brief conversation with Damascelli it was clear that the Italian had been the carrier of hard information rather than some airy speculation on his part. Most crucially, Ronnie Teeman, my lawyer, had established with EEC lawyers that, under new Common Market regulations, with my contract up at Old Trafford I was effectively a free agent. Milan would be required to pay United compensation, which would be less than the fee United had paid Leeds three years earlier. Ronnie had first used his research to stun Arsenal when he conducted the Italian move of another of his clients, Liam Brady.

Soon enough, Ronnie and I were both receiving calls from Italy, including one from the former president of AC Milan, Felice Colombo, who had had to stand down following the bribery scandal. There was no doubt that with Milan's wage offer higher than United's, and the much lower Italian tax levels, a move to Milan would bring a sharp rise in our income. Ronnie's advice was that it was too good an opportunity to miss. Judith, despite the trial of moving with three young children to an entirely new culture, agreed that we might spend the rest of our lives regretting a lack of boldness now. My own feeling was that, apart from the challenge of playing with a top European club, which I had yearned to do ever since Bayern Munich made their first overture, Milan offered us the chance to give ourselves some solid financial foundations.

After meeting an AC Milan official in an Italian restaurant in Leeds, I drove home to Prestbury in a state of great excitement. Judith re-affirmed her support for the idea of moving. She thought the move was important for my career and gave us all a real chance to get ahead. Of course, there would be hazards and difficulties, not least for her, but we were still young and everyone had just one run at life. We agreed there was only one course of action. The following day I told Ron Atkinson that he would have to look for another striker. I was selling my house, cutting my ties and joining another of the great clubs of the football world. My challenge was clear enough. I had to do in Italy what I had done in England; I had to operate successfully at the top of the game.

For Judith, the task was no less daunting. She had to make all our lives work. It may have helped her to a degree that the possibility of my playing in Europe had been moving on and off the horizon from quite early in our relationship, the bid from Bayern Munich having come at a time when it seemed likely that we were heading towards marriage. She had seen how crushed I was when Jimmy Armfield told me that there was no way I was going to get away to Germany and how I had been required to buckle down and get on with my job. Then, as I played my way through my contract at Old Trafford, there was some loosening of the hold clubs had over their players. Registrations, which had previously been held like the papers of inhabitants of Slave Row in some plantation in Alabama, could no longer be held beyond the expiry of a contract, and when Ronnie Teeman established this, the old dream came into focus again. The question was one of timing – had my time of maximum appeal to the big clubs of Europe passed? AC Milan had provided the best possible answer.

As Judith organised the move to our new world, I flew off to Milan for a press conference. Although I was at the most confident point of my career, with Leeds United, Manchester United and two World Cups behind me, I realised there would be new pressures, new trials, and when I arrived at Linate airport in Milan that sense was quite dramatically confirmed. As soon as I got off the plane, microphones were thrust at me and I was immediately swept into a big room filled with flashing cameras and a chorus of questions. Yes, I said through an interpreter, I was looking forward to the challenge. I was honoured to be joining a great Italian club, the winner of two European Cups and the home for so long of so many great players. I would give everything I had to the cause of AC Milan.

Looking back, I was probably more fortunate than some exiles from English football in the way I faced this new phase of my career. Maybe it was because I had always been conscious, right from those first days in Cleland, that success in football demanded huge effort, especially if you didn't happen to be the recipient of great natural gifts. The Italian football culture, I saw instinctively, held this as a fundamental truth. It offered you a wonderful life, a new dimension in terms of rewards and experience, but it wanted a lot back. In fact, it demanded all of you.

This was perhaps never quite grasped by some highly successful graduates of English football – Ian Rush for example, whose scoring feats for Liverpool were so magnificent, Luther Blissett, who could never reproduce in Italy the impact he had first created at Watford, and, perhaps more than anybody, the marvellously gifted Paul Gascoigne. Knowing what I did of Italian football, the atmosphere and attitude, I could only grimace many years later when I saw film of Gazza burping into an Italian TV reporter's microphone. Here was a player whose game was made for Italy – biting, subtle, brilliantly skilled – but Paul plainly didn't understand the wider world of Italian football, didn't latch on to its importance in the minds and the hearts of the Italian people. Football wasn't so much a game as a barometer of life; it was politics, religion and a little bit of war all wrapped into one.

At Naples, Diego Maradona was a different case entirely. He understood, probably better than anyone, the meaning of football in Italy, and no one captured for himself more of its passion and brilliance. In this, he and Napoli, for whom he delivered the first *scudetto*, were made for each other. His great flaw was maybe the city's – he lacked a certain discipline.

For me, the route was the same old one I had been travelling since I was first picked out by Bobby Collins in the colours of Morton. Again, I had to slave at the football – and, as I discovered in my first week of Italian work, more severely than ever before. My regime, as Judith felt her way into her new world, was much harder than anything I had ever faced at Old Trafford or Elland Road. There was the game on Sunday, always a particularly ferocious experience when it was played in the great football cathedral of San Siro; Monday was a day off, a day to regroup and see a little of the family; Tuesday afternoon training; Wednesday and Thursday, all day training and a friendly match against some local opposition; Friday, two training sessions; Saturday, final preparations and going away with the team for the Sunday game. On several days I would leave home at 8 a.m. and get back no earlier than twelve hours later. Subtract eight hours for sleep and family life was at a premium.

Italian football, it seemed to me, had got so many things right – discipline, image, the recognition that although this could be a hugely rewarding, life-changing job, none of these pay-offs would come without absolute commitment. All of this was correct, and on a much superior level to some of the ways football was conducted in England. Diet and training were put on a much more scientific basis, but the schedule of the work, and its intensity, seemed wrong to me. The danger was that too much would be left on the training field, a vital freshness might be lost.

For me, it certainly meant hard going in the early games. I felt I wasn't playing as well as I should have been. I didn't feel as strong or as confident as when I had run out at Old Trafford, with the crowd behind me and an emphatic sense that things would go well. In spite of the new difficulties in Italy, I swore I would do it. It was a matter of the deepest pride, and when I returned to Judith in the evenings, often extremely drained and sometimes a little disheartened, I was determined not to show that I was seriously down. Psychologically, that might have been damaging to Judith because, heavens knows, she had enough in front of her.

She was at all times brilliant, whether it was getting Thomas to a local hospital after he cut his head or just going to a supermarket or filling the car with petrol and generally figuring out the way they did things in Italy. Many of the basic chores of life, per-formed so casually in England, had to be relearned and, like me, she arrived in the new country with hardly a word of the language.

149

Said quickly and in isolation, none of this might sound too demanding, but when I put it all together and tried to see it through Judith's eyes, I knew well enough how lucky I was to have such support. Even the thought of taking three young children through the big airport in Milan on periodic flights home to England when I was away in some corner of Italy, or stuck in our training ground in the hills, was daunting.

Yet when we discussed our new life and all its demands over a late supper, with the children tucked up in bed, Judith and I agreed that this was simply the way it was in Italy; we had made our decision and we had to make the best of it. The best, we already had an inkling, could be quite superb. If it was true that a professional back home would have been spending a lot more time with his family, it was also a fact that if we organised ourselves properly, the time we did have could be spent in some wonderfully rewarding ways.

Monday was the day of enjoyment and adventure. It was often a challenger for the most beautiful day of our lives. One Monday we would drive down to Venice and enjoy the sunshine and the beauty along the Grand Canal. Other days we would go to the lakes at Lugano or Como. Switzerland was just a short drive away, and there were skiing days. Perhaps one Monday we would have a yen to see the sea, so we would drive down to somewhere on the Green Coast near Genoa.

Yes, the professional life was hard and sometimes even on those days of great release from the pressure, the fact that results weren't going so well back in Milan could tug at your spirit as you put your fork into some exquisite spaghetti vongole and sipped a glass of fine, chilled Soave. The vital thing, we told ourselves, was that we were getting through it, working together and building an experience that would surely enhance our lives and enrich our memories when we came to look back on the early days of our life together.

We also noted, as the days flicked by, that our lives were

becoming easier. We enjoyed the quality of life and the new friends we made. There was a certain grace to life that we hadn't known before. We received a lot of help when we first moved in to our new home, a fine, modern house in the village of Burago outside Milan – the club had offered us a choice of six – and that was consistent with our arrival in Italy, when Judith received a personal gift from the president of the club, a beautiful silk scarf. It was a small touch but it was graceful and it made you feel a value was being put on your presence.

Later, when the playing days were over, Judith's attitude to the game would change, though fortunately not towards me and my commitment to it. She could see easily enough why I always wanted to play, what that did for me, but when I became a coach and a manager and certain things happened that she didn't think right, and clearly were not right, she adopted a much harder view of football. She would go wherever I went, she would continue to understand the role of football in my life, but her compliance with all my plans was no longer something I could take for granted. If she would never say it outright, her moods sometimes told me that she wondered why I was still locked so tightly into the ways of football. It was a change that didn't come overnight. It grew with time, accumulating with the wounds, and whenever some passing success came, it was as though she couldn't any longer take it at face value. She saw behind the celebrations of one day's victory.

Never though, right through to this day, has Judith ever stamped her feet and said of football, 'I've had enough.' She has never said that the game, in the way it rewarded success and determined failure, has taken too much out of me and my ability, after the hard days on the field or in a manager's office, to live something approaching a normal life. This, I guess, is because whatever Judith knows about football, she knows more about me. She knows that my pride would not let me hang around football if I didn't think I had something to contribute. Sure it has been hard to lose a job that in all the circumstances you believed you were doing well, or go to an interview and not get even the courtesy of a call back, but I learned, sometimes painfully, that none of that should be a guide to how you see yourself.

You look at the game with what you consider a knowing eye, and you either believe or don't believe that you still have something to offer. I happen to think that all I learned in Scotland, England and Italy down the years, and through my attendance at the latest coaching courses, and my analysis of the modern game, for radio, television or sometimes for a club, can still be put to effective use. It is, anyway, my conviction at this moment and one that I know I am lucky to hold while still in possession of the most vital support of my life – the continued presence of the girl I met in Cinderella's and who agreed to spend the rest of her life with me somewhere around the ball, however it ran.

11

SOMETHING UNACCOUNTABLY MISLAID

Looming before me was the huge arena of San Siro, Milan; behind were the great clubs of Leeds United and Manchester United. With me always, though, lurking at every step I made it often seemed, was something that happened at Anfield a few months before I moved from Elland Road to Old Trafford – something I have to believe now will never go away.

While playing against Wales in a World Cup qualifying game that would carry Scotland to the 1978 finals in Argentina, I went up for the ball in the company of the Welsh defender Dave Jones of Norwich City. It was a routine piece of work, or so it seemed at the time. Then my team-mates cried 'hand ball'. The French referee pointed to the spot. Don Masson, our midfielder, stepped up to convert the penalty.

For Scotland, the door was swinging open to the great tournament and for Wales it was the beginning of the end of another brave but futile campaign, a sad story of failure that stretched back to the 1958 finals in Sweden. Wales would have the chance of redemption four years later but I wouldn't, not in this matter, not in Wales certainly. There, every man, woman and child would soon enough believe that I was the guilty party, the most hated foreigner since an English king strung castles across their country. I had touched the ball with an outstretched arm, they claimed. I was the man the Welsh loved to hate. I had cheated them of their rights.

I denied it then. I deny it today. I will deny it at the moment of my death, which may be necessary if by some cruel fate the sad event should occur in the presence of somebody from Wales.

It was an amazing controversy that seemed to operate on time-delay. The following morning there were no screaming headlines about Wales being conned out of their World Cup destiny, as there were in England when Diego Maradona fisted in Argentina's first goal in the World Cup quarter-final in Mexico City in 1986 – a question mark against the penalty award, some argument about whose hand, if anybody's, had touched the ball, yes, but in the following days the conviction that I was the man grew strongly.

Photographs were analysed. None that I ever saw were conclusive in any way, but the belief that I had indeed handled the ball was soon enough hardened into fact. Even some fellow Scotsmen became convinced. Cynically, some of them still say, 'Aye, Joe, we know it was hand ball but good on you son, it got us to the World Cup.' I could argue the point beyond my innocence on two counts. Although it was an impressive Welsh team, we were undoubtedly the better side on the night, and we played with the confidence that we would win on merit rather than through any trickery. It was also true that we scored more than a dubious penalty. We won 2–0.

Maradona claimed that it was the hand of God that beat England. I say that if the Welsh were honest about it, they would accept that they largely beat themselves. The decision to play the game in Liverpool, for purely financial reasons, was the true Welsh disaster. This still nags at me sometimes when I go over the bridge to Wales from my home in Bristol and encounter the old complaints, sometimes delivered quite aggressively by young people who weren't even alive at the time of the incident. When this happens, and it does with depressing regularity, sometimes when I'm having a meal or a quiet drink, I have to say I'm sorry that it is forty-six years since Wales last qualified for a World Cup, but it is something they have to deal with among themselves. For my part, I'll get on with my life – and with a clear conscience.

If there is a touch of exasperation here, I believe there is good reason. I happen to be proud of my record with Scotland. In all, I played fifty-two times for my country, appeared in three World Cups and scored in every one of them. I played nine out of ten matches against England, and in that ten-year period the only time I missed was when I was on duty for Leeds in a European Cup final. That represented quite a bit of effort and considerable passion, and when all of it is reduced, as it often is, to a question about whether or not in one of a thousand goalmouth incidents I happened to handle when my team was awarded a penalty – one that, as it turned out, was not decisive in itself – I get a little restive. After twenty-seven years, I believe I have a certain right. I've always tried to bring some basic qualities to my football career and in any list of priorities, competitive honesty would always be placed at the top. Of course, there are matters of degree in professional football; you fight to win as best you can, and sometimes you are drawn into battles that take you into grey areas, but if I had indeed handled the ball, there would have been some time, I know, when I would have been required to face up to what I had done. I would like to think I would have had the courage to make a good confession, but before confession you must first have sin.

It is not a matter of denying the truth. It is no hardship to admit that sometimes I played a ruthless game, I fought hard and always with the business of winning uppermost in my mind, but the reason I refuse to own up will always be clear in my mind. I didn't do it, not consciously certainly, and not in any vestige of my memory. I have explored that memory from the moment in the crowded dressing room at Anfield when one voice – the solitary reporter who had worked his way into the middle of our celebration – asked me, 'Did you do the hand ball?' I said no, I didn't. I shrugged the question away and it didn't come again that night.

155

Maybe I should retrace the campaign that took us to Anfield, and made us favourites to beat Wales and qualify again for the World Cup finals, which until four years earlier had seemed as elusive to us as they had been to the Welsh since we had both qualified back in 1958. These were days when there were no second chances in World Cup qualification, no play-off games for second-placed teams. You had to operate on the edge, and we had begun to do it rather well.

As four years earlier, when we fought through to West Germany, the impressive Czechs, reigning European champions, were in our qualifying group. We lost in Prague after Andy Gray was sent off, but at Hampden Park we beat the Czechs 3–1 with something to spare. Rinus Michels, coach of Holland and a man who was being described as the father of 'total football', said that he thought Scotland could well be one of Europe's better bets when the finals were played in Argentina. Another leading coach, Yugoslavia's Miljan Miljanic, was deeply impressed with our victory over the Czechs. He said we were an 'interesting', well-balanced team who could cause some concern among the favourites in South America.

When we beat Wales at Hampden Park, we assumed the return leg would be fought out in front of an impassioned home crowd in Cardiff, Swansea or Wrexham and were staggered to learn that the Welsh had shifted the game to Liverpool in pursuit of a bigger crowd and extra revenue. They had the chance to reach the finals for the first time in twenty years and remind themselves of how well they had performed in Sweden when the superb John Charles and the brilliant Cliff Jones and Ivor Allchurch helped them beat the remnants of the great Hungarian team to win a place in the quarter-finals against Brazil. The Welsh were undone by injury to Charles, whose replacement Colin Webster missed an easy chance as the teenaged Pele scored the only goal. Now twenty years on, they courted their own downfall. They went for the gate money rather than the great prize of a return to the highest level of international competition, and they had to watch Anfield fill up to the seams with Scots.

We had some outstanding players – Kenny Burns, England's current Player of the Year, and Martin Buchan at the back, with Masson and Bruce Rioch good enough in midfield to resist the challenge of Graeme Souness, a choice of John Robertson or Willie Johnston on the left wing, and Kenny Dalglish and Lou Macari vying for one position in attack – but the Welsh had the capacity to give anyone a game, anywhere. They had the menace of big John Toshack, the pace of Leighton James on the flank, John Mahoney and Terry Yorath in midfield and Liverpool's Joey Jones at the back. In front of a Welsh crowd, this was a team sure to generate plenty of aggression, but instead of turning itself into a cockpit of Welsh patriotism, Anfield was decked in tartan. The moment we ran on to the field we realised we were playing at a mini Hampden Park, and that gave us an immediate edge.

The Welsh came at us at the start with some force and our goalkeeper, Alan Rough, was obliged to make a brilliant save from Toshack, tipping the ball over the bar. That, however, was the best the Welsh could do and as the game wore on, we became increasingly confident. At the end, and with no sense of the impending life-long controversy, I felt that we had earned our right to go to Argentina. We had played Wales twice and beaten them twice and it was Wales's fault not ours that we couldn't claim to have done it both home and away.

Judith was at the game and afterwards we were driven home to Leeds by one of our neighbours, Len McCormick. On the way we stopped off at Tunj's club and had a small celebration drink. No one spoke of a hand-ball row. It had not been raised as a major issue, no more than it would be in the morning papers. It was possibly the slowest burning controversy in the history of football, but down the years it has taken hold quite relentlessly.

If I get any amusement from the whole affair, it is only when I hear those comparisons with Maradona's hand of God. Maradona did it with great purpose and, because of the slickness of the operation, he got away with it. This, quite understandably out-raged the English, who were entitled to say, 'My God, he's ripped us off,' but in one way they were like the Welsh. They heaped the fact of their defeat on to the hand of God, conveniently forgetting that the goal that really beat them, the one that tore their hearts out, Maradona's astonishing run at goal while the English defence streamed after him like commuters losing a race for the bus, deserved to win any game. He scored a similar goal against Belgium in the semi-finals, and made the killer pass, despite blanket marking, that killed off the Germans in the final. No player had ever come so close to winning a World Cup single-handedly. However, the English tell themselves that they were cheated out of the great trophy. It is a convenient thing to say, just as it was for Wales to nominate their own scapegoat.

All these years after the event I picked up a newspaper and read that the current Welsh manager, Mark Hughes, was re-porting that Joe Jordan still denied that he had handled the ball. We had met at a coaching course and the subject, maybe inevitably, had been raised by Mark over a pint. He's a good football man and no doubt after his excellent work in recent years, he must have been feeling particularly frustrated that Wales were still in pursuit of a return to the World Cup finals. His mood would not have been improved by the failure of the Welsh FA's attempt to have the Russians thrown out of the last European championship because one of their players, involved in a qualifying game with Wales, had a failed drugs test against his name. Most football insiders considered the Welsh effort ill-advised, especially taking the cost into account, but when a hunger for success is denied over a long period, a little despera-tion tends to creep into your thinking.

As it happened, in a drama that eventually slipped into farce, our own Scottish need to make an impact on the World Cup, to prove that after all the years of under-achievement we could

Feeling at home with new Manchester United team-mates (*left to right*) Martin Buchan,
Stewart Houston, Arthur Albistan and Lou Macari.

Dave Sexton – a great man of football and a great man.

Leading Manchester United – 'When you played at Old Trafford you had the smell of football in your nostrils.'

Another ticket to Wembley: I score against a great Liverpool team in the FA Cup semi-final and my friend Gordon McQueen is plainly just as pleased.

Arsenal's Sammy Nelson stretches to stifle my cross in the FA Cup final.

Sammy McIlroy puts Manchester United level in the FA Cup final when he beats Arsenal's Pat Jennings but we froze at the moment of glory. It is one of my greatest regrets.

Left: Proud house owner – in the doorway of our first house, in the suburbs of Leeds.

Below: The Italian legend Gianni Rivera takes a watching brief as I prepare to negotiate with Milan.

Right: Italian landfall – mobbed by Milan fans at the airport.

Below right: The cathedral of Italian football, San Siro, in 1980.

Family time in Burago. My parents arrive in our new world.

indeed compete with the best teams in the world, brought some disastrous consequences of its own in the wake of the Anfield victory.

Once again, there was huge expectation in Scotland and it was fanned to a hazardous degree by the man who had taken over from Willie Ormond, Ally MacLeod. Although I had been pre-occupied by the challenge of settling down at Old Trafford in the early months of 1978, I could not but be aware that tides of optimism were already running dangerously high back home. MacLeod didn't have the disposition to turn down the rising pressure, declaring that Scotland could win the World Cup. This cry, which when you thought about its effect on the Scottish people had to make your blood run cold, was intensified by the fact that, again, Scotland were the only home nation to make it through to the finals. Wales, who would say it was by my hand, had failed along with England, Northern Ireland and the Republic of Ireland.

Just to nourish the satisfaction of those Scots at whom it still gnawed that England had been crowned world champions twelve years earlier, the demise of Don Revie's team had been particularly inglorious. Despite the presence of such talented players as Kevin Keegan, Trevor Brooking, Mick Channon and Stan Bowles, England were utterly outplayed by Italy in Rome. The Italian captain Giacinto Facchetti delivered the crushing verdict, 'The worst England team I have ever seen . . . disorganised, confused, of only limited ability.'

Meanwhile, Scotland were residing among the stars. Ally made another declaration designed to whip up the frenzy – 'My name is Ally MacLeod and I'm a born winner.' It was around this time that the London sportswriter Hugh McIlvanney, who hailed from Kilmarnock, warned of the dangers of trying to get to heaven in a handcart. He pointed out there was always a danger of the wheels falling off.

In one sense, the Scottish euphoria was a bit pathetic; there was far too much compensating for all the lean years, the barren run from 1958 to '74 irrigated only by the odd victory over England. In another way, and this was the complication when every instinct said we should proceed quietly, it was undoubtedly true that Scotland, after all the years of failure to exploit superb natural talent, were at last making the running. In this context, it was easy for some to believe that Scotland's time had finally come. Going back to 1962, the time Paddy Crerand lamented so bitterly, Scotland could claim tremendous teams. In the forgiving qualifying conditions of today, they might well have made much of the chance to parade their skills on the world stage. In '62 Czechoslovakia blocked Scotland's route to the finals in Chile and, it bears repeating, made it to the final against defending champions Brazil. The Czechs had to fight their way past a brilliant Scottish team in qualifying and the critical judgement was that while the Czechs were strong and well organised, Scotland were a better, more gifted team. At a distance, it seemed like a fair argument; Scotland, after all, could send out players of the quality of Dave Mackay, Slim Jim Baxter and Denis Law.

Those were some of the currents flowing through the country when we assembled for a send-off at Hampden Park. There were tens of thousands in the ground to see us leave. We were put in a lorry and driven round the track. The noise was incredible when we stopped for a presentation. It was quite surreal. Gordon McQueen turned to me and said, 'Christ, what's going on?'

The drive to Prestwick airport was even more staggering. Flags were everywhere. People were hanging out of their windows, crowding on to bridges over the dual carriageway. Among the players, it was particularly hard for me to grasp the extent of the feelings that had come to the surface that day. I had been up to Scotland for a couple of advertising promotions and certainly I had noticed there was a little stirring in the land, but this was leaping off the graph.

Ally MacLeod seemed comfortable, waving to the crowd and,

who knew, perhaps his gung-ho style would have an inspiring effect when it came to the action. I kept an open mind. Certainly, the manager had been very good to me, always filling me with the sense that I was an integral part of his plan to beat the world. He had picked me and suggested that I would be starting the tournament in our first match, against Peru, so of course, in the way of football, he had all my support. It was relatively easy for me to switch off the full weight of the hysteria. I said to Gordon, 'I can let all this fly by me. I can get away from it. I have enough on my mind. I just want to get some focus and that will be easier over there.'

However, that great welling of national passion was extraordinary to see and you had to wonder what bed Ally was making for himself by saying that we were going to win the World Cup, especially when you thought of all the European teams who had gone to South America without success. England had lost to the United States in the Brazilian mining town of Belo Horizonte in 1950 and then returned unavailingly twenty years later as world champions – and with a team many believed to be superior to the one that had beaten Germany in the Wembley final in 1966. You also had to remember how only Brazil and the emerging Pele had travelled the other way to triumph in Sweden in 1958. These unavoidable facts had a sobering effect when you saw Ally MacLeod, arms waving triumphantly, on the way to the hardest battlefield in all of football. I thought to myself, 'Let's board that plane and get out of here.'

We got to our training ground near Cordoba to be greeted with good news and bad. The people in the village of Altogracia, which was not much more than a dot on the rolling pampas, were friendly. Unfortunately, the pitch on which MacLeod's prospective world champions had to train was a potential death-trap.

After the thoroughness of big-match preparations by Leeds and Manchester United, I found this jarring. It was not a question of expecting luxury, as seems to be the case today – Sven Goran

Eriksson, the England coach, had the players and their wives and girlfriends in a luxury hotel in Dubai for a week before the 2002 finals. What we needed on the pampas was a bright but relaxing place with first-class practice facilities. That should have been a priority way beyond the organisation of a farewell parade at Hampden Park.

As it was, Derek Johnstone, my leading rival for a starting position, was betrayed by the surface of the training field and went over on his ankle. Johnstone had been outstanding for Rangers and in the build-up to the World Cup he had been a real threat to my position, doing particularly well in a home international against Northern Ireland. I sat on the bench during that match, and was made a little restive by his energy and his bite. Still, there is always one unerring test of how you stand in the estimation of the Scotland manager. It is whether he picks you for the England game. Ally dropped Derek and put me back into the side. I brought everything I could to that match and the manager made it clear to me that it had been enough.

In the previous year's game against England at Wembley, our victory had been blighted for me by the fact that in the second half I'd pulled a muscle. A week later Scotland were due to go on tour to Chile, Argentina and Brazil and, with the World Cup in mind, I was devastated because I knew the injury would not heal in time for me to play in South America. However, Ally called me at home to say that he knew I wouldn't be fit enough to play but I was very much part of his plans and he wanted me to come along anyway. That, given the attitude of the Scottish FA to players' expenses at that time, was a remarkable gesture. It meant that I would go to South America for the first time, and it also implied a status in the team that was very good for my self-confidence.

Scotland beat Chile impressively, Lou Macari scoring twice, drew with Argentina and lost to Brazil, who on that day were at the top of their expressive form – more evidence that Scotland might just be a coming team.

A year on, I clearly remained high in the manager's thinking and, as I had confidently expected, I was named for the opening match against Peru. Like Ally, we all fancied our chances and looking over our team did nothing to diminish our self-belief, although the great coach, and our admirer, Rinus Michels had warned us against the pace and skill of their wingers Juan Jose Munante and Juan Carlos Oblitas. Yes, Peru's star Teofilio Cubillas was an extremely gifted player but he was an old man. In fact, he was a mere twenty-nine and he slaughtered us with two goals.

We lost 3–1 but, just as easily, we could have won it. I put us into the lead after nineteen minutes, seizing on the loose ball after the Peruvian goalkeeper had stopped a shot from Rioch. Cesar Cueto equalised just before half-time, but we were still playing strongly and the keeper, Ramon Quiroga, had to make a brilliant save from Dalglish. In the second half Masson, who had been so calm at Anfield, missed from the penalty spot, firing it straight at Quiroga. Perhaps out of pure relief, Peru played with a new freedom, Munante and Oblitas overwhelming the full-backs, the inexperienced Stuart Kennedy and Martin Buchan, who was playing out of position at left-back. Cubillas did the rest.

We went back to Altogracia in a state of shock. Just a few days earlier in Scotland we had been cheered to the stars. Now, almost instantly, there was a backlash from those fans who had travelled to South America. Ally had told them that we would win, which of course included beating the Argentinians and the Brazilians in their own corner of the world, the calculating Italians and the brilliant, physically powerful Dutch, who four years earlier in Germany had earned themselves the forlorn title of the best team never to win a World Cup. For many Scottish fans, Ally's pronouncement was intoxicating. Now we were living through a terrible hangover, intensified by the revelation that Willie Johnston had failed a drugs test after the Peru game. Traces of amphetamines had been found in his system. We got the news as we put on our blazers and our most polite faces and attended an official reception. Gordon McQueen and I exchanged the old question over the fruit juice, one that I had first asked myself four years earlier when Jimmy Johnstone had been rescued from the Clyde – 'Christ, what's going on?'

We didn't see Willie again. He was bundled into a car and taken to the airport. Up until this day I do not know what he took or why he took it. I wasn't particularly close to him and, to be honest, my sympathy for a team-mate who had come unstuck on such a huge stage was tempered by disbelief that anyone could take such risks with his career. Also, if it was a terrible blow to him, it was devastating to his manager and his team-mates.

Willie Johnston was an excellent player. He had done well for Rangers and West Bromwich Albion and he brought a direct and effective approach to his work along the left flank. In fact, in some ways he was my idea of a perfect winger. He knew how to use his pace, had great success in going past his full-back, and when you made a big churning run to the far post you could be confident that Willie knew what you were doing – and what he had to do. There was no mystery about Willie Johnston on the field. What you saw was what he delivered. Off the field, at least at that disastrous point of his career in Argentina, it was a different, much more confusing story.

Now Willie was gone and with him went a little more light from the eyes of Ally MacLeod. The man who had proclaimed impending world victory wore his distress on his face. Defeat against Peru had come as a shock to his system and now the Johnston fiasco was another huge blow. There was only one way out of the hole. We had to go out to smash Iran, a team who offered none of the threat of Peru. It was, we told ourselves, just a question of regaining our heads while putting the Johnston business into some kind of perspective. Willie had made a mistake, and he was paying a heavy price for it even now as he flew home to Scotland and into the arms of a no doubt under-impressed nation. At least we could still do something about our situation.

On the day that we were ambushed by the Peruvians, Holland had cruised to a 3–0 win over Iran. We needed to do at least as well. The stadium was just dotted with fans but instead of a rallying, defiant Scottish performance, they saw something quite dreadful, the kind of match that haunts you down the years. Our only goal came from one of their players, the defender Andaranik Eskandarian sticking out a leg and making contact with the ball after he had collided with me. At least the timing was helpful, the goal coming as it did just two minutes before half-time.

Unfortunately, the Iranians, who were by no means a good team, much inferior certainly to the ball-playing Cubillas and his team-mates, refused to be cowed, equalising in the sixtieth minute through Iraj Danaifar, who held off the challenge of Jardine at the near post and squeezed the ball past Rough.

We were all drained at the end of the game – Ally MacLeod looked as though he had been involved in a car crash. At half-time, the sense of crisis had been just about unshakeable. How do we get going, how do we lift ourselves? We just couldn't find a way. A group of disaffected supporters demonstrated against us as we returned to the team bus. Most hurtfully, they sang, 'You only want the money.' This was based on a series of TV adverts we had done with Chrysler cars during the World Cup build-up.

We rode back to Altogracia with a terrible sense of failure resting on our shoulders. It had been my fifth game in the World Cup finals and I had never known anything like this killing feeling – when the challenge was most intense we had come up desperately short of what had been demanded. The sight of those angry faces outside the stadium came back to me that night as I tried to sleep. It felt as though we were trapped in a waking nightmare. The appetite of the fans had become enormous, and they could hardly be blamed for believing that this was going to be the great vindication of Scottish football, rather than another disgrace.

When the media arrived at our headquarters you could almost see the knives flashing in the sunlight. We couldn't really complain. We had flown out, however much it went against some of our instincts, in the fashion of conquerors. Ally said we would beat the world. Now, anxious to put the best possible face on the accumulating disasters, he patted the head of a stray dog as he faced the Scottish press. The dog snarled.

It came straight from the dog's mouth that we were not in any position to make the climb to the mountain top our situation now demanded. Holland had three points from two games, having settled for a draw with Peru after experiencing their potential to score freely. We had to beat Holland, one of the World Cup favourites, by three clear goals to make it into the second round.

Ally said it could be done, but when you looked at the Dutch resources, deep down there was an overpowering inclination to shake your head. Ally, after all, had told Scotland that we were going to win it all. Ruudi Krol, the brilliant defender, had taken over the Dutch captaincy from the great Johan Cruyff, and Holland still had seven of the team that most people believed should have won in Germany in 1974 – goalkeeper Jan Jongbloed, defenders Krol, Wim Suurbier and Wim Rijsbergen, Johan Neeskens in midfield, Johnny Rep and Rob Rensenbrink in attack.

A crowd of 35,000 packed the San Martin stadium in the provincial city of Mendoza to watch the formal progress of the potential world champions, Holland. Scotland were just charging off the highroad of football history yet again.

That belief did hold true – but not before Scotland showed the other side of their football nature. Self-destruction, yes, we could do that better than any nation on earth, but we could also play. We could play football of skill, force and great imagination – we could score a goal that would have graced any World Cup. We beat Holland 3–2 in a superb game that said everything you needed to know about the Scottish knack of straddling football's heaven and hell.

Pushed into the tightest corner of his professional life, Ally MacLeod turned to the man who many thought should have started the tournament, Graeme Souness. He left out John Robertson, who had failed to reproduce the cunning that he had displayed in Nottingham Forest's championship year, and Macari, restored Rioch to the team and sent out Souness, who had been simmering on the touchline during the futile performance against Iran. Souness had created the goal that gave Liverpool the second of their four European Cups a month earlier and his impatience about what had gone before was reflected in the ferocity of his commitment against the Dutch.

We tore at Holland and gave, at last, some evidence of why Ally's hopes had flown so high and the Dutch coach Michels had been so generous about our chances of making a serious impact in Argentina. We needed a three-goal margin to progress, against all expectations, and in the early going we might have had them. Rioch sent a header against the bar, Dalglish had a goal disallowed and, the Welsh may have been gratified to see, I was denied a penalty when I was brought down in the box. In all these circumstances, we might easily have disappeared when the Austrian referee promptly awarded a penalty at the other end, when Kennedy brought down Rep. Rensenbrink scored and Ally, who by now was looking as though he had aged ten years, put his head in his hands.

We were far from beaten, however. Something was flowing in our blood this day, something that had been so sickeningly elusive against Iran – a pure desire to prove that we had more than had been evident these last few weeks. If we couldn't join the élite in the final stages of the World Cup, we could show them that we had something that had been unaccountably mislaid. Souness surged to the fore. He hit a high cross to the far post, where I knocked it down to Dalglish. Kenny had made one of his trademark moves that left him unmarked and he stroked home the equaliser with just a minute to go in the half.

An objective observer might have thought Ally was stretching things when he said during the interval that we could still hit our target of a three-goal victory. Against the Dutch, long respected as the pacesetters of total football? The dispassionate witness would have been excused his belief that he was eavesdropping on another MacLeod fantasy. However, a minute into the second half, Willy van der Kerkhof pushed Souness over in the box and Archie Gemmill coolly converted the penalty. Twenty-two minutes later the little man made the collective heart of Scotland stand still. He scored a wonderful goal, one that in many ways typified the classic values of Scottish football – impertinent and marvellously skilful. He collected the ball on the right of the Dutch penalty area, beat Wim Jansen inside, Krol outside, and nutmegged Jan Poortvliet before chipping the ball over the desperately advancing keeper Jongbloed. One more goal was needed in another twenty-two minutes, and if Gemmill could produce such brilliance, surely there was, with the blood coursing so strongly now, every chance of another strike. It happened in three minutes, but not for Scotland. Johnny Rep hit a long shot and it flew by Rough.

A beaten army never had a longer, more dismal journey home. Perversely, the defeat of Holland heightened our sense of failure. Gemmill's goal was a gem, but its setting, when you balanced all the hopes that had been generated against what had been achieved, could only be seen as shoddy. What did the great goal, and the victory over a team who would go on to the final, really prove? More than anything it said that Scotland still didn't know how to exploit all that was best in their game.

Lou Macari angrily attacked the Scottish FA and the command of Ally MacLeod. He spoke from raw frustration and the price he paid was that he never played for his country again – nor did the captain Bruce Rioch, Don Masson, Tom Forsyth or Willie Johnston. Ally MacLeod, despite a battering in the media, retained his job, but only briefly. The experience weighed on him heavily and he resigned after just one more game.

There was no reception on the Corn Patch this time. I trailed back to Manchester, beaten and bruised and took Judith, who was pregnant and not keen to endure the heat of a Spanish beach in that condition, for a short break in Cornwall. Listening to the sea lap against the shore should have been soothing but when I shut my eyes I could only see the anguished face of Ally MacLeod – and hear big Gordon repeating that terrible question, 'Christ, what's going on?' In Cornwall, it rained every day.

12

WELCOME, LO SQUALO

I HAVE to say right away that my time in Italy was not as I had hoped in my more optimistic moments. There was some glory; a fantastic roar assailed my ears when I scored in the great stadium of San Siro – and I will be able to tell my grandchildren how it was when a squad of carabinieri had to escort me out of the ground because of the rush of admirers. They christened me Lo Squalo, 'The Shark' and even when injuries and differences with the coach hampered my progress at Milan, the fans never turned against me. They saw that I had come to play.

So much was overwhelming in the sweep of AC Milan's demands on my time and my thinking. There were many days when the best of what was left was not much defence against fatigue and doubt. The fact was that for all my commitment to the game, I had always enjoyed a full life beyond the football club and the training field. While in Italy, that is something you have to accept as mostly just a memory. The change of approach required of players from countries where it was possible for them to do their work in the mornings and pick up their lives with their families in the afternoon has always been enormous and, I suspect, always will be. The regime cannot accept any compromise because if it ever started to do that, something utterly essential to its meaning would be lost. Football is not a job but a calling for which few are chosen. Those who are have to live a different, sometimes separate, life.

This reality came swiftly when the first excitement of my arrival in Milan passed. My eyes were wide open with anticipation when Judith and I arrived at Linate airport for the transfer formalities. I asked the president of the club, Felice Colombo, to take me to the San Siro stadium. I had seen it on television, had a sense of the awesome scale of it, but I had to make it real in my own mind. We didn't stop there. We drove by and it was enough to catch the sweep of one of the most demanding arenas in all of football. I just wanted to confirm my sense of a new world. That was evident enough when I was handed my first week's schedule. The change in my style of life was very great, but it was the first sighting of the San Siro that took me to the heart of my new agenda. As at Elland Road and Old Trafford, I had to compete in that huge arena and handle everything that went with it. I had to play against the best players and the best teams and under the greatest pressure and I had to take each day, good and bad, as it came. I also had to make more sacrifices than ever before.

I was reminded of that in the build-up to the 2004 European Championship. Paul Scholes, a superb professional by any standard, was invited by reporters to define his ideal day. He said it was the one he lived every day – he did his training in the morning, picked his young children up from school, played with them, put them to bed and spent the evening at home with his wife. Maybe he would go down to the local supermarket in the afternoon, perhaps have a stroll through the neighbourhood before picking up the kids. That life, no more than the wild partying we read about so often in the tabloids, just couldn't happen in Italy.

The fact that you belong to the club in ways that stretch far beyond your work on the training field and in the matches is made evident on the day you play your first game. There is no sneaking away into your car and heading for the shadows. No, you have to pass through a great salon where the TV cameras and the radio mikes come at you without any restraint. If any branch of the media wants to speak to you, they can do so, and it doesn't matter how you are feeling about what has just happened on the field. You have to give your time and if not your deepest feelings, a certain politeness, because it is part of your job.

John Charles, the great star of Juventus, was still a revered figure when I arrived decades after his glory. He was such a success in Italy, and will always be mourned, because apart from all his marvellous ability he had great respect for the people who gave him such a warm welcome. Charles was the ultimate example to players who wanted to make their mark in Italy. As deeply committed football men, Liam Brady and Graeme Souness also wanted to earn the respect of the Italians. When I think of that kind of determination, which I shared, it puts into some perspective for me the attitude of some modern players who seem to take all they receive for granted. Claude Makelele, who doubled his salary when he moved from Real Madrid to Chelsea, complained about living in London because of the bad weather, unfamiliar food and difficult traffic. I'm not talking about the merits of different cultures but the requirement for every professional to get on with his job. He had accepted his terms, so he had to play. I imagine, even now, the Italian players arriving in the Premiership are stunned by both the drop in their responsibilities and the huge leap in the time they get to themselves and to spend with their families.

Italian football, I discovered, was hard and intense and beautiful all at the same time. In fact, when I thought about it, it was not so surprising that Il Calcio meant as much as it did in a land of both great culture and quick-fire emotion. Anyone from Lanarkshire would recognise its role quickly enough. My strength was that I did. I felt that I was born to play in the atmosphere and the intensity of Italy and that instinct was confirmed when I ran out on the field at San Siro. The thunder of the crowd was moving and inspiring at the same time. However, when the noise of the crowd died, the challenge was a lot more complicated.

I ached to add the great stadium to the list of battlefields where I had found glory – Elland Road, Old Trafford and Hampden Park – but there are so many factors shaping success in football. In the most of crucial of all, the touch of the coach or manager and your ability to avoid serious injury, I had always been lucky. Gigi Radice, my first coach at AC Milan, broke the pattern. One day I had to tell him not to point his finger at me. At the time he was telling me, finger jabbing, that I had to be at the Milanello training ground at a certain hour. 'Yes,' I said, 'I'll be there – but no more of the finger, please.'

Radice had enjoyed success as a Milan player, he was a friend and team-mate of the great coach Giovanni Trapattoni, but now he didn't show so much evidence of being a happily fulfilled professional. Certainly, he didn't extend to me the grace that the club president Colombo had shown when he presented Judith with that beautiful silk scarf as a welcome present. Radice's greeting was rather more harsh. He implied strongly that I had everything to prove, that I came from somewhere outside of his experience and that maybe it was a place he suspected he might not like. The situation worsened when I picked up an injury. Eventually, I had to go to him and say, 'Look, believe me or not, I have an injury – it's something you should know.'

Radice's demands were not a particular problem for me. I would have liked to have been able to tell him in fluent Italian that I always played the game in a certain way, and that if it had been good enough for Revie, Busby and Sexton, it should be good enough for him. I didn't have fluent Italian and I knew well enough that suddenly I was fighting for my career in Italy. I played hard and I faced my responsibilities as a professional – for me, that was the way it always had been. I had never done easy riding and it was a bit late to start now.

I worked out my approach to Radice after carefully noting his style. Milan did things differently from anywhere I had been before. They piled the training into long days but if that was the way it was, they would have no argument from me. They paid my wages and they had given me my chance to experience a new and in many ways fantastic football culture, and I would do everything I could to meet their expectations. The trouble was that in the early going the new, heavy rhythm of training was no doubt taking some sharpness away from me. I was getting to the big game on Sunday a little short of that edge I had always worked for, and I couldn't discuss it with my new boss in the way I might have with Revie or Sexton. To do that you need to have established some level of trust. It was also true that no rebellion of mine was likely to throw over an approach to the game that had been established in Italy for so many years.

Radice was aggressive towards most of the players, and quite unpopular, and later my friend Tony Damascelli, the sportswriter, told me what it was that had made him change so sharply. A few years earlier he had been at the wheel in a crash in which the Italian World Cup winger Paolo Barison had died. Barison had been a powerful, crowd-pleasing player who had the forlorn distinction of scoring one of Italy's only two goals in the 1966 World Cup, when a team that included such great players as Sandro Mazzola and Gianni Rivera were pelted with eggs when they arrived home at Rome airport after losing to Russia and, most shamefully, North Korea. Tony said that the accident, which cost Radice two of his fingers and for a week required him to fight for his life, weighed heavily on the coach.

On another occasion, after the finger-pointing episode, Radice ordered me to run repeatedly around the training track because I had arrived late after being fogbound in Glasgow following a World Cup qualifying game for Jock Stein's Scotland. I had done everything I could to get to Milanello on time; such things were always a matter of professional pride with me, and if that instinct hadn't been there already, it would no doubt have been hammered into me in those first few weeks with Leeds United. In Italy, anyway, discipline was always a high priority for everyone and I was determined from my first day in Milan that I wouldn't do anything to support the belief that foreign players lacked a competitive edge. I did the run, even though I was nursing an injury. I gritted my teeth and got it done. It was an extremely difficult situation, though, especially when I had just a few words of Italian. The club had given me a young interpreter from my first day at the ground, and he did his best to help me. Unfortunately, small but vital nuances of meaning can be lost in translation. Expressing rage through an interpreter is a difficult and dangerous challenge.

I had no alternative but to play on their terms, which at times were extremely harsh, but I never considered sloping away. I promised myself that I would give everything I had, as I had done at Elland Road and Old Trafford. So things were not going as sweetly as I had hoped – it happens. The trick, I told myself driving home from Milanello, was to work away at the things you know are right.

Quite recently, Damascelli, who had played such an important part in my move to Italy, after watching my progress with Leeds and Manchester United on the Swiss television broadcasts he could pick up in his home in Turin, reported on a moment when he believed I was expressing all my frustration. I missed a goal from, as he put it, 'zero yards', heading the wrong side of the post. In more encouraging circumstances, I would have simply knocked the ball into the back of the net. Tony said, 'You took hold of the goalpost and grasped it very hard, as though you wanted to shake it down. You were a great fighter and it was as though you were saying, "What can I do?"'

I don't remember that specific incident but I can recall vividly enough that time I had to battle with my fate, when things were not going so well for me or the team. I just had to slug it out in order to gain a foothold in the Italian game, which, for all the difficulties, I still deeply admired in so many ways.

Tony also reported that at that time he found me a 'closed

man', someone who gave him the impression that he had discovered a new world. In a sense it was true, and maybe I was building a few walls around myself. Apparently, I told him I didn't like wine or spirits and he thought to himself, 'This man is not possible.' Maybe it was at Tony's instigation that Liam Brady, who had settled in well with Juventus, drove over from Turin to give me some encouragement and to talk about his experiences. It was a good gesture and I appreciated it very much – but I also knew that my destiny lay in my own hands. I had to do what I done down all the years. I had to battle on.

In the end, I could look back on three years in Italy, two with Milan and one with Verona, a club and a place I came to adore, and tell myself that I hadn't quit on my stool. Nothing in my career has given me more satisfaction than getting through those years and coming out of them with a young family richer for the experience and a sense that I had met the toughest challenge of my football life. There were times when it would have been easy to pack my bags and run. Sometimes it seemed the long days, my efforts to learn the language, the change in playing philosophy, were all designed to destroy the spirit of self-belief that had always been a central part of my success in the game. At my lowest points, I told myself that nothing I faced in Italy could be as daunting as those first weeks at Elland Road when I arrived after just a few games with Morton. I also remembered what Bobby Collins had said about me all those years ago – I played like a man.

In fact, the dressing-room rituals of AC Milan, in which I was quickly immersed, were relatively gentle. I was whisked away to training camp and, if it was a hard regime, the players were easy with each other and they gave me a good welcome. I recall one night after dinner we took a gentle walk and finished up in an ice-cream parlour, where the trainer footed the bill. It was a brief but soothing interlude and it gave me a sense of how things might be after I'd negotiated these first difficult days of transition. The training in the afternoon was the new element I found most tricky. I was not used to it and, while not afraid of the effort, I worried that it would take away the vital sharpness that is so crucial to a striker's confidence.

I saw, and experienced, all of Italian football in those three years. I lived through terrible upheavals at Milan. I lay flat on the floor of the bus with my team-mates when bricks were coming through the windows after a game that the referee had to leave dressed as a policeman because one of his decisions had so inflamed the crowd. I heard the cheers and the boos rolling down from the vast terraces of the San Siro. I will never forget the cheers, and especially the first wave of them, before the start of my first league season with Milan. We played in the Italian Cup and I scored against the hated enemy Internazionale. It was a good goal, I made some space for myself and met a quickly taken free kick perfectly with my head. The ball flew into the back of the net and the AC fans went mad. After the game I was mobbed and it was then that I had to be escorted from the crowd by the carabinieri. I had a vision of an heroic future. Suddenly, I was Lo Squalo. I thought that it would be the first of many goals, that it was my calling card, but unfortunately, one deadly thrust of a shark doesn't make a season. Looking back, that season was always doomed.

The problems at the club ran deep. They had been put in train by the great bribery scandal that shook the foundations of Italian football in the 1979–80 season. It is remembered now as the Paolo Rossi scandal, but the man who would eventually emerge as the great scoring hero of Italy's World Cup win in Spain in 1982 was just a small part of it. Some players went to prison and the affair cost the president and owner of Milan, Felici Columbo, his proud position at the club that for so long had been the centre of his life.

The police made a synchronised swoop all over the country, at San Siro before a game with Torino. Milan, devastatingly, were sent to *Serie B* – the second division, or, as far as their passionate fans were concerned, the very edge of the earth. It was as though a great cloud had crossed the land. If you couldn't trust your *regazzi*, your boys, to play for the colours, where could you put your faith? Perhaps inevitably, the built-in power and wealth of AC Milan, and the extraordinary talent and maturity of the young Franco Baresi, brought a swift return to the top flight. The crowds, after nursing the wounds, were still enormous and passionate, but what happened had got into the very bones of the club. The battle to reinstate Milan as a front-line force in the Italian game was proving a major struggle. You could see the tension on Radice's face and in his manner, and after a few weeks we were bumping around at the foot of *Serie A*. The complaints from the terraces were growing both in volume and bitterness and it soon became clear that Radice was not going to survive the crisis.

One day, all of the players were summoned to a restaurant on the outskirts of Milan. Radice was nowhere to be seen. The gathering was presided over by the president and his directors. The only people in the restaurant were the players and the directors. With my limited Italian, much of the talk swirled over my head but the point was clear enough. The hierarchy of AC Milan were asking the players what they thought of the coach. Whatever the verdict of the players, that in itself was a professional death sentence for the man who had survived a fatal crash but perhaps not all of its effects.

In that restaurant, you saw all the ruthlessness of the Italian game. Something was wrong in the team and the directors wanted to get right to the heart of the problem. Despite being almost entirely a spectactor, I knew enough to see that it was over for Radice. For me, it was an extraordinary situation to be in. I could never have imagined it happening at Elland Road or Old Trafford. However, whatever I thought of Milan's way of doing business with their coach, it was impossible to mourn Radice. He got it wrong in the most comprehensive way. His greatest weakness was that he wasn't flexible enough. He couldn't grasp that while general discipline was the basis of any club's success, each player was an individual and had to be granted that respect. What pushed him so far to the edge? Maybe it was the effect of the crash, at least to some extent. Perhaps, having been a player at San Siro – in the time of Greaves – he wanted to be a success on his return a little too desperately.

Radice's job passed to Italo Galbiatti, an experienced professional who had worked with the fast-rising coach Fabio Capello, and the morale of the team improved, as did mine when I was able to shake off the effects of a nagging injury. Unfortunately, there was too much ground to be made up and the great AC Milan had to face up to the prospect of another relegation, this time one fashioned on the field rather than the backrooms.

I survived the fall, however, and came to enjoy my football again under the stewardship of Ilario Castagnar, when he took over from Galbiatti, who reverted to the role of assistant. The spirit of the club was re-assembled and playing with Baresi, Batistini, Alberigo Guani, Mauro Tossoti, Oscar Damiani, Francesco Romano and Aldo Serena was something I knew that I could hold forever. They were good team-mates and companions – and excellent guides to the culture of Italian football about which I was still learning and which is often portrayed, at least in my experience, in excessively negative terms. Things changed for the better for both Joe Jordan and AC Milan. I knew I was stronger both as a footballer and a man for surviving that season of trial.

My life with Judith was better because we had been through a tough experience together. We had made it through some difficult days, realising how much strength we could get from each other. To live in Italy, and be under the gaze of the public as a football player, pushed me hard. I have never, before or since, been under such pressure in my career. Obviously, there is pressure everywhere in a competitive business, and there is special weight on managers because they are dependent on so many other factors outside themselves, but I knew, when it was happening to me, that because I had got through the Milan experience, I could handle anything that came along later.

In Italy, the value of defence is given huge weight, but there is a code in which great performance and character are held in the highest respect. I played there for three years and not once was I spat upon; not once did I leave the field thinking, 'Christ, wasn't that cynical, that showed no conscience.' I was done physically three or four times in bad tackles, but I never felt there was anything clinical about it. I never felt victim of anything that was sick or snide, which is something I'm afraid I couldn't always say of the football back home. The Italian player was always aware that he occupied a special place in society. He was a footballer but also a symbol of achievement and he knew that he could not afford to slip below expectations. The idea of attracting the kind of negative publicity that is now so commonplace in English football remains unthinkable in Italy. The society there, at any level, just couldn't support the idea that one of its heroes was not aware of his responsibilities to his club, his followers and also, in the end, himself.

Castagnar had made his name by driving the modestly financed Perugia into second place in *Serie A* while the mighty Milan were forced to scuffle in the second division. Relegation was a terrible blow for everybody, but maybe a line could now be drawn under the worst of the club's times. I had another year on my contract and Castagnar said, yes, he could use me. He cleared out all the older players except the goalkeeper and me. I took my chance, scoring fifteen goals, eleven of them in the League, and providing plenty of strength up front, holding the ball up and making my presence felt in the box, particularly at set-pieces. The crowd stirred again and, with an average 60,000 at home games, we swept to the second-division championship, claiming the title against Lazio. It had been hard, at times desperately so, but at the end of that second season I felt I had rescued my situation. I had achieved the degree of respect that had been my basic ambition when I arrived in Milan. I had also learned enough about the way things worked in Italy not to be surprised when Castagnar called me into his office at the end of the season, thanked me for my efforts but said that the team was being re-cast. What did I want to do? I could return to England with honour restored or I could stay in Italy, several clubs were interested in me, with Verona at the head of the list.

I was thirty-one years old and for the first time I was being told that I was no longer part of a club's plans. Up to now I had always made the decision. Yes, I would join Leeds United, yes, Manchester United would be very much to my liking. AC Milan? Yes, how could anyone with my instincts deny them? Now Milan were telling me that I had to move on. It was something to absorb on the drive home to Burago; something to be sad about because this had been the great adventure of my career and now it was over. It was also something to be proud about. Milan could have easily broken me but I was strong where I had been most wounded and, as I said to Judith when we opened one of our better bottles of wine, I liked the sound and the feel of Verona.

It is a beautiful old city surrounded by a Roman wall and with the remains of an amphitheatre beside the square where they have lovely restaurants and a band playing in the late afternoon sunshine. That kind of appeal, coupled with my determination to get more of the Italian experience and on better, more comfortable terms born out the battles that had gone before, persuaded me to turn down the overtures of Lawrie McMenemy, who was building a successful team at Southampton.

Lawrie felt that I fitted in with his liking for players of experience and proven track records, but I wanted more of Italy – after dealing with the reality that, for the first time, the future had been taken out of my hands. It shook the old certainties and was a reminder that, in football, your fate is ultimately always dependent on somebody else's opinion and the need to avoid serious injury.

We packed up our belongings and drove down the Milan–Venice autostrada to the old Roman city, nestling in a fold of the vine-covered hills. I would never know now what it was to play in those famous red and black stripes when the issue was not survival but some ultimate glory, winning the *scudetto* or a European prize. Clear signs of the club coming together were evident under the canny Castagnar. Milan had gone through some horrendous times; the traumas of relegation and scandal had, for a while, taken residence in everyone's psyche but now you could sense the pressure was lifting. The young prodigy Baresi was improving before your eyes and around him was a growing pool of talent. Evani, Batistini, Romano and Serena would all become accomplished internationalists. The young talent, and one or two clever signings, had made a return to the élite of Italian football inevitable, and in a couple of years, time, when I had returned to England, there would be the great launching of AC Milan's European empire.

I would have to watch that from a distance – and learn the oldest truth in the game, which is nowhere more implicit than in Italy – for the great clubs, a footballer has his time and then he is gone like an old brown leaf in autumn.

13

A YEAR IN VERONA

VERONA was a gift that Judith and I embraced enthusiastically for the beauty of the city and the good, rich life it gave to us. For me, it meant there was another year of playing the game in a great environment – another year in which to learn about a game that, even when it had been at its hardest, had given me a glimpse of the grandeur of a great club. I immersed myself in Verona as enthusiastically as I had ever done at any club and for a little while they were the centre of all my hopes. Naturally, however, to this day I have retained a sharp interest in the affairs of AC Milan. I had been part of their drama for just two years but, as far as I was concerned, it was a lifelong connection.

Silvio Berlusconi, the TV magnate who would eventually become prime minister of Italy, made the move that cemented his role as a national figure, buying the club from Farina and installing the brilliant coach Arigo Sacchi. The Dutchmen Ruud Gullit, Marco Van Basten and Frank Rijkaard were signed and suddenly AC Milan were the team who had it all – the brilliant finishing of Van Basten, Gullit's wonderful athleticism and touch in midfield and the great defensive minds of Franco Baresi and, soon enough, the emerging young Paolo Maldini.

Maldini was a kid in the youth team when I was at Milan. His dad, Cesare, who would later coach Italy with his son in the team, was frequently around the club. Paolo grew to be a great player and a great representative of Italian football. On several occasions while visiting Milan I have met up with him and each time I was struck over all again by his distinguished bearing and gentlemanly manner.

Baresi won a championship medal when he was eighteen but even so it was impossible to know that he would achieve quite such great stature. Yes, he was going to be a fine player, anyone could see that, but what he did in the end was raise and define the position in which he played, something that doesn't fall to many of even the greatest players.

At the start, Baresi was an out-and-out sweeper, a role that was fundamental to the way Italian football was organised and a basic element in Italy's cautious psychology – always cover the ground, always have someone at the back, never take the risk of giving anything away. Sacchi asked the young Baresi to think about the way he played. While the Italian game was built on the principle of safety first, Sacchi wanted Baresi to bring vision to the sweeper's role, to explore every chance of applying pressure further up the field. In embracing the thought, achieving Sacchi's goal, Baresi became a huge influence on Italian football, and the effects can be seen clearly today.

The game there has changed so much from my days, when it was terribly difficult to operate as a forward in an orthodox position. For evidence of this you only have to consider that in my three years in Italy, Michel Platini of Juventus was the top scorer in *Serie A* from midfield. The Frenchman was a world-class player who found plenty of opportunity in the space granted to him by the Italian insistence on deep defence, but the growing Milan influence was built on much more aggression. Sacchi wanted a little more of the British style, which, when I think back, is more evidence that one of the greatest tricks in life is to get your timing right. In retrospect, in terms of my fate in Italy, maybe I was born just a little early. Who knows, in other circumstances I might have been making bullets for Van Basten, surely one of the greatest strikers of all time.

Sacchi wanted his team to intimidate the opposition with the sheer force of their ambition to play the game expansively. In closing down opponents, they would do it in terms of attack as much as defence. They pushed the opposition back, then played from there. Later, Tossoti told me that the result was Milan would go to Real Madrid's Bernabeu, for instance, without a scrap of fear. There would no be jockeying; they would go to win the ball and then use it. It had been quite different before the arrival of Sacchi. I remember Baresi saying to me as I tried to close down a defender, 'Leave it, let them have the ball.' Maybe I had been doing my marking chores and not getting very far, but it was my deeply ingrained habit and it was very hard to forget the way of football I had learned under Don Revie. The young Baresi would be insistent. 'Don't try to win the ball when you're not sure you can really do it – you're using up energy and not really achieving anything,' he would say. It was a difficult point to accept but I did come to realise that, in that part of my game, I couldn't achieve much on my own.

Under Sacchi, Milan refined the process of applying pressure. When the front two were poised to close down the defence, the team did it *en masse*. Nothing was off the cuff, it was a hard, calculated method and the more I watched Milan under Sacchi, the more I admired his achievement.

I met Sacchi a few times and I was fascinated to hear his version of how he set up Baresi as the key man to develop his philosophy of the game. He had said to Baresi, 'Give me three months, Franco. You are the best sweeper in Italy but I don't want you to sit back and read the game and pick off the ball as it comes through. What I'm asking you to do is no less than coordinate everything that is in front of you. We will channel our work through you in the week before the game, and when the time comes, we will play where you dictate us to play – and you will also dictate the positions your team-mates take up.'

Tactics come and go in football, coaches have theories that

sometimes stand the test of time and sometimes don't, but nothing could be more thrilling than to see a young player respond so brilliantly to the urgings of an outstanding football man, a true original. Baresi had much more than a brilliant football brain, however. He had a brilliant football heart. One stage of his career always leaps out at me when I think of him. It was his effort in the 1994 World Cup in America, where Italy came so close to winning their fourth World Cup in the final against Brazil in Pasadena. Baresi missed in the penalty shoot-out and his agony was terrible to see but, in my eyes, it did nothing to diminish his glory.

Baresi was injured in Italy's first group game against Ireland and was told that he would have to have a knee operation. Astonishingly, Baresi had a cartilage operation and recovered in time for the final. Italy, under Sacchi, had been bedevilled by injury and bad luck throughout the tournament and it was staggering that, in all the circumstances, they made it to the final. Most remarkable of all, though, was not that Baresi played in the final but that he performed so superbly. Romario and Bebeto had been the stars of the Brazilian game, quick, darting attackers who had undermined every defence they had faced in the competition – but not Italy's. Baresi pushed them further and further back and took away their lines of supply. In the end, the Brazilian coach Carlos Alberto Parreira and his players were content to settle for the shoot-out lottery. They may have won but Brazil shared in the general awe at the fantastic recovery and performance of the Italian captain.

That affair told you about Baresi the man as much as the footballer. He represented the best of the Italian game and that says something huge indeed. Some years later Baresi achieved another distinction, although it is possibly not one that is constantly in the forefront of his mind. He became my only live television interviewee when I analysed the Italian game for Channel Four television. We covered the build-up to the derby game between AC and Internazionale and Baresi agreed to be interviewed by me – in Italian, I'm proud to say – in the San Siro dressing room. Subtitles were provided for the benefit of the British viewer. An angle of the interview was that I had scored in a Milan derby and Baresi hadn't. He had, however, done just about everything else. An ordinary Italian lad lifted so high by his ability to play football, he had the character to grow with his success. His testimonial match at the San Siro was a fitting tribute to a wonderful career. It seemed that everybody who mattered in Italian football was there, including the great Dutch trio of Gullit, Van Basten and Rijkaard. Baresi donated all the takings to charity. He said he had enjoyed great good fortune in his football career and now he wanted to give something back.

Despite a badly timed injury, my own sense of good fortune remained high in Verona. When we arrived in Milan two years earlier the club had made all the arrangements and looked after us. Now our situation had changed a little, but not in a way that made it difficult to cope. We had been around the Italian block, and we considered our options on where to live quite carefully. Judith was strongly tempted by a beautiful village on Lake Garda, but we decided that with the children so young there would be hazards living so close to the water. In the end, we decided to move into a big old villa on the other side of Verona in the wine-growing Soave district. We could have stayed in the city itself, it was so beautiful, but for a little while we believed we were living in paradise out on the hill among the vineyards and the fruit trees.

Life at the football club was so much easier than it had been in the first year at Milan. I could speak decent Italian now and although the injury was depressing at such a point in my career, it didn't weigh me down as it might have done under the Radice regime at the San Siro. There was a great feeling about the place, the strong sense of a team coming through.

The injury of a senior player always has the potential to open the door to someone else's ambition, and just as I benefited initially from the knee problems of Mick Jones at Leeds, Giuseppe Galderesi moved into my boots with impressive certainty. Galderesi had been fighting to make an impact in *Serie A*, having come from Juventus on loan. He took his chance so well at Verona that eventually he made it into the Italian national team. Galderesi formed an excellent partnership with Maurizio Iorio, who had come down from Roma after winning a championship medal but then having to fight for his place. Iorio just blossomed at Verona, enjoying new responsibility – and the confidence of the coach that it implied.

Iorio and Galderesi worked so well together that although I fought back to fitness, I could do no better than operate on the fringes of the team. Galderesi simply exploded and after I left the club they refused to give him back to Juventus. There was quite a row between the clubs but Verona were emphatic – they would not surrender their local hero to the old giant Juventus. Eventually, he moved to AC Milan.

I would come in and do well enough, exert my strength and experience, and in that way I was valuable to the squad. It was not quite what I had in mind for my Italian farewell but the coach, Osvaldo Bagnoli, was a good man and, unlike Radice, he always made it clear that he was aware of my commitment to the club.

Bagnoli had played for Milan in his time but he put down new roots in Verona and a few years ago, his football career over, he returned to the city, where he owns the second biggest hotel. After his stint at Verona, during which he won the fabled *scudetto* title – the year after I left – he could have gone anywhere in Italy. He chose Internazionale Milan, where I visited him and watched his training, and then he moved to Genoa. In 2003 the Verona club had its centenary and I was invited to join the celebrations. Bronzed and fit, Bagnoli met me at the airport. It was good to see how a decent man had come through football so unscathed, and had been able to prosper so well after separating himself from something into which he had put so much of his life.

Under Bagnoli, it seemed to me, Verona represented everything that was good about the game. They had standards, they
played good, clean football and when you ran out in their blue
and gold you felt you were representing more than just another
football club. You were also playing for a set of values.

Bagnoli was particularly impressive in his handling of the
players. He never lost his head. He understood the difference
between bad form, perhaps brought on by injury or some other
problem in a player's life, and a lack of commitment. Verona's
attraction was a little odd in that the seeds of it were sown in one
of my first games for Milan. We played them in the Cup and they
beat us. Defeats have to be banished from your mind but this one
lingered in mine. I noted Verona's style, and reckoned that this
was a team undoubtedly on the up and up. You could see it in the
snap of their play, their good discipline, their attention to detail –
all the signs of a team on the move.

Bagnoli explained to me his basic ideas on attack. He wanted a
big centre-forward who was sharp enough to do some damage
apart from leading the line and holding up the ball. He'd always
tried to have a powerful striker – someone strong and uncom-
plicated. He made it all sound very simple but when I looked at
his team and saw the rhythm of their play, one thing above all
struck me – each round hole had a round peg.

They weren't all exceptional players but there was a good
level of talent and a genuine star in Piero Fanna, who was a
glowing advert for Bagnoli's brand of buying. Fanna, like
Domenico Volpati, was a versatile player. He had pace and
skill and he could operate on both flanks but he was best on the
left side of midfield. He did extremely well for Verona in their
championship year and was then sold to Milan. It was an
example of the Bagnoli touch, one he displayed in so many
shrewd transfer deals.

I can happily while away some time remembering that phase of
my career. The goalkeeper, Garela, went on to Napoli, and the

good sweeper, Roberto Tricella, to Internazionale. Luciano Marangon played on the left and pushed on as a full-back. Silvano Fontolan was a big, dour stopper central defender from Como. Beside him, Feroni was less imposing physically but sharp and with plenty of vision. He reminded me of Liverpool's tremendous, rugged defender Tommy Smith. Luigi Saccheti played in the middle of the park. He had a mean streak – a touch of Souness without that depth of ability. Antonio Gennaro, from Florence, was the playmaker, clever and unshowy, a coach's player who rarely wasted the ball.

My particular pal, my Italian version of Gordon McQueen, was Volpati, a superior utility player who, like Bagnoli, always planned to make a professional life outside the game. He became a dentist when he retired, having earlier suspended his studies to give himself a real chance in the professional game. He got himself a practice in Cavalese in the Alps and also bought a house over the border in France. I get calls from him occasionally, usually at Christmas time, and during the centenary year we spent a few days together, having a few glasses of wine and sharing some good memories.

The surging partnership of Galderesi and Iorio, and the fact that I was thirty-two, meant that the Italian adventure was inevitably drawing to a close. I reckoned I had two or three decent years left as a player and had reason to believe that I would continue to play in the first division when I returned to England or Scotland. It was time to savour the last drops of Italian wine and I did so with the philosophical approach that is so essential in an ageing pro. You take what you can and always work not to let yourself down.

In fact, there was, for me, a late flurry of action on the field. Verona had a good run in the Italian Cup and I scored a goal in the semi-final against Bari. I made it to the final, which was played home and away. We lost 1–0 to Roma. My last game in Italy was played in the Olympic stadium, which stands beside the Tiber

The Shark bites – I score against one of our great rivals, Juventus.

Gigi Radice, the troubled – and troubling – Milan coach. He was wary of me, and maybe of all foreigners.

Franco Baresi of Milan and Italy – one of the true greats.

My new Milan team-mates – fine individual players, they were kind in the worst of times.

Domenico Volpati, Verona's Jack-of-all trades who became a dentist and one of my close friends.

Osvaldo Bagnoli, a fine football coach of Verona – and a gentleman of the world.

Fighting for the Verona cause in the place that mattered most, in front of goal.

The Jordan bunch – Lucy, Caroline, Thomas and Andrew enjoy the Italian beach life.

Back on the home front, duelling with Everton's Derek Mountfield in the new colours of Southampton.

Joe Jordan the manager. In a sweet moment of victory, Bristol City beat Chelsea 3–1 in the fourth round of the FA Cup in 1990.

Another managerial pose, and more sombre, at Hearts in September 1991.

Fighting the dying of the light in one of the last battles on the field at the age of thirty-six – for Bristol City against Walsall in the third division play-off final in 1988.

Liam Brady and I look on the brighter side, briefly. My smile died when Liam decided to quit the struggling Celtic.

Another start. Launching a new regime with Lawrie McMenemy (*centre*) and Pat Jennings with Northern Ireland – great company, but it was a hopeless task.

Fighting for survival, again – this time with my friend Lou Macari at Huddersfield Town in 2001.

After the battles, Gordon McQueen, Eddie Gray and I dress up for dinner.

After the storm, a home match for the winning team. Whatever the fortunes of football, Judith has always been there.

The Jordan bunch, 2004 – Thomas, Lucy, Andrew and Caroline.

with cedar trees lining the surrounding hills like sentinels – not a bad place to say *arrivederci*.

For all the frustrations, I was at the end of an adventure that would come back to me so warmly at the most unexpected of times. In some of the struggles back on the lower rungs of the English game, when the budget strings could be tightened suddenly on the most basic of expenses, one great memory was of Bagnoli taking the players out to lunch. Everybody came, the doctor, the masseur, the physiotherapist, the kit man. It wasn't a 'bonding' session with the drink spilling all around. Bagnoli would pick a restaurant and a leisurely lunch would be taken. Bottles of wine would be produced but often not drained. Everyone would take a glass and the talk would flow with the good wine and the fine food. Mostly the talk would be of football, of the ebb and flow of our season. Sometimes the discussions would be heated, but always there was a sense of great companionship and a shared challenge. One ritual was that when we were due to play Fanna's old club, he would cry, 'Boys, win today and I'll buy all of you dinner.'

Of course, the life would have been so much richer if I had been playing regularly, but I had my time and chances. Galderesi and Iorio took theirs. It is the classic way of football. One player is ambushed by fate, another runs into the vacancy, and if he does well enough, he can make an unanswerable demand on the place you thought was your own. Always you have to prepare yourself for the time when you are no longer in charge of your career, when the injury comes or a new manager wants something that you can no longer offer. I had done that preparation as well as I could and if it didn't take away the hurt when Milan told me that they were looking for somebody to put in my place, it wasn't as though the blow had caught me off guard. I'd gone along the road quite a way in my own mind.

Not long before we returned home to England I was sitting at home watching TV after dinner when the bell at the front gate sounded. It was a surprise at that time of night when you are not expecting casual visitors. I looked out and saw a man dressed in the Verona playing kit. I went down to the gate and talked with him for a while. He was, if there is such a thing, a gently fanatic supporter of Verona. He said he had recently found out where I lived and just wanted to talk to me about my career and his team. He didn't want to bother me, he said, but it seemed so important to him and we talked for a few minutes. Then he said, 'Thank you, I'll let you go now.'

I sometimes think of that gentle fellow when I read of hooligans rampaging across the country and the continent. He reminds me of the true power of football, its ability to affect so many lives in the simplest way. I think, too, of that first time I scored in the San Siro and how the crowd lifted me up and took me to the heart of my dream. Yes, Italy was tough but it drew so much out of me as a football player and a man. As Judith and I packed our bags for home, we knew that we would always carry a little part of Italy in our hearts.

14

A THIRD WORLD CUP

I N the rush to leave for Italy I remembered to make a phone call to the man who will for ever represent the best and most glorious values of Scottish football, the man who achieved with the raw talent of the land – well, let's be precise, the environs of Glasgow – unprecedented success. I called Jock Stein, who was now manager of Scotland, to say that although I would be out of his sight in Italian football, I hoped I wouldn't be out of his mind. I suppose I was looking for a little reassurance. I had enjoyed two World Cup campaigns with Scotland but as I approached my thirtieth birthday I was reluctant to believe that I had pulled on the blue shirt for the last time.

When I was first called up by Tommy Docherty, I never made it my ambition to play in three World Cups. That it could be fitted into the career span of a player who looked after himself and enjoyed freedom from serious injury was obviously a possibility, but it had to be something that unfolded with the years. You needed luck, you needed to play on through all circumstances. Playing for Scotland, at whatever age and in whatever circumstances, was always to me a compelling goal. It had driven me on at the worst of times. Now the Big Man held the key.

He wished me well in Italy, said that I should be careful not to get too involved with all 'the carry-on' with Italian defenders. He said he had managed many teams against the Italians, and although they were excellent players they could easily wrap you up in their tactics, and the result was often yellow and red cards. As to my chances of making it to a third World Cup, Jock was non-committal, as I might have expected. I had made a courtesy call, in effect, and I always knew that, with him, the determining factor would be how well I performed out on the field. There were not so many absolute laws in football, but nobody needed to tell me this was one of them.

Today, so many years after his death, Stein represents in the mind and the spirit of Scottish football exactly what he did back in 1967 when his Celtic team – the Lisbon Lions – so magnificently overcame the power and, we were told, sophistication of the great coach Helenio Herrera's Inter Milan. Celtic were the first British team to win the European Cup, of course, but the mere deed was lifted so far above the detail of success by the nature of the performance. Celtic did more than win; they invigorated a whole nation in their belief that they could play football as well as anyone.

Picking up the phone and calling Jock Stein, for someone with my background, was no light chore, even after the years I had accumulated at the top of the game. As I placed the call, the memory flared vividly of the day when John Delaney, cousin Joe and I had travelled into Glasgow to be part of the great mob that welcomed home the Celtic heroes. The pulse of the streets was amazing. I had seen all of the home European ties and now was the moment of delirium. Glasgow can, of course, do football delirium as well as any city on earth.

What that Celtic team, and the man who shaped them, had meant to me all down the years from that day of jubilation to the time I called the great man was a source of constant refreshment, a standard to set yourself – the knowledge that if you had enough spirit, if you could produce all of your talent, there was no limit to what you could achieve. I suppose of all those Celtic players, Jimmy Johnstone, brilliant, ill-starred Jimmy, was the one who had always touched me most. If that brief time I roomed with him during the build-up to the great catastrophe on the Clyde was too much of a distraction to me at that age – and probably would have been ten years later – it is still something I cherish. The abiding memory was of great players such as Danny McGrain and Kenny Dalglish coming up to see Jimmy, partly to chat, partly to pay homage. Stein made more than a team – it was a force of nature.

Bobby Murdoch, with his great barrel chest, probably never got the ranking he deserved beyond the borders of Glasgow and Scotland. He had a problem in that, with his body type, if he didn't look after himself, he would be in trouble very quickly, but he was a superb player – the one who really made Celtic play. There were so many great characters in the team, quite apart from their superb ability to perform in the big games – Billy McNeill, Tommy Gemmell, Tommy Craig, Bobby Lennox. Today they would play for Scotland for ever, soaring past the one hundred cap mark, but then the pressure for places was so great, so relentless.

Even in my own time the pressure was particularly hard, and nowhere more so than in midfield. I reflected upon that quite bitterly last year when I travelled to Cardiff and watched Scotland, under their German manager Berti Vogts, lose 4–0, against a background of talk of drafting into the team the Italian-born and bred Lorenzo Amoruso. My epoch started with Billy Bremner and Graeme Souness, went through players of the quality of Lou Macari, Asa Hartford and Archie Gemmill, and dwindled away with the last easily identified Scottish midfield craftsmen, Gordon Strachan, Gary McAllister and Paul McStay.

Souness and Bremner were definitive midfielders of their day. Questions had to be asked at the outset of a game. What is it we have to do today? Are we going to play football right away, or do we need to dig in for half an hour, do we need to absorb a bit of the battle? Some of that happens today, but not so blatantly. The attitude now is let's get in their faces, let's get tight with people, curse them, harass them, don't let them play, but in the conditions of the modern game, you can only go so far with that. The limit is preventing your opposite number lifting his head, getting time on the ball and space to see what's developing around him. In the days of Bremner and Souness, there was a wee bit more to it than that. An opponent could go through you, making physical contact and often leaving his foot in, so the great, even the merely effective, midfielder had to say to himself, 'Whichever way they want to play it, I can handle it.' For so long, Scotland's midfielders always could.

The competition for a place in the Scottish team was hard. I'm thinking of Jim Bett, who played for Rangers and Aberdeen and had a spell in Belgium. He won three caps. Today he would be a staple of the Scottish team.

Where did the Scottish footballer go? Sometimes you think that maybe the images of wealth, the big houses and driveways with the Ferraris and Porsches, might provoke the old ambition to play football in the same way that, it is said, the lure of wealth drives American basketball and baseball players out of the ghettos, but in Scotland even that motivation does not seem to exist. However, I don't believe that Scottish football, as a serious force, needs to die. The administrators of the game have to look at Holland, the Czech Republic and other small countries – even Latvia, who performed impressively in the 2004 European Championship – and ask what are they doing that we are not?

There has to be an injection of interest and real organisation. Back in the fifties, Hungary produced a whole generation of brilliant footballers, and people asked how can this small nation carry such weight? It was because sometimes the smallness of a country can work to its advantage. For one thing it should mean that nothing passes you by. You have a small population, so make sure you are getting the best of it and developing and encouraging it properly.

Such thoughts came jumbling into my head the night Wales cut Scotland to pieces in Cardiff. I hadn't intended to make any public comment, but in the pain of that humiliating defeat I found myself voicing my thoughts, and frustrations, when somebody stuck a microphone into my face.

At first I told the interviewer that I didn't really want to discuss the matter. It was all a bit raw, all to near some of my deepest feelings about the game, but then I thought what Scottish football meant to me and all my people. I thought of Jimmy Delaney at the bus-stop and all the great players I had seen wearing the Scottish shirt, and all the ones I had been lucky enough to play with. I thought of the night I went on the town in Glasgow with Denis Law and Billy Bremner after scoring the goal against Czechoslovakia that took us back to a World Cup after all those years. I thought of what it meant to score a goal against England, and how it was when you heard the sound of the crowd at Hampden, both as a young kid on the great terraces and down on the field as a player. I had nothing against this boy Amoruso, but let him play for Italy, let him relate to his own past. Scotland, no doubt, had reached a low point in their game, but that was a reason to fight harder, to organise, rather than surrender. For me, there was something ethically wrong in importing foreign players to wear the Scottish shirt; it was an insult to the past and it made a nonsense of the future. So there was the microphone and my thoughts came spilling out, hot and angry. 'It's ludicrous, ridiculous,' I stormed.

It was something of a breaking point. I had just seen Scotland beaten 4–0 by Wales, quite effortlessly, in a terrible indication of how poor Scotland had become. This was not a comparison with some distant place, Moldova or Slovakia, even Brazil. It was with Wales, a few hundred miles down the road. Why had they become so much better than us? Wales hadn't qualified for the European Championship but they were in a different league from us. You had to look beyond the bad performance and ask some questions. The meaning of that defeat, above all, was that we had run out of talent. You had to ask the questions and look for some answers.

The answer is certainly not signing up foreign mercenaries for the team, somebody who may have earned his living in the country for two or three years. That means nothing. We have to find a way back to the situation of 1978, when a player of the quality of Souness has to fight to get into a World Cup team. Go back to Cleland and recall how it was that we could produce players good enough to play anywhere in the world, and how all the other villages could do the same. When you come from a corner of a country that produced Busby, Delaney and Jimmy Johnstone, you don't go to visitors and hope they'll accept your offer of a game.

Later, I was told that Scotland had no serious intention of exploiting European regulations and selecting foreign players who were filling up the leading club sides. However, the fact that the idea was given plenty of space in the Scottish media seemed to be highlighting new levels of dismay about where the game was going. On the field, the Scottish team were completely outplayed by a Welsh side that had suffered a rash of withdrawals in the days before the game. Yet still they were able to toy with the men in the blue shirts. Inside, you felt as though you had suffered a small death.

Scotland had been trailing away, signing up the former German coach and World Cup player Berti Vogts after the resignation of Craig Brown and expecting him to understand the Scottish mentality and deal with the decline, which had been relentless. You had to think of the slide in expectations. In Argentina we lost to Peru, drew with Iran and beat Holland, won four points, and came back to be slaughtered, admittedly after expectations had been raised by some of Ally MacLeod's less considered statements. Craig Brown took Scotland to France twenty years later, lost to Brazil and Morocco and drew with Norway. That was one point and there was scarcely a whimper when that Scotland team returned. The decline was in the bones of the nation then. This isn't a criticism of Brown, who is a clever man. He understood the limitations of the players he had his disposal and, of course, he could work with officials. He was a diplomat and a bureaucrat and because of that he was able to handle a lot of the pressure that was inevitably building up. In the end, it couldn't disguise the degree of the underachievement of all of Scottish football.

Back in 1981, when I made my call to Big Jock, there was certainly no call for foreign legionnaires. I have a picture of myself and some of my rivals for the shirt I had worn in Argentina and Germany – Steve Archibald of Spurs and then Barcelona, Alan Brazil and Kenny Dalglish. It was a formidable set of runners, and there were others on the edge of the race. Derek Parlane and Johnstone were still in the frame, and new claimants included Dixie Deans and Joe Craig of Celtic and Ian Wallace, a tricky, hard-shooting little striker who did very well for Coventry City – and always, it seemed, there had been my rivalry with Andy Gray. At times he was the manager's choice, at times he was injured, and the same was true of me – the old story of football. For me, the good luck was that I was always fit, and playing well enough, at the right times in the World Cup cycle. My remarkable good fortune was to stay healthy around three World Cups; and three managers, completely different in so many ways, all saw enough in me to take me to the greatest football show of them all.

It has to be said, though, that Jock had been less than totally convinced by my form. He had dropped me for a while but, fortunately, he felt he needed me in a couple of qualification games and I did well enough to keep myself around the forefront of his mind when it came time to pick his squad for the World Cup in Spain. He had called me up to the squad before a qualifier with Sweden and when I arrived he gave me one of his famous hard looks and asked me if I was fit. 'Aye, I'm spot on, Jock,' I said and so he played me. We won 2–0 and I got the first goal, a low diving header from a free kick John Robertson sent in to the near post. I played well and was full of running – it was as though I was breaking away from the pressure of Milan – but with the going hard in Italy, and with the reviews not so good, I had to accept that my place was far from guaranteed and, worryingly, Stein left me out of a few games. So it was with great relief that I took a call from him.

'How are you doing?' he asked.

'Not bad,' I said, with as much enthusiasm as I could.

He said he wanted me to play in a friendly against Holland at Hampden Park. The Dutch fielded a strong team, including Rudi Krol, who was playing for Naples at the time, but we took the game to them and won quite convincingly, 2–0. I didn't score but I was delighted with my performance. The pressure building around the need to produce was getting stronger all the time. I had to show that I was still operational at the international level, still Scotland's best centre-forward.

So I played my game and returned to Italy, where I promptly got injured while playing for Milan in an away game. A bad tackle put me down and gave me ligament damage. It wasn't the worst of injuries, but with the World Cup coming up on the horizon it was badly timed. I had strapping on for several weeks, and when it came off I had to push myself to the limits to get fit.

Jock had a detailed plan for his World Cup campaign after carefully studying the opposition. Scotland had been drawn with the brilliantly emerging Brazilian team of Socrates, Falcao and Zico, New Zealand and the Soviet Union. Jock said he intended to play me against the Soviets – apparently a case of a strong horse on a tough part of the course.

As expected, the first game against New Zealand, which I watched from the bench in the sizzling heat of Malaga, was something of a romp. However, after Kenny Dalglish had given us an early lead and John Wark had headed in two more goals, a couple of defensive mistakes brought an unnecessary crisis. With less than twenty minutes to go we were leading 3–2 only; with the Brazilians and Russians to come that was hardly the goals ratio we wanted. Fortunately, Gordon Strachan was playing well along the right, and late goals from John Robertson and Steve Archibald gave us a three-goal winning margin. A 5–2 win looked impressive enough, but Stein had reckoned on a bigger cushion of goals with the prolific Brazil our next opponents and the Soviets presenting an obvious threat in the third game.

The Brazilians who came at us in Seville were everything that Jock had feared they might be. It was all there – the lovely passing, the subtle movement. Socrates and Falcao used the ball with swaggering confidence and it was easy to see why the manager had sacrificed Alan Brazil and Kenny Dalglish and attempted to crowd the Brazilians in midfield with the inclusion of Asa Hartford and David Narey. It seemed like nothing so much as optimism, though, as the Brazilians rolled towards our goal. I settled into my seat in the bleak certainty that I would be watching a siege, but in the eighteenth minute something extraordinary happened – Scotland scored.

Souness sent a long ball to the right side of the Brazilian goal area, Wark got up to head it across the goal and Narey came in to clatter home his shot – 1–0. The reality we feared had been suspended but, as we might have guessed, not for too long. Goals came from Zico, a beautifully flighted free kick, and the big defender Oscar, who met a corner from Junior at the near post. Then Eder, a brilliant forward with a reputation for fierce shooting, ran at goalkeeper Alan Rough, who nerved himself to deal with a powerful shot. Instead, Eder produced the purest touch of Brazil, chipping the goalkeeper with outrageous skill. Finally, the long-striding, elegant Socrates outstripped the left side of our defence before cutting the ball in to Falcao, who struck the ball home with great confidence with just three minutes left.

We went into our last group game, against the Soviets, needing to win. They had lost by a mere 2–1 to Brazil and had beaten the New Zealanders 3–0. A formidably organised team with fine players, including captain Aleksandr Chivadze and Oleg Blokhin, Jock didn't need to tell us that we faced a great challenge. The

Russians and Ukrainians have never caused much of a stir in the World Cup but they have a fine record in the European Championship, winning the first one in 1960 by beating Yugoslavia, and reaching two more finals, against the hosts Spain four years later and the brilliant Dutch team of 1988. They have never been easy opposition and they were certainly tough opponents on that hot day in Malaga. Jock was as good as his word; after nursing me to fitness, he sent me into the Soviet game and gave me my chance to create the record of scoring in three World Cups.

The record was mine within fifteen minutes as the Soviets failed to cover a long ball by Narey. We had made a lively start and I was able to get on the ball and bear down on the goalkeeper Renat Desayev, putting the ball past him with some ease. We led fifteen minutes into the second half, when Chivadze put in a loose ball. The effects of my battle for fitness began to tell in the heat and my legs began to go. Jock hauled me off in the seventy-first minute. Thirteen minutes later we were finished off by one more piece of Scottish misadventure. Our central defenders Alan Hansen and Willie Miller both went for a long high ball and collided. Ramaz Shengali collected the ball and, swerving past Alan Rough, put it into the net. Graeme Souness lashed in a late goal but by then we knew we were heading home.

I had my third World Cup and my scoring record, but there was also the familiar feeling of anticlimax that comes when leaving in the middle of the great football show. I joined Judith and the children in Marbella and the McQueens came along too. It was a time, again, to nurse the wounds and as part of that process Gordon and I went to Malaga airport to see if we could get a flight to Madrid for the final. With my Milan connections, I was confident of getting a couple of tickets for the final when Italy, having beaten that brilliant Brazilian team with goals from Paolo Rossi, reached the final against Germany. The ticket clerk said that she could put us on a plane leaving for Madrid immediately. It was our only chance. All other flights were solidly booked. We boarded the plane in T-shirts, shorts and flip-flops, which guaranteed us a rather cool reception from the immaculately clad Italians. However, the important objective was to see the match and I was proud of the Italian effort. Under their coach, Enzo Bearzot, they had played more expansive football after surviving their ordeal by Brazilian fire in Barcelona and I leapt to my feet when Marco Tardelli drove home the winning goal. Someone wrote that Bearzot had released the 'caged bird of Italian football'. It was a nice phrase, but a hard and brilliant victory.

Naturally, we had a few drinks to celebrate the Italian victory before retiring to our hotel. We went to the airport the next morning and I was sitting in the airport lounge while waiting for the flight to the coast when I was startled by screams and a terrible commotion. A young child had crawled along a balcony overlooking the lounge and slipped through the rails. The baby fell on me and in my relaxed state I provided a relatively soft landing. Maybe if Hansen and Miller hadn't collided, maybe if we hadn't surrendered those goals against New Zealand, I might have been at a banquet celebrating World Cup triumph instead of stretching out on that airport couch. Maybe a litter of pigs will one day fly over the Clyde. However, a baby's life had been saved and, at the time, that seemed miracle enough, although perhaps not quite enough of one to deflect the reproaches of our wives when Gordon and I finally returned to the holiday villa in need of fresh clothes and a little more sleep, not necessarily in that order.

For me, that World Cup signified the end of something that had been such a key part of my existence. At thirty-one I could not realistically expect to play in another one and, denied that possibility, I could hardly expect to add to my collection of Scottish caps. I could only reflect on my good fortune down the years – and express disbelief when I read of the complaints of some players that Jock never called them up to thank them for their services. Surely, when it is over you know it in your bones, and why would a manager have reason to thank you? He had already thanked you by handing you the Scottish jersey.

Jock had stood by me under the weight of a lot of competition. He dropped me for a while, gave other players their chance, but he came back to me when he thought I could do a specific job against the Soviets. He knew what he wanted and he knew what he was going to get. I'd delivered the best way I could. The account was square, with the great man and with Scotland. Indeed, from my point of view, I could only marvel at the time I'd had playing for my country – fifty-two caps, three World Cups and all those games against England. Many great players had had nothing like such a run. Paddy Crerand, that beautiful passer of the ball, had sixteen caps; Stevie Chalmers and Bobby Lennox had a handful between them; and Billy McNeill, who had led Celtic to all that glory, had a mere thirty.

It makes me believe that my career with Scotland was a great gift, something to cherish always, and it is because of this that I do feel a rush of the old blood when the discussion turns to the current plight of the national side and the prospects for the future. The Czechs were a powerful force in the 2004 European Champion- ship as the major nations, France, Germany, Spain, Italy and England, left them to fight it out with Portugal, Holland and Greece. Scotland should note the example of that performance, and also that of the previously ill-considered Greeks, who showed what can be done with a coach who understands the international game. At the start, you have to get the structure right and have a proper system of development. If you are a small country, you must hunt down every bit of available talent. That pursuit is the least that Scotland can do in recognition of some of the best of its past.

Towards the end of my playing career, when I was playing for Southampton, I was asked to work as a commentator at another Scotland–Wales qualifying game, this time at Ninian Park in Cardiff. I took my father and got him his seat in the stand before going off to the commentary box. Jock Stein was still in charge of

Scotland, putting all his knowledge and hard passion into the game. At the end, I heard on the earphones that he had collapsed and went down to the tunnel where I saw a knot of officials whispering to each other. Someone said that Jock had died. I collected my father and we drove away from the crowd. We didn't have a lot to say, but we had a lot of thoughts. We both knew that we had lost one of the great men of our game and our lives – and we had to wonder what would happen to Scottish football now.

——15——
SETTLING FOR THE POSSIBLE

I F Scotland's future was in doubt when the great Stein died, my own might have seemed to be blowing in the wind when I came back from Italy without a club or a house, but it wasn't the reality. I was sure of that. I knew my value. I knew what I was capable of and that my story as a player was some way from over. I felt confident enough to wait and let football people come to me.

That wasn't arrogance. It was just an old pro's instinct for where he truly stood. I had looked after my body and my confidence was far from broken. Italy may have been a turbulent experience but overall it had been a good and toughening one. Some parts of me were still drawn to the Italian game, I admired its culture and style, the way they saw things there, but other factors had to be taken into account, which Judith was not slow to draw to my attention. Most importantly, the children were coming up to school age and when Judith and I discussed the future in Marbella we decided it was time to go home. Although nothing had been arranged, I was confident that my services would be required at a good level of the English or Scottish game. I reckoned I had at least three years left.

Confirmation that I was right not to be worried came quickly enough. We stayed first in Leeds with my sister, where I trained with my old club, and then with my parents back in Cleland, where I trained with Motherwell. I felt good. The years did not feel heavy on me, although when I trained with my old team-mate Eddie Gray's players in Leeds I did realise that I was a little bit behind in the work. My basic fitness was not in doubt, though, and the calls began to accumulate. In the end, it came down to a decision between Celtic and Southampton, a team who had been skilfully guided by their manager Lawrie McMenemy to the upper reaches of the first division. I was still a football property and not an old gun, mooching around in the hope of being hired. Had Celtic come to me when I was younger they would have been very hard to resist. I talked with their manager, the former Celtic and international midfielder David Hay, and he had ambition, but deep down I had a feeling for Southampton. They had built on the foundations left by the sound old football man Ted Bates, and McMenemy had displayed a particularly good touch in getting the best out of experienced players. Southampton were not Arsenal or Manchester United, but they were a very well run club and McMenemy was producing a high level of entertainment and sound football. Most importantly, he had put together a set of standards that would have graced any club at any time.

Ideally, he would have gone for the pick of a younger crop of players, but his financial situation was the same as Tony Waddington's at Stoke City twenty years earlier. McMenemy had shrewdly based a lot of his work on the pattern of Waddington, who brought in local hero Sir Stanley Matthews when he was in his late forties. That was an emotional move aimed at regenerating some local passion for the club in the Potteries from where the genius of Matthews had sprung. Other initiatives were based on a clever calculation of what could be drawn from the last reserves of fine players such as Jimmy McIlroy, Jackie Mudie and Peter Dobing. McMenemy, as a young football man, had seen the point of that and at Southampton he invested in two things that in football never lose their value – hard experience and knowledge. He had signed Peter Shilton, Kevin Keegan and Mick Mills – and now he was coming for me.

Hay and McMenemy offered me roughly the same money but the clinching factor for Lawrie was that he was offering me a three-year contract. That was perfect. It would carry me into my mid-thirties and offer me the chance of a good, slow ride home from the glory of Leeds and United, Milan and Verona, and Scotland. It also helped that I would have team-mates of real accomplishment and I would be playing for a man I liked and who had shown great trust in both my ability and my professional character.

I hadn't grown wealthy from my days at Leeds and Manchester United. The Italian phase had helped a bit, but it was comforting to be more or less guaranteed what in those days was just about the ultimate ambition of a professional – to finish his career healthy and able to pay off his mortgage and, as a final bonus, have a pension. The way football is today no doubt makes such hopes seem paltry, but back then it was some kind of measuring stick for how well you had done. In my day, many players who had excellent careers – and didn't live the high life to which some big names were drawn – still had to scrape for a decent living when they could no longer play. I was lucky in that I had a very good chance of playing into my mid-thirties and when I came back from Italy I wasn't desperate. I could sit and wait for the phone to ring – at least for a little while. It was a luxury that many of my contemporaries just couldn't afford.

I thanked David Hay for his interest after deciding that South-ampton had far more appeal for me at that stage of my career and life. It was a lovely corner of England and a good place for the children to start their education. Lawrie McMenemy showed us around the area and was delighted when I said I wanted to sign. He had a striker who had proven himself at the highest level of the game – and one who was obviously still in good condition. He said he would happily pay the £150,000 transfer fee to the gentlemen of Verona.

His reward came soon enough. I had an excellent season,

scoring seventeen goals, and the team was further strengthened by the signings of Dave Armstrong, a winger who had done extremely well for Jack Charlton's Middlesbrough, and Jimmy Case, Liverpool's talented and tough veteran midfielder. They brought a further edge of both experience and ability. By the time we flew to Bilbao for a pre-season friendly game against Atletico I felt I was well on the way to catching up my new team-mates in preparation for the season. I didn't score, but I fitted in well. The team had all the basic requirements for a successful season – a sound defence anchored by the goalkeeping brilliance of Shilton, plenty of craft – and iron – in midfield and good width and bite along the flanks.

Unfortunately, all of that optimism was not confirmed by our opening league match at Sunderland – we were beaten and failed to score. The journey home was made all the more depressing for me by the fact that I had two goals disallowed, unfairly I thought. One was called off for offside and the other for what I thought in my bitter mood was a case of excessive protection of the goalkeeper. He swore that the ball was already in his hands when I stroked it into the net. I said it was a loose ball, a legitimate target for a predator keen to make his first kill for his new club. The referee, as seems to become ever more a formality with every new season, agreed with the goalkeeper. At that point we were temporarily back in Leeds with my sister and it is fair to say that my mood on my return did not exactly light up the house.

The next game was at home to Manchester United, and although we again failed to score, we managed a draw and I felt that we had looked full of promise. I was happy with the way I was settling into the team and I particularly enjoyed it at the old Dell ground. It had an excellent playing surface and the crowd, never vast, was close to the action and could be quite intimidating for the visiting team. With Leeds and Manchester United, I'd always felt that Southampton was a hard place to go. The goals came soon enough, as did an effective partnership with Steve Moran, a prolific goalscorer. Football might have heard a lot more of him if he had taken up an option to tour South America with England under Bobby Robson during the build-up to the 1986 World Cup in Mexico. It was one of those decisions that can heavily influence a career, and reminded me of my old Leeds colleague Paul Madeey who, years earlier, opted against joining Sir Alf Ramsey's squad for that first World Cup in Mexico in 1970. Mark Hateley took Steve Moran's place and established himself during the tour. John Barnes shot to prominence with a memorable goal in the Maracana stadium in Rio, but was shockingly subjected to racist abuse from some England 'supporters' on the plane home.

In the domestic game, Moran made a significant impact and he was an important reason for the club's high ranking in the League and contributed to Lawrie McMenemy's fast rising reputation as a manager of imagination and fine instinct for players who could deliver the best of themselves in the twilight of their careers.

There were some setbacks, including an FA Cup defeat by Barnsley, managed by my old football mentor Bobby Collins, and the Uefa Cup place I had inherited when I joined the club was quickly swept away by defeat by Hamburg. Overall, however, the sense of a club going forward was strong, and we re-stated our right to play in Europe with another qualification for the Uefa Cup. Unfortunately, that achievement was quickly stripped of value by the rioting at Heysel stadium in Brussels during the European Cup final between Liverpool and Juventus, and the tragic death of so many Juventus supporters. Uefa promptly, and in the circumstances inevitably, banned English clubs from competing in Europe. It may have been hard on the innocent but English football was obliged to live with the ban and struggle on as best it could.

Soon enough, I had a private battle of my own. Out of a clear, blue summer sky Sunderland moved to sign McMenemy on terms he couldn't resist. Whenever the manager who signed you goes, it is in the nature of the game that you have to re-establish yourself all over again with the new man. You weren't his idea, his investment, so there is no guarantee that the virtues that commended you to the old boss will necessarily be appreciated by the new man. McMenemy was succeeded by Chris Nicholl, a former player at the club who had been working for Grimsby. I didn't know him and I didn't get to know him. My circumstances, which had seemed so favourable while settling in under McMenemy, were suddenly made even more difficult when I was injured in pre-season training. I challenged for a ball with reserve goalkeeper Phil Kite, went down first and he landed on top of me. He opened my knee joint. I knew I had tweaked something but the club doctor said just to let it settle down for a few weeks. I did some weight work to try to strengthen the muscle but I kept tweaking it and as we moved into October I was beginning to realise that something was not right.

'I've done enough weights,' I thought to myself. 'This isn't getting me anywhere.' I demanded to see a specialist after talking things over with a doctor friend. The specialist told me that I had torn a cartilage and would have to have an operation. It was Christmas by the time I came out of hospital with my leg in plaster. On Christmas Eve Judith and I went to midnight mass. We sat in the back row, so I could more easily hobble out of the church at the end of the mass. Unfortunately, I had placed myself in the path of a man who had clearly been celebrating a little too vigorously. The moment I saw him I feared the worst. He lurched and wobbled and, of course, landed on top of my wounded knee. The moral of the story – don't go to midnight mass with your leg in plaster.

As I fought to get fit again I had very little contact with Chris Nicholl. The club signed Colin Clarke, a useful striker who helped them to the semi-finals of the FA Cup. For a player of any age, it is the worst of times carrying an injury and watching a season unfold without you. For someone who is ticking off the last days of his career, and begining to think more deeply about the future when the playing has to stop, it is even more tormenting.

I hated the lost time. At thirty-three I was desperate to keep the sharp edge of my game. I depended on my quickness, the ability to turn a defender, and to be out for so long was a heavy blow. Stamina was no problem, I was still in the best of general fitness, but a striker needs that extra step from which he gains the confidence that he can get into a dangerous position with some freedom.

I played just a few games that season, and I was never right. After the bleakest of summers, I returned to pre-season training with no sense of being part of the manager's plans. The confirmation of my unpromising situation came quickly enough – and it was hard. While the first team went off to Portugal on tour, I was sent to a game in Winchester with the young academy boys.

It was a lovely summer's night – I will never forget it. After all I had experienced, the graduation from Morton, the emergence at Leeds, the Manchester United experience, the Italian adventure, the World Cups, there I was in a game echoing with the shouts of the young players. My dad stood on the touchline. I don't know what was going through his mind. I never asked him. I played my game. I didn't sulk because I know only one way to play football, but I didn't think it was right. In my own mind at least, I believed I still had a lot to offer the first-team squad. I thought my situation might have been given a little more consideration. I just didn't see the benefit, for anyone, of my playing that game.

Humiliation wasn't the problem. I enjoy every game I play. I would never mess about in a game. I've been anxious before games for Scotland and Southampton reserves, but once the referee blows the whistle I'm away. A football game is a football game – you play it and you act like a professional, especially alongside young boys who need some kind of example whenever they are in the company of older players. No, the memory of that night in Winchester flares so strongly because of the deep frustration I felt. I'd had a bad injury but I had fought my way through it, even to the point of playing a few games at the end of the previous season. I had done some work in the close season and got through all the pre-season training without mishap. I had conducted myself properly. No, you wouldn't forget that, playing against local lads while the first team were off in Portugal.

Of course, you cannot throw all the toys out of the pram. You get on with the work and you help the lads around you. That wasn't a difficult chore with a boy who was brought on at half-time to play up front with me. I liked the look of the kid immediately. He was tough and smart and very confident. He did everything with a hard purpose. He was born to play the game professionally and I thought right then, 'This boy could go to the top of the game.' His name was Alan Shearer and if anyone had asked me if I had seen some promising talent, I would have borrowed a phrase from Bobby Collins. I would have said, 'Yes, there's a kid in Southampton. He's only a boy but he plays like a man.'

When the game was over I got changed quickly and drove my dad to a little pub I knew from when we had first moved to the area. We had a meal and talked about everything but the match I had just played with a bunch of lads. My father wouldn't dwell on my situation; he wouldn't want to upset me. There was no question of him saying something along the lines of, 'Son, what the hell are you doing winding up here on a little field in the backwoods of football?' Maybe we were both a little more thoughtful than usual.

A few months earlier I had a chance to move from South-ampton to West Bromwich Albion, where Nobby Stiles was manager, having taken over from John Giles, who had done a second spell at the Hawthorns and, he told me, almost immedi-ately regretted it. Nobby had seen me play for Southampton reserves against Crystal Palace at Leatherhead. I scored a goal and Nobby was impressed enough with my showing to put in a bid. The move had some appeal, given the way things were going with the new manager, but it troubled me that Nobby might be buying himself trouble – it was before my knee had been properly diagnosed – so I called him up and said I was worried about joining him, and maybe getting a signing bonus, and then failing to deliver. I told him I didn't think that would be right. Nobby thanked me for my honesty. I said that I didn't want to put him – or me – in an embarrassing position. I had always prided myself on being worth the money any club was prepared to pay. I didn't want to break that pattern now.

As it happened, I might well have been a good signing for Nobby. A decade or so on from when he was forced to leave the game with shattered knees, medical science had moved on at a considerable pace and when I had completed my rehabilitation from the operation, I was able to think of myself again as undamaged goods. The problem was the loss of the year at a time when I needed to be in constant action.

I played a few more times for Southampton after the first-team squad returned from Portugal but my relationship with the manager remained quite distant. I made no attempt to change that; I tried to get on with my season and my career, and all the time I knew that my playing days were drawing in. I was thirty-five now, still fit, still wanting to play on and do the thing that had always been at the core of my life, but I was growing a little anxious about my ability to do it on terms I would find acceptable.

There had been several offers for me but all of them were pointing me down the leagues. The reality that had first touched me in Milan was now a fact of my professional life. I still had a value, no doubt, but it was a shifting one and I knew it would inevitably present me with the need to make a compromise – I could play on, but at a level I had never known before as a professional. This is the final uncertainty for the professional footballer. How does it end? At what point do you say, 'Now, I have come far enough down the ladder.' I was at that point in the debate in my own mind when my old Leeds team-mate Terry

Cooper phoned to ask me to join him at Bristol City in the third division.

I was pleased to hear from Terry, but I didn't jump at his offer. I was very conscious of its implication; it meant that Joe Jordan of Leeds United, Manchester United, AC Milan and Scotland would suddenly be Joe Jordan of the third division. Bristol were a good club and had made progress under Terry, coming up from the fourth division, but I had to expel a few demons. I had to accept where I was rather than where I still wanted to be. I had to remember that good pros had played down in the lower leagues, they had let the string run out there, and if I wanted to play some more, if I still wanted to feel the thrill of preparing for a new season, not as some careworn manager but somebody doing what will always be the best of it, the playing and having that rush of blood when the action begins, maybe I had to settle for what was still possible.

Terry, fortunately, was insistent and said that I should drive down one Sunday and bring Judith. We could get a feel of the place, see what a fine city Bristol was and maybe, after we'd had a good talk, my attitude to the move might warm a little. Terry was a good salesman – and a guide – and eventually I agreed to join City on loan. My signing received quite a lot of attention in the local media and I got off to a good start. I moved into digs in Bristol with David Moyes, a fellow Scot and now the manager of Everton. We were natural companions, Moyes having played for Celtic. He also shared my passion for the game and we spent long nights discussing our place in it when our playing days finally ran down.

Already, I had rediscovered how life could be outside the élite of the game. My first game for City was against Brentford in the Freight Rover Cup. I always like to be thorough in my approach to a game and that morning I drove over to Bristol, did my training and told Terry that I wanted to have a sleep in the afternoon. Terry said there was no way the club would pay the half-day rate for a hotel. I was a little shocked when he said that the only solution was for me to go over to his house and use the spare bedroom. Suddenly, I was back in the corridor at Morton, waiting for my wages, sensing what a great battle it was to keep a football club of the lower orders in business. It was clear that City were inhabiting equally perilous ground. They had gone through administration and had only just avoided going bust.

However, Terry had gathered together a useful team, with some good young players, and with David Moyes and me battling away with great enthusiasm, we were Wembley bound. We lost the Freight Rover final to Mansfied in a penalty shoot-out but we had acquitted ourselves well enough and for the first time since that opening burst in Southampton I was enjoying my football again. It was all a bit hectic, especially when compared with the Italian game, with a lot more loose balls to chase down, but I was getting through it and my knee was standing up well to the new physical pressure. At the end of that first season I was judged by Terry to have done well enough to be offered a permanent contract. The money was not great but I had a good feeling for the club and despite the financial difficulties I said I was interested in moving my family down to the West Country. I went to the boardroom to discuss details with Terry and the directors and everything went well enough until I mentioned that I expected the club to pay my removal charges from Southampton. One of the directors said, 'Oh, we don't do that – you'll have to do your own moving.'

So there I was right down to the basics of my new situation – no deputations led by Sir Matt Busby, no tours of the villas of Burago or Soave, not even a removal van for the possessions we had accumulated down the years in Leeds, Manchester and Italy. At first I was shocked into silence, as I had been when I was told the club wasn't up to paying less than £30 for a hotel room for my pre-match siesta. Then I had a little surge of old pride. I said there was no way I was moving my own stuff. It had been across Europe with my family and it had a certain value. Terry and Clive Middlemass, the assistant manager, intervened.

'We'll do the moving for you,' Terry said.

'We've done it before.'

Apparently, when Alan Walsh was signed from Darlington, they had gone up to the north east, hired a van and brought down his furniture. I told them Judith would never permit such a non-professional job. I would get three estimates, one from Pickfords' and two others, and they could take their pick, but I was adamant. If I was to go down the ladder – as I had to do – it would not be with broken furniture. Maybe that was not the greatest issue I had ever confronted in my career, but suddenly its importance loomed very large. I suppose I was marshalling my pride as well as protecting some of the good things that I had won for myself at the top of the game.

In my second season at Bristol it became clear to me that when Terry had picked me as a player he was also thinking about the future and a possible coaching role. In the past, I had always kept my distance from the manager in the belief that I was at the club to play, and it was only on that basis that my contribution should be judged. It was different with Terry. He asked me my opinion on team matters from time to time and, given our shared back-ground at Leeds, I felt able to talk freely enough. My mind was, finally, turning towards the days when I would no longer be able to play. I was pushing thirty-seven now. The playing days, nobody needed to tell me, were finally wearing down.

16

A PROPER SETTING

I T was always going to be the day I would hate; the day when
the cheering stopped, when the adrenaline rush finally ebbed
away and I recognised it was time to put away the boots for the
last time. However, the glimmerings of another kind of football
life at Bristol City were drawing me along in a way I was
beginning to like. For all their difficulties, City still had the aura
of a real football club. They operated in a big, fine city and the
Ashton Gate ground was a place that you always felt could provide
a proper setting for a successful team.

Terry Cooper was gradually but very surely involving me in the
thinking about how we should play and develop as a team. After
Friday morning training, Terry, Clive Middlemass and I would go
to an Italian restaurant and discuss the way things were going and
how we might approach the game the following day. Terry and
Clive did most of the talking, which was appropriate and maybe
inevitable. I'm not the most voluble talker by nature and these
were the guys who were running the team, but of course I had my
views and I was always willing to give an opinion when invited.

The 'brains trust' broke up when Clive was tempted away to
manage Carlisle United and Terry gave me the duties of assistant
manager and coach as well as player. Unfortunately, City were
losing some of the momentum created by the drive to Wembley
of the previous season. The team were becalmed in the middle of

the third division, and after the sharp rise in expectations, pressure was building around Terry.

He had done well, taking the team to two Freight Rover Cup finals, winning one, and lifting them up a division without spending much money; but one the oldest truths in football is that, as a manager, everything you do, good and bad, is another nudge towards the day you are sacked. Des Williams was a good and appreciative chairman, one of those who remembered what his manager had achieved, but some of the other board members were not so patient and the local media were getting a little restive. Terry had been a good housekeeper, had some success on the field and could claim to have made City a few bob. At any level of the game, however, the more you succeed, the more you bring pressure on yourself. You might complain about it and fight it but it is the way of the game, the way of the life.

What happened was a classic little story of the game. Terry had put in all his passion for the game, all the lessons he had learned under the master manager Don Revie. He had even hauled furniture for his new players, but there came a point when he had simply had enough. One knocking piece in the local paper, one barbed comment from the board, you never quite know when the breaking point arrives, but there he was on the day of a game telling me he was leaving. I was quite stunned. We were not setting the heather on fire but we were a solid enough team and, with a signing or two, we might move ahead again. Terry resurfaced later at Exeter City, a little further down the football social scale. No doubt, he carried his own football furniture, his own belief in a new start and the old dream that if you believe in yourself enough you can beat the odds.

I was offered the caretaking job and accepted it with more than half an eye on the future. This was a good place to try out as a manager. Although Terry had felt it necessary to resign, the pressure had not been vicious, or even unusual. He would have been the first to accept that, and for him, it had been more a question of time. He had been at Ashton Gate for a few years and maybe some impatience had crept into his bones.

There was no doubt now that I wanted to stay in the game and I considered myself fortunate to have been able to play with some success at Bristol and also learn the rudiments of the manager's job under a football man I liked and respected. What I learned mostly from Terry was detail, the need to take care of matters that might have easily been pushed on one side. For instance, Terry always made a point of returning calls from anyone in the game. When you are pressed for time, it is easy not to do that. Terry's sound belief was that you just didn't know what was around the corner. One phone call might yield a player on the right terms who might just make all the difference to your season.

This was not a glamorous part of the job but Terry stuck to it admirably. It defined for me the difference between being a player and a manager. When you play you are utterly self-absorbed. Of course, a good professional wants to fit in with the team but his preoccupation inevitably is with himself, his game, his fitness, his prospects. After training, Terry would go to his office and map everything out – players he needed to look at, games he had to attend and preparation for training. A lot of this work was to do with the future. You had a list of players to watch, which you had to do more than once, and then, if you were convinced, you had to check with their clubs at the end of the season. One day after training in Bristol, we drove up to see a Queen of the South match in Dumfries. It was hard driving but, as Terry said, it was a vital part of the job. It was clear to me that Terry was doing the job properly, setting a pattern that, whatever else I could bring to the new challenge, I would do well not to forget.

Terry left with a couple of months of the season still to go. Much of our work together, when we weren't preparing the team, had been to do with the transfer market – the key to any success at any level of the game. We would balance the value of our current players against what we would have to pay for new men, always trying to measure the difference and anticipate what the bottom line of the other clubs would be when we came to make our offers. Terry was giving me his insight into the transfer market, how to handle it and smell your way through it.

Already, I had made my investment in the future of the club, buying a lovely, roomy house in a leafy corner of the outskirts of the city. The house had a big, sculpted garden and great privacy. We have lived there, on and off, for nearly twenty years now and it has proved an excellent place to bring up the children – and sometimes retreat from the worst bruises that football can deliver.

I was told I had the job for a three-month trial period and during that time, other names were being put up in the press. I was in quite a vulnerable position; with the need to continue playing, it wasn't so easy to get an overall picture of the team. I realised that I had to step back a little from the action, but the difficulty was that the club said they didn't have the money for me to sign a new striker who could take some of the pressure off me and perhaps make a claim for the future. Whether that was entirely the situation, or whether the directors thought they would hold on to their 'war chest' until they decided on a permanent appointment, was not the point. For me, there was only one available option. I had to make the most of what I had and sign a player on loan.

I settled on Colin Gordon, a Reading reserve who had found his way on to the shopping list drawn up after our many scouting journeys across the country. I went to watch him again to confirm that first favourable impression and I wasn't disappointed. He was not quick but he was hard-working and he knew how to lead a forward line. With Colin's help, we suddenly surged forward, winning games and moving strongly towards a play-off position. Colin and I played together in several games and he scored a couple of vital goals but I soon learned how tough the job can be. His loan period was expiring and, of course, Reading were aware of our changed situation. They said that if we wanted to carry on using him, we would have to buy him outright. I went to the boardroom and pleaded to retain this vital ingredient in our success. The directors said we didn't have the money and we weren't going to be pressurised by the opportunism of Reading. I argued that this was the way of football and we had to think of what was at stake. We needed the play-offs. If we got through them, we could count on much greater revenue, a fact that was confirmed when, with the Gordon deal aborted, we still made it to the play-off action. In our first home-and-away tie we drew second-division Sheffield United, managed by Dave Bassett. We won 1–0. Alan Walsh, who was extremely good and should have been playing at a higher level, got our goal amid tremendous excitement.

Eventually, and rather bitterly, I had to sell Walsh to Gordon Milne, the former Liverpool and England player who was managing in Turkey. We could ill afford to lose a player of his quality but the board said they needed the money. It wasn't much but, as I had already discovered, the margin between life and death behind the imposing facade of the big old football ground was fine indeed.

Walsh's goal was enough to get us through. We battled out a scoreless draw at Bramall Lane to reach the play-off final, and another home-and-away tie, against Walsall. Again, we played the first game at home but this time with disastrous results. Walsall won 3–1. You wouldn't have given much for our chances in the second leg but somehow we got ourselves together again. I'd played in all the play-off games and I was delighted with the way the lads had responded to the challenge. Now I said, 'You've done yourselves proud so far, you've exceeded all expectations. Now just go out and give it everything you have. None of us have anything to lose.' We won 2–0, and then had to toss a coin to decide where the decider would be played. We lost the throw and had to return to the Midlands. After the hard season and a brilliant run that had rescued our situation, that was one journey too far. There was nothing left the in locker and Walsall won with a couple of goals to spare. I couldn't have been persuaded so in the first few minutes after the match but it was probably just as well. We weren't ready for the higher division. In fact, we might have suffered disaster.

For me, though, they had been precious months. The run had given me the job – my permanent appointment was promptly confirmed – a promising relationship with the players and I knew I had learned a lot. One reason for my early impact, I reflected, was that I had been able to use an excellent piece of advice from Alex Ferguson. He had said to me, 'Remember, Joe, when you send out a team you always have to give them a cause to fight for.'

I remembered what Ferguson said before a match at Fulham soon after Terry Cooper had left the club. I said to the lads, 'Look, we all owe a lot to Terry in different ways. He believed in us, he signed us, and now that he's gone, let's show he was right to put his faith in what we represented to him as a group of players. Terry kept the club, and our jobs, going and he only left because of the pressure. Well, pressure sometimes can produce results, so let's make it so today. He brought you together as a team and it didn't quite work. But we're still his team so let's make it work today. I think we owe it to him and ourselves.' We didn't leave a blade of Craven Cottage grass uncovered that day. We got a draw and you could tell in the dressing room afterwards that everyone was delighted. It was the basis of everything we did for the rest of that season. It started there, as, I realised later, did my managerial career.

I was given a two-year contract and I reckoned I could do something in that time. I could strengthen the club and, maybe, I could make a bit of a reputation. Perhaps it wouldn't be the same as playing; maybe I would never get that same jolt of life as when I ran out at Elland Road, Old Trafford or the San Siro, but I knew already that I was involved in something that could be both absorbing and fulfilling for the rest of my working days. I had already experienced some of the extremities of the job. The sensations that came with the draw at Fulham, the defeat of Sheffield United and the temporary rescuing of a lost cause at Walsall had been tremendously exhilarating – balanced by the feeling that came at Mansfield when we lost, one of the few occasions in the spell that carried us to the play-offs. A City director had patted me on the back and said, 'Don't worry, Joe. It's only a game,' and I grunted a non-committal reply when really I was thinking, 'Is it hell only a game.' No it wasn't just a game. If you were a football man, it shaped your life. One result could lose you your job and make the roof fall in. How could it ever be just a game?

As you go along in the game, you acquire debts and the one I owed Fergie was of the more significant variety. We first met casually on holiday in Spain and went out to dinner. Naturally, we discussed football at some length. After that, we spoke from time to time on the telephone. I would do the school run, drop the kids off and then call Fergie at around 8.30, when he was starting his day at the old Manchester United training ground at the Cliff in Salford. He was always there, with a few minutes to discuss a specific point. I never called him simply to chat but on a point of advice or perhaps to check on a player. He gave me his time – and a sense that he was pleased to hear from a fellow Scot and centre-forward.

Ferguson's theory about the value of a cause had been proved by my own experiences but in the new season I realised it would take more than clever psychology to move the team up that vital notch to win promotion, an achievement that could be built upon. My suspicion that the board were holding back on money until the appointment of a permanent manager was not immediately confirmed. The stuff really was in short supply. I was able to confirm this to my satisfaction by regularly consulting with Jean Harrison, the club secretary, and her assistant Marcia. They were always willing to show me the books and the truth was that despite some success in the FA Cup – and a run to the semi-finals of the League Cup, where we fought a tremendous scrap with

Brian Clough's Nottingham Forest – the margin between acceptable debt and developing disaster was as fine as ever.

Before meeting Forest we faced an away quarter-final against
Bradford, who had claimed the impressive scalps of Everton and
Tottenham. I told the board that this was a tie we could win but
only if we invested in the necessary preparation. I said I wanted
the team to have the kind of built-up that was routine in the top
flight, training in Yorkshire and a stay in a first-class hotel. The
board who a couple of years earlier deemed it too extravagant to
hire a hotel room for me to have an afternoon sleep before a
game, agreed that we could stay in Craiglands, a hotel that Don
Revie had frequently used with Leeds United before big home
games. We had a perfect built-up and a perfect game, winning 1–
0. The following morning I was awakened by a call from Ferguson. 'You got a fantastic result – well done,' he said. It was a good
feeling to be called by a top manager. It gave a powerful sense of
belonging in this new and demanding club where membership
could so often hang on the result of a single game.

In the semi we drew 1–1 in Nottingham and then at Ashton
Gate in the last five minutes, with the score still level, Walsh got
the chance to put us through. He sent the ball through the
goalkeeper's legs – only to see it bounce against the post and then
roll clear of the line. That was our last shot at victory. In extra time
we had to mop up a lot of pressure but Forest scored a late, killing
goal. I'd played in both the games and gone the distance in this
last one, the full 120 minutes. Defeat was sickening but also
instructive. As a club manager, I needed some more firepower. As
a man, it was perhaps time to show a little mercy to my body.

Fergie's phone call was the highwater mark of my season
because soon enough it was clear that the League Cup run
had not prevented some rumblings in the boardroom. Jim
Rosenthal, the TV journalist, had come down to interview me
before the Forest game and he said to me, 'I don't really grasp
why, but despite your great run in the League Cup and the fact

that you're not struggling in the League, there's quite a bit of discontent here.' My honest reaction was that I wasn't really aware of it. I had been playing, immersing myself in the action and the team. Maybe if I'd been a more experienced manager I would have had more of a sense of danger. The fact was that Rosenthal was right. There was indeed danger.

After the close run the previous season, the expectation had been that we would complete the job in the new campaign. In fact, we were back in the middle of the League, which to me was no great surprise. We hadn't been able to invest in the team, and just maintaining our position seemed to be a reasonable achievement. I learned that there might be a move against Jimmy Lumsden, my assistant manager, in one of those boardroom manoeuvres that are designed to test out the manager. Lumsden, who had played at Leeds, was a good friend and a good football man and I was not prepared to sacrifice him. Instead, after being alerted, I decided to go on the offensive. I said if the team was to make any progress I needed to strengthen, and most pressingly in the striking department. I said I needed to sign Bob Taylor of Leeds United. Taylor was a natural goalscorer and this was the prime need of my team.

Eventually we put together a deal that was both expensive and risky. We would pay Leeds £240,000, a vast amount of money for a club in City's position, and throw in Carl Shutt, who was a favourite with the crowd. If Taylor didn't click quickly, if the crowd got restive, Taylor's signature might as well have been on my professional death warrant – at least in Bristol – but another lesson I had learned was that in football you can't always play it safe. If you decide things need changing, you have to do it with some conviction, and you have to follow your instincts.

The worst possibility didn't happen – well, not quite. Taylor played well enough in his first game for us and we won. Unfortunately, he didn't score, which is always a disappointment when a big-money striker comes in to introduce himself and you are the guy with your neck on the block. Still, I was happy enough until one of the directors came up to me and said, 'Well done, Joe, good performance tonight. Oh, by the way, Carl Shutt scored three for Leeds.'

Taylor was paying his way, and with interest, soon enough. His most dramatic impact came with perfect timing. Although we were playing well in the League and edging up the table, the rumblings were still to be heard and I formed the impression that the board were indeed trying to get rid of Lumsden. It was necessary to give some firm indication that the team were building to a better future and, as my key signing, Taylor was the man who could do it with maximum effect. Right on cue, he scored a hat-trick in a runaway win against Huddersfield Town. In fact, he was everything I believed him to be when I urged the directors to make the big investment and sacrifice a crowd-pleasing player.

With the budget stretched, there was not a lot I could do in the way of transfer dealing, but after that crash course from Terry Cooper I was able to work the market quite well, moving in a few new players, parting with some I felt lacked the necessary edge to move us up a division, and all the time keeping the accounts pretty much balanced. The result fulfilled almost all my hopes. We went into the 1989–90 season with great assurance and Taylor repro-duced his form against Huddersfield with tremendous consis-tency. He maintained his sharpness throughout the season, finishing with a total of thirty-four goals – an output that brought us promotion. Really, we should have won the division title but second place spared us the ordeal of another play-off campaign. The place was buzzing. Crowds had swollen beyond the 20,000 mark on a regular basis and there was a strong feeling that, after the years in the wilderness, the club might just have the potential to make another run for the first division.

I was, naturally, in the best of spirits that summer when we holidayed in Italy at the time of the World Cup there, spending some time on the Mediterranean coast where we had first been taken by the president of AC Milan, Felice Colombo. I felt there was reason to believe I had built the foundations of a successful managerial career. I was on good terms with Alex Ferguson and back home in Bristol a new two-year contract from City awaited my signature. Doug Ellis, the chairman of Aston Villa, swiftly entrenched my mood of well-being. He was in Italy watching the World Cup, and wrestling with the fact that he was about to lose his manager Graham Taylor, who, with Bobby Robson already committed to the Dutch club PSV Eindhoven, had been offered the England job.

Ellis invited me to a meeting in Rome. I met him and his son and the talks went well. They asked me if I fancied the move and I put a series of questions to them about my terms and how I would be able to operate at Villa Park. Of course, I was excited by the prospect of taking over a club that had always had the potential to be one of the leading forces in English football. Indeed, just eight years earlier they had won the European Cup as part of that flood tide of English success on the Continent, one that was reversed only by the horrendous events at Heysel. However, there was a lot to think about. Ellis had a formidable reputation in the game and was not famous for the delicacy of his relations with managers. His nickname 'Deadly Doug' had not been lightly earned.

I had plenty to think about as I travelled back up the coast to rejoin my family. It was, I suppose, one of the classic dilemmas of any professional life. Do you ride on an early tide of success and go for a main chance at the first opportunity, or do you build up, learn your business as well as you can as quickly as possible, and then strike when you feel you are perfectly ready? In the mean-time, how do you guarantee continued success, especially in a business like football, and how can you be sure doors will be open when you reckon it is the right to time to move on? Ellis's reputation for eating up managers was an additional complica-tion. His ruthlessness and his care for profit margins were among the legends of the game.

The arrangement was that we would meet again in England when the World Cup was over. As the tournament unfolded, and I had to suffer the twin shock of seeing Scotland lose to Costa Rica and England threatening to win a second title after somehow surviving an ambush by Cameroon, I did quite a bit of agonising about the future. I had bedded in well at Bristol and maybe I would now have something of a comfort zone to develop my ideas about how a club should be run. As always, Judith said she would support me in whatever I decided. In the end, Deadly Doug made it relatively easy for me to tell City that I was ready to sign up again. I told Ellis that, as is common in football, I wanted to bring with me the people I trusted. That meant Jimmy Lumsden getting the assistant manager's job and Tony Fawthrop coming along as chief scout. The Villa chairman did not receive my proposals with too much enthusiasm. In fact, the vibes were not good at all whenever I returned to the subject, which was to my mind quite vital to any decision I made. In all other respects, Villa had made me a decent and flattering offer, but if you feel that something as fundamental as choosing your own staff is not a formality, you have to worry about the future. You have to wonder whether that would be the first of many points of disagreement.

I told City that I would sign their new contract on two conditions. I wanted a new car, a good Mercedes, and a clause added to the effect that I would be able to talk to any clubs that might come in for me. City agreed on both counts and the deal was done. I didn't have any regrets about turning down the big club. Villa offered brighter football lights, the chance to operate at a higher level of the game, but I had looked at myself carefully and reached the conclusion that I wasn't ready to deal with a man who plainly liked to have everything his own way. Certainly, I wanted to move up the football ladder, but at my own pace. I thought it was just a little too early to run the risk of being slapped down.

17

A FINE LINE

S O I said no to Deadly Doug, but in one of those moments
that condition the rest of your life, I said yes to Wallace
Mercer, the entrepreneurial chairman of Heart of Midlothian. If
you are wise, you bury such occasions among the debris of your
experience; you shrug your shoulders and make the best of what is
before you. It is more difficult when you are obliged to look back
and can see, as if drawn on a map, where your journey went amiss.

Mercer came to me early in the 1990–91 season at a time when
my profile as a young football manager was at its most promising.
We had made a good start to our new life in the second division,
the crowds were good and a surge of confidence had been
provided by an early win at home to Blackburn Rovers, when
Bob Taylor had electrified Ashton Gate – again – with two late
goals. My name was being linked with big clubs. In the Sunday
football columns I was listed among the coming managers of the
game. If I had believed everything I read, I would probably have
gone a little daft, but there was certainly more than a little
momentum to my career. I had a name from my playing days,
and the signs were that I knew how to run a team. In the armchair
of reflection it is easy enough to see what my strategy should have
been. I should have maintained the approach I had adopted in the
talks with Villa. I should have waited for the offer I couldn't
refuse, when the terms and the prospects were concrete and

spelled out entirely to my satisfaction. I had a position of strength that I would never quite enjoy again.

The negotiations went very swiftly, Mercer saying that he was anxious to make the deal as quickly as possible. Armed with the clause in my contract, I felt free to talk with him but I said that I couldn't sign right away. I owed it to City to talk it over with them, even though I knew deep down that the call to Scotland was very strong. Hearts, I believed, had great potential, Edinburgh was a fine city, and, who knew, I might with some success put myself in line for the managership of Scotland. That, after all my World Cup experience, had for some time been one of my ambitions and I had noted that in the past there had been a tendency to appoint former Scottish internationals, Willie Ormond for instance, and Ally MacLeod.

I went to see Des Williams at his home. He had always treated me very decently, and I explained my situation and my instinct to move. I told him that I wouldn't be going without some pangs of regret. The team was well set up and we had had some good times together. He said he understood my thinking, I was a young manager and it was the way of the game that young football men in my position had to take their opportunities.

Mercer had painted me a picture of an expanding club and I thought that, with my knowledge of players both in England and Scotland, I would be able to put together a competitive team. Judith loved the city and the move north was filled with excitement. That mood didn't last too long. It was soon clear that Mercer's picture of the future and reality did not exactly converge. Immediately, there was an added complication. Bristol City complained that they had lost their manager through an illegal approach. Although I was cleared of any wrongdoing by a Football Association inquiry, it was found that Mercer had not gone through the correct channels. Hearts were ordered to pay £80,000 compensation and on the drive back to Edinburgh Mercer told me, 'Joe, it means you have to sell a player.'

I felt as though someone had just kicked me in the pit of my stomach. I was in a hole and the only thing that came into my head was that I would just have to do the best I could. In any football situation you expect to have to do a bit of wheeler dealing – buy some players, yes, but first move a few out, let's try to balance the books, keep the bank happy – but this was football on the breadline. Selling a player to cover my own move into the manager's office was a long way from what I had in mind when I left the going concern of Bristol City.

However, the job had been taken and it had to be done. I had to put a few things in place. I was taking over from the former Rangers player Alex McDonald. He had done a good job and won the club a place in Europe, but I had a strong sense that he had got everything out of the team that was possible. There were some good players, but some of them were not quite as good as they imagined. I knew quite a bit about contemporary Scottish football but I didn't know it all and I moved for Frank Connor, the former Celtic goalkeeper who was now managing Raith Rovers. John Calderwood, who had worked in Scotland for Tottenham, joined me as chief scout. These appointments would prove to be the cornerstones of my work at Hearts. They were real football men who provided unflagging support and in-depth knowledge.

I knew the extent of the challenge but I was also aware that it would be a mistake to rush into changing too much, too quickly. I had a nucleus of experienced players to work with – John Robertson, a regular goalscorer, David McPherson, captain and centre-half, two other fine centre-halves, Craig Levein and Alan McLaren, and an experienced midfielder, Gary Mackay. I realised that for the moment I would have to get by with a squad of players who had been around for years – some of them for too many years, I concluded, as we battled through that first season around mid-table.

Eventually, I was able to bring in some new players, including two free transfers from England, Glynn Snodin from Leeds and John Miller from Blackburn. When I negotiated for and bought Ian Baird, a striker from Middlesbrough, I was told these wasn't the money to pay for him, so before the deal could go through, I had to sell another player, John Colquhoun. Somehow, by getting the team to play a little differently – having inherited three good centre-halves I played all three of them with wing-backs – and with the injection of some fresh blood, we began to take some effective shape. The second season was a success; we led the League going into the spring before being caught by Rangers, a team fuelled by big money and the experience of Walter Smith.

I had rescued my situation to a degree I would never have believed possible in those grim early days of doubt, when I feared that in one stroke of a pen I had put my career into crisis. It should, all these years on, be a time to recall with pleasure and satisfaction and, of course, there is some of that, but I'm afraid it will always be clouded by the knowledge that, even in those moments of success, I was locked into a professional relationship that was destined to do me and my career damage that in some ways would be irreparable.

One moment you have a destiny, the next you do not, and that was always my nagging sense when I worked at Hearts. It was confirmed in the third season, at the start of which I had made a potentially killing mistake. I told a press conference that if Hearts were to develop, if they were going to qualify for Europe regularly and truly compete with Rangers and Celtic, there had to be more serious investment. We had to be square with our following, I thought, but apparently that was something to think and to tell Mercer privately, not something to say in public. We were knocked out of the Scottish Cup by Rangers in the semi-final and I was fired three games away from the end of the season, after a bad defeat by Falkirk. The secretary of the club gave me the news, reading from a fax received from Monte Carlo, where the chairman was in tax exile.

The Falkirk result I reflected afterwards, may have been a product of the fact that I was unable to mask my feelings about how I saw the future. We were struggling to the finishing post, still with a chance of a Uefa place – which was eventually achieved – but I think some of the boys sensed my doubts about where we were going as a club. Maybe they switched off for that game, and the consequences were fatal.

One of the sadnesses was that the team had played for me after I had faced the problem of dealing with people who had been playing for one manager for a long time and one whom they felt had been looking after their best interests. McDonald had done very well, but often in football you get a situation where everything goes dead. The players have been there too long and so has the manager, so who goes? Most conveniently, it is the manager.

Recently, I worked on a coaching course in Scotland where some of my old Hearts players were trying for their badges. The scoring hero John Robertson went over some of the old days. He asked me about the changes in training and routine I made when I arrived, and whether they were to do with my experiences abroad.

'Yes, John,' I said, 'but it was more to do with the fact that I thought you guys were a little set in your ways. I wanted to take you in different direction – and I wanted to feel that you were with me.'

I recalled the time I had persuaded the chairman to let me bring in a chef from a local restaurant to prepare some pasta for the players in the wee canteen where we had our meals. I told John how I noted a certain resistance initially.

'You looked at the pasta,' I said, 'you touched it but you didn't accept it, so of course I backed off for a little while. You were used to minced steak pie and tatties. The trick was to coax you along rather than batter you with my ideas.'

In the end, and it is the most satisfying aspect of the job, I felt we had reached the right level of understanding. I was the boss, and I always had to be so, but it is so much better if progress flows from an acceptance that you have sound ideas and that you have given the challenge before you a little thought.

The bitterness I felt when I was fired still lingers. We had led all of Scotland for a while, we had qualified for Europe, the reserve team won their League and the boys won the Scottish Youth Cup. The feeling of confidence around the place gave me great pride. Looking back, the anger flares again not just because of what happened but also because of what it led to, what it created in my own mind and perhaps in the minds of those who, in the future, would decide on my ability to do the job.

If you go somewhere and make a mess of things, it is not so difficult to acknowledge that you got things wrong – perhaps deep down Brian Clough would admit to this when he thinks of his brief time at Leeds United – but it is not so easy to accept the sack when you feel that you did all you could and it was good work. When someone comes along and says you're finished, it's hard to take. It was then and it is now. My passion for the game, and its place in my life, remains as strong as ever, but I do know how it is that Judith sometimes says that she would be happy if I never went near a football ground ever again. Of course, if it's in your blood, you cannot shake it off, and in the aftermath of my sacking there was reason to believe that my stock had not gone down completely.

Jim McLean, the knowing old boss of Dundee United, called me to say that he had been impressed by my work and asked if I was interested in taking over his club. At the same time Ken Bates, then owner of Chelsea, called me to say that he was in Edinburgh and wanted to talk about the young centre-half McLaren, a good player who would eventually join Rangers. Could I come down to the Balmoral Hotel where he was staying? Could he pick my brains? He was wearing a robe when I joined him in his suite and while we talked about McLaren – I assured him he was an excellent player – I had the impression that Bates was appraising me as a possible manager at Stamford Bridge, the job being held at the time on a temporary basis by the club's former full-back Dave Webb.

I will never know the truth of my suspicions because when I left Bates, after he had peppered me with a hundred questions that stretched far beyond the virtues and the weaknesses of a young defender, I had a call from Liam Brady, who was battling as manager of Celtic. Would I join him at Parkhead as his assistant manager? I had told McLean that I had had enough of Scottish football, that I was heading back to England, but I knew Liam, I respected him and Celtic was, after all, Celtic. It meant that I would no longer be running my own club, which, for all the difficulties, was something I had got used to and liked, but after the Hearts experience I felt it would be good just to work with the boys again for a while. The fact was I felt very raw and embittered. I felt I had been played for a mug. In a way, Liam represented some of the best of my past in football; we had had good contacts when we were both in Italy, and since then we had stayed with each other occasionally. He had a huge challenge at Parkhead under the dominance of Rangers and he said he had been impressed with my work with Hearts. I took over from Mick Martin, the former Newcastle, Manchester United and Ireland player. Liam said he would continue to pick the team but I would be in charge of training and coaching and team talks. Surrendering the power of selection was something of a problem because it is at the heart of the job, and if Celtic hadn't been such a big club – and if I hadn't liked so much the chance to work with Liam to return it to better days – I probably wouldn't have done it.

Unfortunately, the chance to make some kind of impact at the club that had been so much a part of my life and coloured so much of what I believed was most exciting about the game, was over almost before it began. Liam had been fighting for several seasons under the pressure of Rangers' success and the relentless belief on the Parkhead terracing that the club's destiny was always to be the best. Something went out of him when we lost to St Johnstone.

Coming back on the team bus, I could see he was depressed. Celtic are not supposed to lose to anyone in Scotland and defeat by St Johnstone was obviously going to bring the usual clatter of criticism and big black headlines.

'I'm going,' he told me. 'I can't do this any more.'

I tried to talk him out of it, but he said his mind was made up. It wasn't as though I could bombard him with positives. The fact was that we were short of players and short of financial resources. The only thing we had in abundance was pressure, the old expectation that had been built into the psyche of the club over the years and most dramatically in the years of Jock Stein.

It took me just twenty-four hours to prepare the week's training schedule, pick up my coat and walk out of the doors. I didn't feel it would be right to take over from Liam. I had gone there to help him, as his friend as well as professional assistant, and when he resigned I felt bound to do the same. I had joined him to form a team and I thought that we should go out that way. I wished he had stayed. I thought we might have been able to turn things around to some degree, but Liam had been living with the problems for a lot longer than me, and I could see that there was no point in trying to change his mind.

From my perspective, it was another blow to that sense of being a young manger with the world of football beckoning in almost every direction. In fact, I didn't have to wait too long for another job but when it came it was not a foundation on which I could easily rebuild my career. Lou Macari was given Liam's job and I took over Lou's at Stoke City. As it turned out, what I was doing at the Victoria Ground was keeping Lou's seat warm while he became the latest victim of the battle to make Celtic a great club again.

Lou had done good work at Stoke and was very popular, and in the ten months I was there my old Scottish team-mate was always a shadowy companion. I was happy with the response of the players who were available to me, but I always had the sense that I was in the wrong place at the wrong time. When Lou lost his job at Parkhead and it was all over the local press, the implication could not be missed. At no time did I lose belief in my ability to do the job but I had already been around football management long enough to know that sometimes you cannot win. I was in and out at Stoke and my CV, which had read so promisingly, was now marked by another blotch.

At Stoke, as at Hearts at the end, I never felt that I would have the resources to carry through my best hopes for the club. Lou had done well, lifted them up into the old second division, but he had been forced to sell the club's best asset, striker Mark Stein, who had gone to Chelsea for £2 million. Naturally, most of that money was absorbed in the running of the club and it was only after some heavy pleading that I was able to bring in a new forward. I signed Paul Peschisolido, who knew his way to goal but in the course of his career tended to win most publicity by marrying, Karren Brady, the managing director of Birmingham City. He did well at Stoke but it wasn't to my benefit. He had played just six games by the time I was fired.

Peter Coates, the chairman of Stoke, no doubt did what he thought was right when Lou came back into the market. He paid up my contract and said he was sorry that the situation had developed as it had. He said he thought he was doing the best for the club. I looked at my performance closely, as you always do in those circumstances, and felt that I had done reasonably well. At the end of the first season we were close to the play-offs for the old first division. With three games to go, the right combination of results would have taken us into the post-season action but we didn't get them. Over the first six games of the following season, we had an average start, not triumphant, not a disaster, but when the news came in that Lou had been fired by Celtic it was plain that I had become history.

The pattern was disturbing now; since those foundation stones had been laid at Ashton Gate I had lost three jobs, two by sacking, one by resignation. In each case, I could tell myself that I had acquitted myself well – particularly so at Hearts – and yet I was accumulating the badges of defeat. It wasn't supposed to be like that. Perhaps, I thought, a return to the starting point would bring a return of some of the old certainties. My old chairman at Bristol City, Des Williams, had died but the majority of the old board were still in place and my good work was remembered when, a few months after I left Stoke, they decided they needed a new manager. I liked the place and the people, and we still had the house in Bristol, but in strictly football terms it was not the most inviting of engagements. City were bottom of the old second division and it was clear I wouldn't be able to buy myself out of trouble.

I joined around November and although the boys fought hard, we couldn't turn it around. The next season we were back in the third division from which I had led the club five years earlier. We battled around mid-table; neither the club nor I seemed to be heading anywhere quickly. My situation was worsened by the arrival of some new directors, led by Scott Davidson, whose family were in publishing and who had got involved in the music business. Quite early on I formed the impression that this new blood at the club wanted their own manager, their own appointment. I was told that they were revoking my contract – I had signed for two years plus a roll-over year – and giving me a new deal, but it was no great surprise when they fired me soon afterwards. Friction had been growing between Davidson and me and some of it was created by my angry reaction to his intervention in a move I was making for Kevin Davies, who eventually moved from Southampton to Blackburn for millions of pounds.

I had been negotiating with the Chesterfield manager John Duncan and it had been going well. When Duncan said the club were sticking out for a certain fee, I said I wasn't sure I would get the deal past my chairman. It was the way of the game, but when I went back to Bristol and told Davidson what was happening he said, 'I'm already talking to the chairman.' It was a classic case of a chairman wanting to get involved in the action and pushing the professional football man to one side. It was an extremely bad sign for the future.

One afternoon I got a call at the club from Lou Macari. He asked me how things were going. I told him they were not too good, adding, 'In fact, I think I'm going to get the bullet any day now.' Maybe the news hit a raw spot with Lou, who by now was familiar with the violently shifting fortunes of a football man. 'Get out of there, Joe,' he said. 'Just piss off. Don't let them have you on a string. Don't make it easy for them.' He was tapping into a build-up of frustration.

'Aye, Lou, you're right. I'm off home,' I said.

Training was over, I wasn't inconveniencing anyone that day if I left early and I felt a powerful need to get out of the place, partly as a reaction to the fact that earlier I had been told, 'The chairman wants to see you.' There was no time or date, just that vague announcement, which in a football club in a state of some tension can mean one of only a very few things. The chairman was looking for me, they said. I let the office phone ring out a few times, then I picked up my jacket and car keys and walked out of the ground.

At home the phone rang out some more. I talked things over with Judith. For some time Judith had been telling me that my time at the club had passed, that I was a goner. She had read between the lines of the chairman's comments and the drift of press opinion. She had read the smoke signals, she said, and they were not good. I supposed I had been a little too buried in the job to get quite such a clear picture.

Eventually, I answered the phone and it was someone at the club saying, 'Can you come down and see the chairman?' It was around 6 p.m. when I got to the ground and the car park was all but deserted. I saw the cars of a few of the directors – and one in which a local reporter, no doubt having been tipped off, was sitting or, as I felt at the time, lurking. I thought the tip-off was a bit tacky. The directors told me that they were going to end my contract. I said of course that was their right but because I had had a little time to think about it I wanted to ask them a few questions. I wanted them to give me some idea, after considering all aspects of the club's situation, where they thought I had failed. The sense was that they just thought it was time for a change. My instinct was that the new men wanted their own manager and more hands-on control of transfer deals. I could have lived with that principle, as long as I had been able to nominate my own players, but we had moved past that point. The club appointed John Ward as my successor, and he was able to do a good job for a while. He got them into the play-offs and then the following year they won promotion.

Linked with my fate at Hearts and Stoke, it was another blow to my profile, but not a fatal one to my confidence. I still believed I had a feel for the job, that from all my experience I had learned valuable lessons about how to handle players and develop a team. One of my difficulties, on reflection, was that I couldn't come away from the ground and put the job down. I lived it, and sometimes it cost me some sleep.

After the break with City, Channel Four offered me some respite from the day-to-day strains of management. I worked on their coverage of the Italian game, which gave me the chance to revisit the land and the life I had grown to love. I appreciated the break, but I also knew the draw of football would never leave me and I was glad to respond to my old boss Lawrie McMenemy's request that I work with him and Pat Jennings, the great Irish goalkeeper, in his latest role as manager of the Northern Ireland team. It was a tough assignment, Northern Ireland's pool of players being so small, but we did the job properly. Lawrie picked the team and I coached them and went scouting on the opposition. We were drawn against Germany, Finland, Turkey and Moldova in the qualification group for the 2000 European

Championship. It was good to work with Lawrie again but it wasn't what I really wanted. I needed to be back in the day-to-day challenge of the game.

The boys worked hard. Iain Dowie, who would later emerge impressively as the coach of Crystal Palace, driving them to the Premiership, was particularly committed, but after we failed to qualify for the finals in Belgium and Holland Lawrie wasn't offered a new contract. I was back in the market and, even if I might have still been carrying the odd wee bruise, delighted to get another call from Lou Macari. He had taken the job at Huddersfield in succession to Steve Bruce. Following a lot of buying, the club had slid down the first division. When Lou and I arrived the situation could scarcely have been less promising. All the money had gone – the club chairman and benefactor Barry Rubery was taking a lot of stick from the crowd despite investing millions of his own money – and the team had gleaned just eight points from eighteen games. The club was in free fall. We had to sell players and at the same time fight relegation. All we could do was gather the players together and tell them that, as a group of professionals, we just had to work as hard as we could to protect our reputations. Maybe the situation was hopeless, but that didn't stop us fighting. The least we could do was show some pride. It almost worked. The players responded brilliantly and from the remaining twenty-eight games we won 41 points. Having been hopelessly adrift, we went down in the last game of the season – and then, we all agreed, only because of a dodgy goal by Crystal Palace.

It is odd to feel a certain exhilaration when you have gone down, but both Lou and I felt that way. We had been obliged to sell off the nucleus of the team – a pattern that had started under Bruce when he was obliged to part with the excellent goalscorer Marcus Stewart – but the boys who had come in, most notably teenager Nathan Clark, who arrived a little later, did extremely well.

The following season the financial pressure was still heavy, forcing us to sell one player, Clyde Wijnhard, at the transfer deadline. The reason was it would save on his wages until the end of the season, but at the end of that season we had made it to the play-offs and we needed all the bodies we could muster.

The young team had produced a tremendous reaction on the terraces and despite the need to sell players, there was a sense that the club had come alive again. I headed off to Spain for a holiday with Judith with that old feeling of belief in the future. Before I left, Lou told me that a new contract would be awaiting me on my return. There was no discussion of terms, but Lou suggested I would be happy.

In Majorca I had a good, easy time as I recovered from much delayed hip operations that I had finally submitted to at the end of the season. One afternoon I was resting in the apartment in Puerto Pollensa when I was awakened by the sound of the mobile phone. It was a reporter from the *Yorkshire Post*. He wanted to know my reaction to being sacked. There had been a change in the boardroom, the old chairman had resigned and the new people wanted to make a fresh start. I said I had no reaction. I told the reporter I didn't know anything. I called home and my son Andrew said the news was running on Sky television. When I told Judith I saw the anger in her eyes. I felt numb. Football had given me so much of what I had wanted in life, but if it gave, it also took away. Loving it was one thing, making sense of it quite another.

EPILOGUE

O NE summer morning, two years after being fired so unexpectedly by Huddersfield Town and wondering for the umpteenth time if football had finally passed me by, I received a phone call from Harry Redknapp, the manager of Premiership team Portsmouth. He asked me what I was doing. I said not a lot. I had gained some more coaching certificates, done a little broadcasting, attended the odd interview and then read somewhere that someone else had been appointed. I'd coached a team of British pop stars against one representing Italy for a big charity match in Florence. Paul Gascoigne had come along and behaved himself extremely well, going to bed early, which made me speculate, like any other football lover, what might have happened if he had done that a little more often when his talent could so easily have blazed across the heavens.

I didn't give Harry a sob story. I simply told him how it was when your name is out of fashion and all the work you did, all the ideas you had, all the hopes you had nourished down the years, might have happened on another planet. I wasn't telling Harry anything he didn't know.

Harry asked me if I would like to come down to Fratton Park, one of the famous old grounds of England, and talk to him about helping to coach his team against the likes of Manchester United, Arsenal and Chelsea. I would work alongside my old team-mate at

Southampton, Kevin Bond. I could put a few of my theories into practice. I could again be in the company of top-flight players.

I said I would be delighted – and I think I kept the excitement out of my voice. At fifty-two years of age, the compulsion of football was, of course, as strong as ever. However many times it knocks you down, it always has the potential to lift you up. When I told Judith about Harry's call, maybe a touch of ambivalence crept into her eyes but I could see that she was happy for me. I would again be doing the thing that had most powerfully co-loured all my days – for how long, well, who could say?

If Harry's call had not come, I would have had no reason to regret my lifelong commitment to the game, no more than I would to discourage my sons Andrew, who plays for Hartlepools, and Thomas, who as I went off to Portsmouth was hoping to continue his professional career with non-league Woking. For every blow football has delivered, it has given my family and me a good life and a thousand memories. My daughter Lucy has a good career in management and Caroline is on the point of graduating from Birmingham University. We still have that lovely house surrounded by greenery and the sense of a wider world, one that could have been gained, for a boy from Cleland, only by the sweep of a top-flight football career.

I like to think that these words are simply by way of a provisional report. In football, you never draw down a curtain on your hopes, and if you doubt that, look at Sir Bobby Robson fighting his battles until so recently at Newcastle and my friend and confidant Sir Alex Ferguson at Old Trafford. They have gained so much from the game, including their knighthoods, but has their appetite for it diminished? Have they wearied of the game that takes as randomly as it gives?

It is impossible for an old footballer to be impressed with all he sees in the modern game. I hate some the excesses of today's football. Sometimes I wonder how a lad can keep his focus when his driveway is littered with flash cars and, if he chose not to, he wouldn't have to work for another day in his life. I speculate sometimes on how that kind of largesse would have affected my own generation, back when it seemed every game was a branch of warfare. Would going to Elland Road, Old Trafford or the San Siro have moved me quite so much if all the materials of a good and luxurious life had been guaranteed so early and so irrevocably? Would arriving at the station in Leeds or at Milan airport have been such an excitement if all my bills had been paid for ever?

Despite my suspicions, I cannot say because I lived in my own time and, looking back, it is hard to imagine how anything could have been more fulfilling than a confirming slap on the back as you came in wearing the colours of Scotland or Leeds, Manchester United or AC Milan.

Football, like life, may have changed dramatically these last few years but some values are eternal, even if they slip from sight from time to time. The need to perform, to express everything that you have inside you, is not likely to die. As long as that is true, the game that I made my life will no doubt survive and continue to touch every corner of the world. Like Jimmy Johnstone, one of its greatest exponents, it will find its way back to the shore.

Index

AC Milan 145–50, 170–8
  bribery scandal 177
  Internazionale 4
  San Siro stadium 153, 171
  v Leeds United 59, 111–12
Adams, Dr 31
Ajax 123
Alberto, Carlos 74
Allchurch, Ivor 156
Amoruso, Lorenzo 195, 197
Archibald, Steve 199, 201
Armfield,, Jimmy 103, 106–8, 114–
      24, 128, 147
Armstrong, Dave 209
Arsenal 60
  v Leeds United 57, 61
  v Manchester United 134, 136
Astle, Jeff 22
Aston Villa 228–9
Atkinson, Ron 132, 137, 144, 146
Attenborough, Sir Richard 65

Bagnoli, Osvaldo 188–91
Bailey, Gary 137
Baird, Ian 233
Bailey, Mike 57
Bajevic, Dusan 86
Ball, Alan 30
Barcelona, v Leeds United 55, 108–
      10
Baresi, Franco 178–9, 182–7
Barison, Paolo 174
Barnes, John 210
Bartram, Per 20

Bassett, Dave 222
Bates, Ken 235
Bates, Ted 207
Batistini 179, 182
Baxter, Jim 78, 160
Bayern Munich, v Leeds United 107,
      110–11
Bearzot, Enzo 203
Bebeto 186
Beckenbauer, Franz 107, 111
Beckham, David 138–9
Berlusconi, Silvio 183
Best, George 60
Bett, Jim 196
Black Sabbath 47
Blackley, John 88
Blanchflower, Danny 97
Blantyre Vics 16–17
Blissett, Luther 148
Blokhin, Oleg 201
Bloor, Alan 65
Bogicevic, Vladislav 86
Bologna 145
Bond, Kevin 48, 245
Bowles, Stan 159
Bowyer, Lee 36
Boyd, Lee 40
Brady, Liam 136, 146, 172, 176, 236
Brazil, v Scotland 74, 86
Brazil, Alan 199, 201
Bremner, Billy
  bribery allegation 61–2
  and Clough 91
  goals 23, 42, 58, 71, 109

Hull City 121
and JJ xvii 197
Leeds captain 37
Leeds United 23, 27–8, 31–2, 39,
    59, 63–6, 78–9, 97, 102
Scotland 69, 71, 74–6, 85, 87, 88,
    195
Brennan, Joe 3, 8, 9, 23–5, 29, 41,
    88
bribery scandals 61–2, 177
Bristol City 121–2, 218–27
    v Blackburn Rovers 230
    v Bradford 225
    v Huddersfield Town 227
    v Leeds United 66
    v Mansfield 216
    v Nottingham Forest 225
    v Sheffield United 222
    v Walsall 222
Brooking, Trevor 159
Brown, Craig 198
Brown, Laurie 125
Brown, Tony 132
Bruce, Steve 242
Buchan, Martin 126, 134, 157, 163
Burns, Kenny 157
Busby, Sir Matt 37, 144
    European Cup 68
    Manchester United 2, 125, 127,
    130

Calderwood, John 232
Callaghan, Ian 60
Capello, Fabio 179
Carey, Johnny 37
Case, Jimmy 48, 209
Casey, Peter 7, 10, 12
Castagnar, Ilario 179, 180, 182
Celtic 236–7
    European Cup 194
    v Leeds United 23, 29
    v St Johnstone 236–7
Celtic Supporters Club 10
Ceulemans, Jan 145
Chalmers, Stevie 204
Channon, Mick 159
Charles, John 156, 172
Charlton, Bobby 60, 79
Charlton, Jack 31, 33, 36–7
    England 69
    injuries 42, 57

Middlesbrough manager 57, 66
Chivadze, Aleksandr 201, 202
Clark, Nathan 242
Clarke, Allan 31–2, 55–6, 59, 66, 79,
    109, 111
Clarke, Colin 211
Cleland 1, 43, 52, 88
Clodoaldo 74
Clough, Brian 84
    Leeds manager 91, 97–102, 235
Coakley, Tommy 30
Cocker, Les 31, 36, 113
Collins, Bobby, Barnsley 210
Collins, Bobby xvi 22–3, 25–6, 30,
    36–7, 47, 117, 176
Colombo, Felice 171, 177, 228
Colquhoun, John 233
Comfort, Michael 8
Connelly, George 23
Connor, Frank 232
Conroy, Terry 65
Cooke, Charlie 64
Cooper, Terry 31, 54, 58, 121, 215–20
Coppell, Steve 132
Coventry City, v Leeds United 28–9
Craig, Joe 199
Craig, Tommy 195
Cramer, Dietmar 110, 115–17, 119,
    120
Crerand, Paddy 77–8, 160, 204
Cruyff, Johan 108, 110, 166
Cubillas, Teofilio 163
Cueto, Cesar 163
Cup Winners' Cup (1973) 59
Currie, Tony 122–3
Cussins, Manny 91
Czechoslovakia, v Scotland 74–5

Dalglish, Kenny 48, 70, 128, 135,
    143, 195, 201
    goals 167, 200
    Scotland 70–5, 82–3, 86–8, 157,
    163, 167, 199, 200
Damascelli, Tony 145, 174–6
Damiani, Oscar 179
Danaifar, Iraj 165
Davidson, Dave 239–40
Davies, Kevin 239
Deans, Dixie 199
Delaney, Jimmy 1–3, 37, 58, 88, 118,
    125, 127, 197

Delaney, John 3, 8, 24, 25, 41, 88, 194
Delaney, Patsy 3
Dempsey, John 64
Derby County 61, 64
Desayev, Renat 202
Djazic, Dragan 86–7
Dobing, Peter 207
Docherty, Tommy 70, 71, 125, 133, 193
Dougan, Derek 57, 61
Dowie, Iain 242
Duncan, John 239
Dwyer, Kathy 51

Eastham, George 118
Eder, 201
Edwards, Louis 125
Ellis, Doug 228–9
England
   v Poland 79
   v Scotland 72, 82–4
Eriksson, Sven Goran 162
Eskandarian, Andaranik 165
European Championship (1960) 202; (2000) 241–2; (2004) 171, 196, 204
European Cup 67, 103, 107–13, 210
Evani 182
Everton 29–30
v Leeds United 54

FA Cup final (1963) 37; (1965) 60; (1970) 64; (1972) 61; (1973) 54, 57, 59–60; (1979) 134, 136
Facchetti, Giacinto 159
Fairs Cup (1971) 41
Falcao 200, 201
Fanna, Piero 189
Fawthrop, Tony 229
Ferguson, Sir Alex 3, 105, 223–5, 228, 245
Feroni 190
Ferry, Bryan 11, 47
Finney, Sir Tom 118
Flynn, Brian 123
Fontolan, Silvano 190
Forsyth, Tom 168

Galbiatti, Italo 179
Galderesi, Giuseppe 188, 190, 191

Galvin, Chris 55
Garela 189
Gascoigne, Paul 148, 244
Gemmell, Tommy 195
Gemmill, Archie 102
Gennaro, Antonio 190
Giles, Johnny
   and Bremner 61
   and Clough 97–8, 100, 102
   Ireland 70
   Leeds 23, 31–2, 37–9, 63–4, 66, 103, 106–7
   Manchester United 37, 38
   and Revie 92–4, 96–7
   Vancouver Whitecaps 40
   West Bromwich 97, 115, 121–2, 137
Gillies, Matt 15
Gledhill, Mrs 41, 46
Goligey, Jim 8
Gordon, Colin 221
Graham, George 71
Gray, Andy 123, 156, 199
Gray, Billy 30
Gray, Eddie 28, 30, 32, 35–6, 76, 79, 99
Greenhoff, Brian 135
Greenhoff, Jimmy 125, 128, 135
Guani, Alberigo 179
Gullit, Ruud 183, 187

Hansen, Alan 128, 202
Harris, Ron 'Chopper' 64
Harrison, Jean 224
Hartford, Asa 195, 201
Harvey, Colin 30
Harvey, David 67, 79, 88, 112
Hateley, Mark 210
Hay, David 88, 207–8
Haynes, Johnny 38
Heart of Midlothian 230–5
Hegen, Danny 61
Herrera, Helenio 194
Hill, Jimmy 126
Hinton, Alan 98
Holton, Jim 75
Hong Kong Rangers 10
Houllier, Gerard 60
Huddersfield 242
Hudson, Alan 64
Hughes, Mark 158

Hunt, Roger 60
Hunter, Ally 75
Hunter, Norman 39, 79, 100, 121–2
Hutchison, Tommy 87

Internazionale Milan 4, 177, 187, 188
Iorio, Maurizio 188, 190, 191
Ipswich Town, v Leeds United 57
Italian Cup 177, 190
Italian football 149, 170–92
Italy
  bribery scandal 62, 177
  v Brazil 186
  v Germany 202–3
  v Ireland 186

James, Leighton 157
Jansen, Wim 168
Jardine, Sandy 81, 165
Jennings, Pat 136, 241
Johanneson, Albert 60
Johnston, Willie 157, 168
  drugs 163–4
Johnstone, Derek 123, 162
Johnstone, Jimmy 4, 16, 143, 194
  Scotland 71, 80–4, 89, 199
Jones, Mrs 46
Jones, Cliff 156
Jones, Dave 153
Jones, Joey 157
Jones, Mick 32, 55, 66, 102, 188
Jongbloed, Jan 166, 168
Jordan, Andrew (son of JJ) 145, 243, 245
Jordan, Caroline (daughter of JJ) 245
Jordan, Elizabeth (sister of JJ) 10, 11, 44, 51–2
Jordan, Frank (father of JJ) 3, 10–11, 15, 18, 25, 51–2, 57–8, 76–7, 88, 125, 127
Jordan, Joe
  CHARACTER xi-xiii
  CHILDHOOD 1–13
  FOOTBALL
    Blantyre Vics 16–17
    North Motherwell 17
    Morton 17–23
    Leeds 22–5, 27, 53–68, 104–5
      goals 54, 55, 57, 64, 65
      Injuries 28–9
      salary 32

Scotland 69, 72, 74–6, 82, 84, 204
  goals 76, 87
  hand ball claim xii 153–4, 157–8
Bayern Munich offer 115–20, 146, 147
offer from Ajax 123–4
Manchester United 124–45
  goals 129, 135
  injury 134
  Italian interest 145–6
  Player of the Year 137
  transfer fee 126
Milan 145–50, 170–82
  goals 177, 180
  injury 200
Verona 176, 181, 183–92
  injury 187
Southampton 48, 204, 207–14
  goals 209
  injury 211
Bristol City 215–18; manager 219–29
Aston Villa offer 228–9
Heart of Midlothian manager 230–5
Celtic assistant manager 236–7
Northern Ireland coach 241
Stoke City manager 237–8
Huddersfield 242–3
Portsmouth coach 244–5
World Cups 70, 74–5, 85–7, 155, 165, 194, 204
  goals 76, 85, 87, 199, 202
Jordan, John (brother of JJ) 10, 11, 44–52
Jordan, Judith (wife of JJ) 46, 117, 138, 140–52, 235, 240, 245
  Milan 146–51, 179
  Verona 187
Jordan, Lucy (daughter of JJ) 145, 245
Jordan, Mary (grandmother of JJ) 11
Jordan, Mary (mother of JJ) 10–11, 15, 18, 21, 25, 51–2
Jordan, Thomas (son of JJ) 47, 145, 149, 245

Kane, Georgie 'Purdie' 4–5, 8, 32
Karesi, Stanislav 87

Kay, Tony 62
Kazadi 85, 87
Keane, Roy 105
Keegan, Kevin 73, 119, 159, 207
Kendall, Howard 30
Kennedy, Stuart 163
Kidd, Brian 36, 133
Kite, Phil 211
Krol 166, 168, 200

Law, Denis 60
    and JJ xvii 4, 197
    Scotland 71, 85–8, 160
Layne, David 62
Leeds United 33–9, 63, 90–3, 127
    1974 Division One title 66
    directors 92–4
    European Cup 107–13
    FA Cup Final xvii
    record run of undefeated games 64
    v AC Milan 59, 111
    v Arsenal 57, 61
    v Barcelona 55, 108–10
    v Bayern Munich 107, 110–11
    v Bradford City 54
    v Bristol City 66
    v Celtic 23, 29
    v Chelsea 64
    v Coventry City 28–9
    v Everton 54
    v Ipswich Town 57
    v Juventus 41
    v Liverpool 60
    v Manchester United 123
    v Stoke City 64–5
    v Sunderland 54, 57, 59–60
    v West Ham 113
    v Wolverhampton Wanderers 57
Lennox, Bobby 74, 195, 204
Levein, Craig 232
Lindley, Maurice 31, 36
Liverpool
    v Borussia Moechengladbach 128
    v Leeds United 60
    v Manchester United 135
Lorimer, Peter
    goals 109, 111
    Leeds 28, 32, 35, 70, 76, 80, 99,
        109
    Scotland 70, 72, 85, 88
Lumsden, Jimmy 226–7, 229

McAllister, Gary 7, 195
Macari, Lou 73, 240, 242
    Celtic manager 237–8
    goals 162
    Huddersfield 242–3
    Manchester United 126, 134
    Scotland 157, 167–8, 195
    Stoke City manager 237–8
McCormick, Len 157
McCourt, Pat 17
McCreadie, Eddie 64
McDonald, Alex 232
McFarland, Roy 98
McGovern, John 101
McGrain, Danny 80, 89, 195
McIlroy, Jimmy 207
McIlroy, Sammy 134, 136
McIlvanney, Hugh 159
Mackay, Dave 78, 99, 160
Mackay, Gary 232
McKenzie, Duncan 101
McKenzie, John 83
McLaren, Alan 232
McLaren, Father Isaac 5–9, 143–4
McLean, Jim 235–6
MacLeod, Ally 159–68, 231
McMenan and Brown 18, 21, 69
McMenemy, Lawrie 181, 207–10, 241
McNab, Bob 129
McNeill, Billy 2, 195, 204
McPherson, David 232
McQueen, Gordon 79, 95
    friendship with JJ 48, 67, 95, 113,
        140–1
    Leeds 46, 58–9, 79, 91, 110, 113,
        116–17
    Manchester United 133, 136
McStay, Paul 195
Madeley, Paul 32, 39, 65, 210
Mahoney, John 157
Makelele, Claude 172
Maldini, Cesare 183
Maldini, Paolo 183–4
Manchester City
    v Leicester City 37
    v Manchester United 129
Manchester United 60, 129, 134
    FA Cup Final 134, 136
    v Arsenal 134, 136
    v Leeds United 123
    v Liverpool 135

v Manchester City 129
v Newcastle 129
v West Bromwich 132
Maradona, Diego 148, 154, 157–8
Marangon, Luciano 190
Marcia 224
Marinho 109
Martin, Mick 236
Masson, Don 153, 157
  Scotland 153, 157, 163, 168
match fixing 62–3
Matthews, Sir Stanley 118, 207
Mazzola, Sandro 174
Mercer, Joe 78
Mercer, Wallace 230–1, 233
Michels, Rinus 156, 163, 167
Middlemass, Clive 217–18
Middlesbrough 5, 57
Milan see AC Milan
Miljanic, Miljan 86, 156
Miller, John 233
Miller, Willie 202
Mills, Mick 207
Montgomery, Jim 59
Moore, Bobby 70, 113
Moran, Steve 209–10
Morgan, John 95
Morgan, Willie 76
Morton 17–23, 26
Motson, John 82
Moyes, David 215–16
Mudie, Jackie 207
Muller, Gerd 111
Munante, Juan Jose 163
Murdoch, Bobby 195

Narey, David 201, 201, 202
Neeskens, Johan 108, 166
Newcastle, v Manchester United 129
Nicholl, Chris 211
Nicholson, Bill 97
North Motherwell 17

Oblitas, Juan Carlos 163
O'Brien, Terry 8–9
O'Farrell, Frank 70
O'Hare, John 98, 101
O'Leary, David 36
Olive, Les 125, 127
Ormond, Willie 71, 75, 81, 84–6, 89,
  159, 231

Osgood, Peter 64
Owen, Syd 29, 36, 111
Ozbay, Tunj 76

Paisley, Bob 73, 128–9
Parlane, Derek 123, 199
Parreira, Carlos Alberto 186
Partick Thistle 17
Peacock, Alan 60
Pearson, Stuart 125, 128
Pejic, Mike 65
Pele 38, 74, 156
Peschisolido, Paul 238
Platini, Michel 184
Poortvliet, Jan 168
Professional Footballers' Association
  126

Quiroga, Ramon 163

Radice, Gigi 173–4, 178
Ramsey, Sir Alf 79, 84, 92
Rangers 25
Rankin, Stan 21
Redknapp, Harry 244–5
Rensenbrink, Rob 166, 167
Rep, Johnny 166–8
Revie, Don
  discipline 114
  England manager 104
  Leeds manager 22, 30–46, 53–67,
    79, 90–6, 99–100, 127, 140,
    219
Richards, John 57
Rijkaard, Frank 183, 187
Rijsbergen, Wim 166
Riley, Harold 137
Rioch, Bruce 157, 163, 167–8
Rivera, Gianni 174
Roberts, Bob 127
Robertson, John 157, 167, 199, 201,
  232, 234
Robson, Bryan 105, 132
Robson, Sir Bobby 210, 228, 245
Romano, Francesco 179, 182
Romario 186
Rosenthal, Jim 225
Rossi, Paolo 62, 177, 202
Rough, Alan 157, 165, 168, 201, 202
Rubery, Barry 242
Rush, Ian 128, 148

Sacchi, Arigo 183–6
Sacchi, Luigi 190
Sager, Alan 44
St Aidan secondary school 7, 12, 45
St John, Ian 4, 60, 78
St Mary's Boys Guild 6–7, 45
San Siro stadium 153, 171
Sanderson, Jimmy 83
Scholes, Paul 171
Scotland 155–6, 193–200
   v Argentina 162
   v Brazil 74, 86, 162, 201
   v Chile 162
   v Czechoslovakia 74–5, 160, 197
   v Denmark 70–2
   v England 72, 82–4
   v Holland 166–8
   v Iran 165
   v Italy 159
   v Peru 163
   v Russia 201–2
   v Spain 200
   v Switzerland 74
   v Wales 153–4, 156–7, 196–7, 204
   v Yugoslavia 86–7
   v Zaire 85–6
   World Cup xvii 70, 160, 193–8
Serena, Aldo 179, 182
Sexton, Dave 64, 125, 127–30, 133–5, 137, 144
Shankly, Bill 60, 129
Shearer, Alan 213
Shengali, Ramaz 202
Shilton, Peter 79, 83, 207
Shutt, Carl 226–7
Smith, Denis 65
Smith, Eric 19–21
Smith, Tommy 190
Smith, Walter 233
Snodin, Glynn 233
Socrates 200, 201
Sorensen, Erik 20
Souness, Graeme 128, 135, 157, 167–8, 172, 195, 201
Southampton 48, 204, 207
   v Manchester United 209
   v Sunderland 209
Sprake, Gary 23, 30, 67, 140
Stapleton, Frank 136
Stein, Jock 2, 4, 16, 72, 83, 204–5
   European Cup 68

Scotland 193, 199–200
Stein, Mark 238
Stevenson 9
Stewart, David 112
Stewart, Hal 19–20, 24, 26, 30, 71
Stewart, Marcus 242
Stiles, Nobby 3–4, 70, 112, 213
Stoke City, v Leeds United 64–5
Stokes, Peter 238
Stokoe, Bob 59
Storrie, Jim 60
Strachan, Gordon 195, 200
Stuart, Brian 40, 48
Sunderland, v Leeds United 54, 57, 59–60
Sunderland, Alan 137
Suurbier, Wim 166
Swan, Peter 62
Sweeney, Gerry 30

Talbot, John 136
Tardelli, Marco 203
Taylor, Bob 226–7, 230
Taylor, Graham 228
Teeman, Ronnie 123, 146, 147
Thomas, Micky 135
Thompson, Peter 60
Todd, Colin 98
Tomaszewski, Jan 84
Toshack, John 157
Tossoti, Mauro 178, 185
Tostao 74
Trapattoni, Giovanni 173
Tricella, Roberto 190
Tunj 141, 144, 157

Valdomiro 87
Van Basten, Marco 183, 184, 187
van der Kerkhof, Willy 168
Venables, Terry 70
Verona 176, 181, 183–92
Vieira, Patrick 105
Vogts, Berti 74, 195, 198
Volpati, Domenico 189

Waddington, Tony 65, 207
Wagstaffe, David 58
Wales, v Scotland 153–7, 196–7, 204
Wallace, Ian 199
Walsh, Alan 217, 222, 225

Ward, John 241
Wark, John 200, 201
Webb, Dave 30, 236
Webster, Colin 156
Wenger, Arsene 105
West Bromwich, v Manchester United
        132
West Ham, v Leeds 113
White, John 78
Wijnhard, Clyde 243
Wile, John 132–3
Williams, Des 219, 231, 239
Wolverhampton Wanderers, v Leeds
        United 57
Woodgate, Jonathan 36

World Cup 155–61
World Cup (1954) 156; (1958) 75,
        156; (1962) 78; (1970) 22;
        (1974) 70, 74, 83–9; (1978)
        153, 159; (1982) 202–3;
        (1986) 154, 210; (1994)
        186

Yeats, Ron 60
Yorath, Terry 40, 102, 121, 157
Yugoslavia, v Scotland 86–7

Zagallo, Mario 74
Zaire, v Scotland 85–6
Zico 145, 200, 201